BUSINESS ECONOMICS IN A RAPIDLY-CHANGING WORLD

THE USE OF BIG DATA

BENEFITS, RISKS, AND DIFFERENTIAL PRICING ISSUES

BUSINESS ECONOMICS IN A RAPIDLY-CHANGING WORLD

Additional books in this series can be found on Nova's website under the Series tab.

Additional e-books in this series can be found on Nova's website under the eBooks tab.

BUSINESS ECONOMICS IN A RAPIDLY-CHANGING WORLD

THE USE OF BIG DATA

BENEFITS, RISKS, AND DIFFERENTIAL PRICING ISSUES

DIANA SIMPSON
EDITOR

nova publishers
New York

Library of Congress Cataloging-in-Publication Data

ISBN: 978-1-63485-318-7

Published by Nova Science Publishers, Inc. † New York

CONTENTS

PREFACE

As the use of online technologies and digital engagement by consumers has expanded, the amount of consumer data that flows throughout the economy has increased. The analysis of this information can guide the development of products and services but concerns have been raised about whether certain uses of big data analytics may harm consumers. This book discusses the benefits and risks created by the use of big data analytics, the application of equal opportunity and consumer protection laws to big data, considerations for business and policy considerations raised by big data research. The book also discusses big data and differential pricing.

In: The Use of Big Data
Editor: Diana Simpson

ISBN: 978-1-63485-318-7

Chapter 1

BIG DATA: A TOOL FOR INCLUSION OR EXCLUSION? UNDERSTANDING THE ISSUES*

Federal Trade Commission

EXECUTIVE SUMMARY

We are in the era of big data. With a smartphone now in nearly every pocket, a computer in nearly every household, and an ever-increasing number of Internet-connected devices in the marketplace, the amount of consumer data flowing throughout the economy continues to increase rapidly.

The analysis of this data is often valuable to companies and to consumers, as it can guide the development of new products and services, predict the preferences of individuals, help tailor services and opportunities, and guide individualized marketing. At the same time, advocates, academics, and others have raised concerns about whether certain uses of big data analytics may harm consumers, particularly low-income and underserved populations.

To explore these issues, the Federal Trade Commission ("FTC" or "the Commission") held a public workshop, *Big Data: A Tool for Inclusion or Exclusion?*, on September 15, 2014. The workshop brought together stakeholders to discuss both the potential of big data to create opportunities for consumers and to exclude them from such opportunities. The Commission has synthesized the information from the workshop, a prior FTC seminar on

* This is an edited, reformatted and augmented version of a report issued by the Federal Trade Commission, January 2016.

alternative scoring products, and recent research to create this report. Though "big data" encompasses a wide range of analytics, this report addresses only the commercial use of big data consisting of consumer information and focuses on the impact of big data on low-income and underserved populations. Of course, big data also raises a host of other important policy issues, such as notice, choice, and security, among others. Those, however, are not the primary focus of this report.

As "little" data becomes "big" data, it goes through several phases. The life cycle of big data can be divided into four phases: (1) collection; (2) compilation and consolidation; (3) analysis; and (4) use. This report focuses on the fourth phase and discusses the benefits and risks created by the use of big data analytics; the consumer protection and equal opportunity laws that currently apply to big data; research in the field of big data; and lessons that companies should take from the research. Ultimately, this report is intended to educate businesses on important laws and research that are relevant to big data analytics and provide suggestions aimed at maximizing the benefits and minimizing its risks.

Big Data's Benefits and Risks

Big data analytics can provide numerous opportunities for improvements in society. In addition to more effectively matching products and services to consumers, big data can create opportunities for low-income and underserved communities. For example, workshop participants and others have noted that big data is helping target educational, credit, healthcare, and employment opportunities to low-income and underserved populations. At the same time, workshop participants and others have noted how potential inaccuracies and biases might lead to detrimental effects for low-income and underserved populations. For example, participants raised concerns that companies could use big data to exclude low-income and underserved communities from credit and employment opportunities.

Consumer Protection Laws Applicable to Big Data

Workshop participants and commenters discussed how companies can use big data in ways that provide benefits to themselves and society, while minimizing legal and ethical risks. Specifically, they noted that companies should have an understanding of the various laws, including the Fair Credit Reporting Act, equal opportunity laws, and the Federal Trade Commission Act, that may apply to big data practices.

1. Fair Credit Reporting Act

The Fair Credit Reporting Act ("FCRA") applies to companies, known as consumer reporting agencies or CRAs, that compile and sell consumer reports, which contain consumer information that is used or expected to be used for credit, employment, insurance, housing, or other similar decisions about consumers' eligibility for certain benefits and transactions. Among other things, CRAs must implement reasonable procedures to ensure maximum possible accuracy of consumer reports and provide consumers with access to their own information, along with the ability to correct any errors.

Traditionally, CRAs include credit bureaus, employment background screening companies, and other specialty companies that provide particularized services for making consumer eligibility decisions, such as check authorizations or tenant screenings. Some data brokers may also be considered CRAs subject to the FCRA, particularly if they advertise their services for eligibility purposes. The Commission has entered into a number of consent decrees with data brokers that advertise their consumer profiles for employment and tenant screening purposes. Companies that use consumer reports also have obligations under the FCRA.

Workshop panelists and commenters discussed a growing trend in big data, in which companies may be purchasing predictive analytics products for eligibility determinations. Under traditional credit scoring models, companies compare known credit characteristics of a consumer—such as past late payments—with historical data that shows how people with the same credit characteristics performed over time in meeting their credit obligations. Similarly, predictive analytics products may compare a known characteristic of a consumer to other consumers with the same characteristic to predict whether that consumer will meet his or her credit obligations. The difference is that, rather than comparing a traditional credit characteristic, such as debt payment history, these products may use non-traditional characteristics—such as a consumer's zip code, social media usage, or shopping history—to create a report about the creditworthiness of consumers that share those non-traditional characteristics, which a company can then use to make decisions about whether that consumer is a good credit risk. The standards applied to determine the applicability of the FCRA in a Commission enforcement action, however, are the same.

Only a fact-specific analysis will ultimately determine whether a practice is subject to or violates the FCRA, and as such, companies should be mindful of the law when using big data analytics to make FCRAcovered eligibility determinations.

2. Equal Opportunity Laws

Companies should also consider a number of federal equal opportunity laws, including the Equal Credit Opportunity Act ("ECOA"), Title VII of the Civil Rights Act of 1964, the Americans with Disabilities Act, the Age Discrimination in Employment Act, the Fair Housing Act, and the Genetic Information Nondiscrimination Act. These laws prohibit discrimination based on protected characteristics such as race, color, sex or gender, religion, age, disability status, national origin, marital status, and genetic information.

Of these laws, the FTC enforces ECOA, which prohibits credit discrimination on the basis of race, color, religion, national origin, sex, marital status, age, or because a person receives public assistance. To prove a violation of ECOA, plaintiffs typically must show "disparate treatment" or "disparate impact." Disparate treatment occurs when a creditor treats an applicant differently based on a protected characteristic. For example, a lender cannot refuse to lend to single persons or offer less favorable terms to them than married persons even if big data analytics show that single persons are less likely to repay loans than married persons. Disparate impact occurs when a company employs facially neutral policies or practices that have a disproportionate adverse effect or impact on a protected class, unless those practices or policies further a legitimate business need that cannot reasonably be achieved by means that are less disparate in their impact. For example, if a company makes credit decisions based on consumers' zip codes, such decisions may have a disparate impact on particular ethnic groups because certain ethnic groups are concentrated in particular zip codes. Accordingly, the practice may be a violation of ECOA. The analysis turns on whether the decisions have a disparate impact on a protected class and are not justified by a legitimate business necessity. Even if evidence shows the decisions are justified by a business necessity, if there is a less discriminatory alternative, the decisions may still violate ECOA.

Workshop discussions focused on whether advertising could implicate equal opportunity laws. In most cases, a company 's advertisement to a particular community for a credit offer that is open to all to apply is unlikely, by itself, to violate ECOA, absent disparate treatment or an unjustified disparate impact in subsequent lending. Nevertheless, companies should proceed with caution in this area. For advertisements relating to credit products, companies should look to Regulation B, which is the implementing regulation for ECOA. It prohibits creditors from making oral or written statements, in advertising or otherwise, to applicants or prospective applicants that would discourage on a prohibited basis a reasonable person from making or pursuing an application. With respect to prescreened solicitations, Regulation B also requires creditors to maintain records of the solicitations and the criteria used to select potential recipients. Advertising and marketing practices could impact a creditor's subsequent lending patterns and the terms and conditions of the credit received by borrowers, even if credit offers are open to all who apply. In some cases, the Department of Justice has cited a creditor's advertising choices as evidence of discrimination.

Ultimately, as with the FCRA, whether a practice is unlawful under equal opportunity laws is a case-specific inquiry, and as such, companies should proceed with caution when their practices could result in disparate treatment or have a demonstrable disparate impact based on protected characteristics.

3. The Federal Trade Commission Act

Workshop participants and commenters also discussed the applicability of Section 5 of the Federal Trade Commission Act ("FTC Act"), which prohibits unfair or deceptive acts or practices, to big data analytics. Companies engaging in big data analytics should consider whether they are violating any material promises to consumers—whether that promise is to refrain from sharing data with third parties, to provide consumers with choices about sharing, or to safeguard consumers' personal information—or whether they have failed to disclose material information to consumers. In addition, companies that maintain big data on consumers should take care to reasonably secure consumers' data. Further, at a minimum, companies must not sell their big data analytics products to customers if they know or have reason to know that those customers will use the products for fraudulent or discriminatory purposes. The inquiry will be fact-specific, and in every case, the test will be whether the company is offering or using big data analytics in a deceptive or unfair way.

Research on Big Data

Workshop participants, academics, and others also addressed the ways big data analytics could affect low-income, underserved populations, and protected groups. Some pointed to research that demonstrates that there is a potential for incorporating errors and biases at every stage—from choosing the data set used to make predictions, to defining the problem to be addressed through big data, to making decisions based on the results of big data analysis—which could lead to potential discriminatory harms. Others noted that these concerns are overstated or simply not new, and emphasized that rather than disadvantaging minorities, big data can create opportunities for low-income and underserved populations.

To maximize the benefits and limit the harms of big data, the Commission encourages companies to consider the following questions raised by research in this area:

- **How representative is your data set?** Companies should consider whether their data sets are missing information about certain populations, and take steps to address issues of underrepresentation and overrepresentation. For example, if a company targets services to consumers who communicate through an application or social media, they may be neglecting populations that are not as tech-savvy.
- **Does your data model account for biases?** Companies should consider whether biases are being incorporated at both the collection and analytics stages of big data's life cycle, and develop strategies to overcome them. For example, if a company has a big data algorithm that only considers applicants from "top tier" colleges to help them make hiring decisions, they may be incorporating previous biases in college admission decisions.
- **How accurate are your predictions based on big data?** Companies should remember that while big data is very good at detecting correlations, it does not explain which correlations are meaningful. A prime example that demonstrates the limitations of big data analytics is Google Flu Trends, a machine-learning algorithm for predicting the number of flu cases based on Google search terms. While, at first, the algorithms appeared to create accurate predictions of where the flu was more prevalent, it generated highly inaccurate estimates over time. This could be because the algorithm failed to take into account certain variables. For example, the algorithm may not have taken into account that people would be more likely to search for flu-related terms if the local news ran a story on a flu outbreak, even if the outbreak occurred halfway around the world.

- **Does your reliance on big data raise ethical or fairness concerns?** Companies should assess the factors that go into an analytics model and balance the predictive value of the model with fairness considerations. For example, one company determined that employees who live closer to their jobs stay at these jobs longer than those who live farther away. However, another company decided to exclude this factor from its hiring algorithm because of concerns about racial discrimination, particularly since different neighborhoods can have different racial compositions.

The Commission encourages companies to apply big data analytics in ways that provide benefits and opportunities to consumers, while avoiding pitfalls that may violate consumer protection or equal opportunity laws, or detract from core values of inclusion and fairness. For its part, the Commission will continue to monitor areas where big data practices could violate existing laws, including the FTC Act, the FCRA, and ECOA, and will bring enforcement actions where appropriate. The Commission will also continue to examine and raise awareness about big data practices that could have a detrimental impact on low-income and underserved populations, and promote the use of big data that has a positive impact on such populations.

I. INTRODUCTION

The era of big data has arrived. While companies historically have collected and used information about their customer interactions to help improve their operations, the expanding use of online technologies has greatly increased the amount of consumer data that flows throughout the economy. In many cases, when consumers engage digitally—whether by shopping, visiting websites, paying bills, connecting with family and friends through social media, using mobile applications, or using connected devices, such as fitness trackers or smart televisions—companies collect information about their choices, experiences, and individual characteristics. The analysis of this consumer information is often valuable to companies and to consumers, as it provides insights into market-wide tastes and emerging trends, which can guide the development of new products and services. It is also valuable to predict the preferences of specific individuals, help tailor services, and guide individualized marketing of products and services.

The term "big data" refers to a confluence of factors, including the nearly ubiquitous collection of consumer data from a variety of sources, the plummeting cost of data storage, and powerful new capabilities to analyze data to draw connections and make inferences and predictions.[1]

A common framework for characterizing big data relies on the "three Vs," the volume, velocity, and variety of data, each of which is growing at a rapid rate as technological advances permit the analysis and use of this data in ways that were not possible previously.[2] Volume refers to the vast quantity of data that can be gathered and analyzed effectively. The costs of collecting and storing data continue to drop dramatically. And the ability to access millions of data points increases the predictive power of consumer data analysis.

Velocity is the speed with which companies can accumulate, analyze, and use new data. Technological improvements allow companies to harness the predictive power of data more quickly than ever before, sometimes instantaneously.[3]

Variety means the breadth of data that companies can analyze effectively. Companies can now combine very different, once unlinked, kinds of data—either on their own or through data brokers or analytics firms—to infer consumer preferences and predict consumer behavior, for example.

Together, the three Vs allow for more robust research and correlation. Previously, finding a representative data sample sufficient to produce statistically significant results could be very difficult and expensive. Today, the present scope and scale of data collection enables cost-effective, substantial research of even obscure or mundane topics (e.g., the amount of foot traffic in a park at different times of day).

Big data can produce tremendous benefits for society, such as advances in medicine, education, health, and transportation, and in many instances, without using consumers' personally identifiable information. Big data also can allow companies to improve their offerings, provide consumers with personalized goods and services, and match consumers with products they are likely to be interested in. At the same time, advocates, academics, and others have raised concerns about whether certain uses of big data analytics may harm consumers. For example, if big data analytics incorrectly predicts that particular consumers are not likely to respond to prime credit offers, certain types of educational opportunities, or job openings requiring a college degree, companies may miss a chance to reach individuals that desire this information. In addition, if big data analytics incorrectly predicts that particular consumers are not good candidates for prime credit offers, educational opportunities, or certain lucrative jobs, such educational opportunities, employment, and credit may never be offered to these consumers. Some fear that such incorrect predictions could perpetuate existing disparities.

To examine these issues, the Federal Trade Commission ("FTC" or "the Commission") held a public workshop, *Big Data: A Tool for Inclusion or Exclusion?*, on September 15, 2014.[4] In particular, the workshop explored the potential impact of big data on low-income and underserved populations. The workshop brought together academics, government representatives, consumer advocates, industry representatives, legal practitioners, and others to discuss the potential of big data to create opportunities for consumers or exclude them from such opportunities. The workshop consisted of four panels addressing the following topics: (1) current uses of big data; (2) potential uses of big data; (3) the application of equal opportunity and consumer protection laws to big data; and (4) best practices to enhance consumer protection in the use of big data. The Commission also received sixty-five public comments on these issues from private citizens, industry representatives, trade groups, consumer and privacy advocates, think tanks, and academics.

The Commission has synthesized the discussions and comments from the workshop—along with the record from a prior FTC seminar on alternative scoring products[5] and recent research—to create this report, which focuses on the impact of big data on low-income and underserved populations. The report is divided into four sections. First, the report describes the "life cycle" of big data and how "little" data turns into big data. Second, it discusses some of the benefits and risks created by the use of big data. Third, it describes some of the consumer protection laws that currently apply to big data. Finally, it discusses certain research in the field of big data and lessons that companies should take from the research in order to help them maximize the benefits of big data while mitigating risks. Importantly, though the term "big data" encompasses a wide range of analytics, this report addresses only the commercial use of big data consisting of consumer information.[6]

II. Life Cycle of Big Data

The life cycle of big data can be divided into four phases: (1) collection; (2) compilation and consolidation; (3) data mining and analytics; and (4) use.[7]

As to the first step, not all data starts as big data. Rather, companies collect bits of data from a variety of sources.[8] For example, as consumers browse the web or shop online, companies can track and link their activities. Sometimes consumers log into services or identify themselves when they make a purchase. Other times, techniques such as tracking cookies,[9] browser or device fingerprinting,[10] and even history sniffing[11] identify who consumers are, what they do, and where they go. In the mobile environment, companies track and link consumers' activities across applications as another method of gathering information about their habits and preferences. More broadly, cross-device tracking offers the ability to interact with the same consumer across her desktop, laptop, tablet, wearable, and smartphone, using both online and offline information.[12] Companies also are gathering data about consumers across the Internet of Things—the millions of Internet-connected devices that are in the market.[13] Finally, data collection occurs offline as well, for example, through loyalty programs, warranty cards, surveys, sweepstakes entries, and even credit card purchases.[14]

After collection, the next step in the life cycle of big data is compilation and consolidation. Commercial entities that compile data include online ad networks, social media companies, and large banks or retailers.[15] One important category of commercial entities that compile and consolidate data is data brokers. They combine data from disparate sources to build profiles about individual consumers. Indeed, some data brokers store billions of data elements on nearly every U.S. consumer.[16]

The third step is data analytics. One form of analytics is descriptive—the objective is to uncover and summarize patterns or features that exist in data sets.[17] By contrast, predictive data analytics refers to the use of statistical models to generate new data.[18] Developing and testing the models that find patterns and make predictions can require the collection and use of copious amounts of data.[19] In a market context, a common purpose of big data analytics is to draw inferences about consumers' likely choices. Companies may decide to adopt big data analytics to better understand consumers, potentially by using data to attribute to an individual the qualities of those who appear statistically similar, e.g., those who have made similar decisions in similar situations in the past. Thus, a retail firm might use data on its customers' past purchases, web searches, shopping habits, and prices paid to create a statistical model of consumers' purchases at different prices. With that model, the retailer could then compare a prospective consumer's characteristics or past purchases, web searches, and location information to predict how likely the consumer is to purchase a product at various price points.

The final step in the life cycle of big data is use. The Commission's May 2014 report entitled *Data Brokers: A Call for Transparency and Accountability* focused on the first three steps in the life cycle of big data within that industry—collection, compilation, and analytics.[20] It discussed how information gathered for one purpose (e.g., paying for goods and services) could be compiled and analyzed for other purposes, such as for marketing or risk mitigation. In contrast, this report focuses on certain *uses* of big data. It examines the question of how companies use big data to help consumers and the steps they can take to avoid inadvertently harming consumers through big data analytics.

III. BIG DATA'S BENEFITS AND RISKS

Companies have been analyzing data from their own customer interactions on a smaller scale for many years, but the era of big data is still in its infancy.[21] As a result, mining large data sets to find useful, non-obvious patterns is a relatively new but growing practice in marketing, fraud prevention, human resources, and a variety of other fields. Companies are still learning how to deal with big data and unlock its potential while avoiding unintended or unforeseen consequences.[22]

Appropriately employing big data algorithms on data of sufficient quality can provide numerous opportunities for improvements in society. In addition to the market-wide benefits of more efficiently matching products and services to consumers, big data can create opportunities for low-income and underserved communities.[23] Workshop participants and others have noted that big data is already being used to:

- **Increase educational attainment for individual students.** Educational institutions have used big data techniques to identify students for advanced classes who would otherwise not have been eligible for such classes based on teacher recommendations alone.[24] These institutions have also used big data techniques to help identify students who are at risk of dropping out and in need of early intervention strategies.[25] Similarly, organizations have used big data analytics to demonstrate how certain disciplinary practices, such as school suspensions, affect African-American students far more than Caucasian students, thereby partly explaining the large discrepancy between the graduation rates of these two groups.[26]
- **Provide access to credit using non-traditional methods.** Companies have used big data to provide alternative ways to score populations that were previously deemed unscorable.[27] For example, LexisNexis

has created an alternative credit score called RiskView.[28] This product relies on traditional public record information, such as foreclosures and bankruptcies, but it also includes educational history, professional licensure data, and personal property ownership data. Thus, consumers who may not have access to traditional credit, but, for instance, have a professional license, pay rent on time, or own a car, may be given better access to credit than they otherwise would have.[29] Furthermore, big data algorithms could help reveal underlying disparities in traditional credit markets and help companies serve creditworthy consumers from any background.[30]

- **Provide healthcare tailored to individual patients' characteristics.** Organizations have used big data to predict life expectancy, genetic predisposition to disease, likelihood of hospital readmission, and likelihood of adherence to a treatment plan in order to tailor medical treatment to an individual's characteristics.[31] This, in turn, has helped healthcare providers avoid one-size-fits-all treatments and lower overall healthcare costs by reducing readmissions.[32] Ultimately, data sets with richer and more complete data should allow medical practitioners more effectively to perform "precision medicine," an approach for disease treatment and prevention that considers individual variability in genes, environment, and lifestyle.[33]
- **Provide specialized healthcare to underserved communities.** IBM, for example, has worked with hospitals to develop an Oncology Diagnosis and Treatment Advisor. This system synthesizes vast amounts of data from textbooks, guidelines, journal articles, and clinical trials to help physicians make diagnoses and identify treatment options for cancer patients. In rural and low-income areas, where there is a shortage of specialty providers, IBM's Oncology Diagnosis and Treatment Advisor can provide underserved communities with better access to cancer care and lower costs.[34]
- **Increase equal access to employment.** Companies have used big data to help promote a more diverse workforce.[35] Google, for example, recognized that its traditional hiring process was resulting in a homogenous work force. Through analytics, Google identified issues with its hiring process, which included an emphasis on academic grade point averages and "brainteaser" questions during interviews. Google then modified its interview practices and began asking more structured behavioral questions (e.g., how would you

handle the following situation?).[36] This new approach helped ensure that potential interviewer biases had less effect on hiring decisions.

While recognizing these potential benefits, some researchers and others have expressed concern that the use of big data analytics to make predictions may exclude certain populations from the benefits society and markets have to offer. This concern takes several forms. First, some workshop participants and commenters expressed concerns about the quality of data, including its accuracy, completeness, and representativeness.[37] Another concern is that there are uncorrected biases in the underlying consumer data.[38] For example, one academic has argued that hidden biases in the collection, analysis, and interpretation stages present considerable risks.[39] If the process that generated the underlying data reflects biases in favor of or against certain types of individuals, then some statistical relationships revealed by that data could perpetuate those biases. When not recognized and addressed, poor data quality can lead to inaccurate predictions, which in turn can lead to companies erroneously denying consumers offers or benefits. Although the use of inaccurate or biased data and analysis to justify decisions that have harmed certain populations is not new,[40] some commenters worry that big data analytics may lead to wider propagation of the problem and make it more difficult for the company using such data to identify the source of discriminatory effects and address it.[41]

Second, while big data may be highly effective in showing correlations, it is axiomatic that correlation is not causation.[42] Indeed, with large enough data sets, one can generally find some meaningless correlations. For example, in eighteen out of the past twenty U.S. Presidential elections, if the Washington, D.C. professional football team won its last home game before the election, the incumbent's party continued to hold the presidency; if the team lost that last home game, the out-of-office party unseated the incumbent party.[43] Other examples of spurious correlations abound.[44] If companies use correlations to make decisions about people without understanding the underlying reasons for the correlations, those decisions might be faulty and could lead to unintended consequences or harm for consumers and companies.

Ultimately, all of these concerns feed into the larger concern about whether big data may be used to categorize consumers in ways that can result in exclusion of certain populations. Workshop participants and others have noted how potential inaccuracies and biases might lead to detrimental effects for low-income and underserved populations.[45] According to these commenters, particular uses of big data may:

- **Result in more individuals mistakenly being denied opportunities based on the actions of others.** Participants raised concerns that big data can lead to decision-making based on the actions of others with whom consumers share some characteristics.[46] Several commenters explained that some credit card companies have lowered a customer's credit limit, not based on the customer's payment history, but rather based on analysis of other customers with a poor repayment history that had shopped at the same establishments where the customer had shopped.[47] Indeed, one credit card company settled FTC allegations that it failed to disclose its practice of rating consumers as having a greater credit risk because they used their cards to pay for marriage counseling, therapy, or tire-repair services, based on its experiences with other consumers and their repayment histories.[48] Using this type of a statistical model might reduce the cost of credit for some individuals, but may also result in some creditworthy consumers being denied or charged more for credit than they might otherwise have been charged.[49]
- **Create or reinforce existing disparities.** Participants raised concerns that when big data is used to target ads, particularly for financial products, low-income consumers who may otherwise be eligible for better offers may never receive them.[50]
- **Expose sensitive information.** Participants also raised concerns about the potential exposure of characteristics that people may view as sensitive.[51] For example, one study combined data on Facebook "Likes" and limited survey information to determine that researchers could accurately predict a male user's sexual orientation 88 percent of the time; a user's ethnic origin 95 percent of time; and whether a user was Christian or Muslim (82 percent), a Democrat or Republican (85 percent), or used alcohol, drugs, or cigarettes (between 65 percent and 75 percent).[52]
- **Assist in the targeting of vulnerable consumers for fraud.** Unscrupulous companies can use big data to offer misleading offers or scams to the most vulnerable prospects.[53] According to public reports, unscrupulous companies can obtain lists of people who reply to sweepstakes offers and thus are more likely to respond to enticements, as well as lists of "suffering seniors" who are identified as having Alzheimer's or similar maladies.[54] Big data analytics allows companies to more easily and accurately identify such vulnerable prospects.

- **Create new justifications for exclusion.** Big data analytics may give companies new ways to attempt to justify their exclusion of certain populations from particular opportunities. For example, one big data analytics study showed that "people who fill out online job applications using browsers that did not come with the computer . . . but had to be deliberately installed (like Firefox or Google's Chrome) perform better and change jobs less often."[55] If an employer were to use this correlation to refrain from hiring people who used a particular browser, they could be excluding qualified applicants for reasons unrelated to the job at issue.
- **Result in higher-priced goods and services for lower income communities.** Some commentators have raised concerns about potential effects on prices on lower income communities.[56] For example, research has shown that online companies may charge consumers in different zip codes different prices for standard office products.[57] If such pricing results in consumers in poorer neighborhoods having to pay more for online products than consumers in affluent communities, where there is more competition from brick-and-mortar stores, these poorer communities would not realize the full competition benefit of online shopping.[58]
- **Weaken the effectiveness of consumer choice.** Some researchers have argued that, even when companies offer consumers choices about data collection, the companies may still use big data to draw inferences about consumers who choose to restrict the collection of their data.[59] Indeed, using data from consumers who opt in or decline to opt out, big data algorithms can still be employed to infer information about similarly-situated individuals who chose not to share their data.[60]

As these examples show, big data offers companies the opportunity to facilitate inclusion or exclusion. Companies can use big data to advance education, credit, and employment opportunities for low-income communities or to exclude them from these opportunities. They can use big data to target products to those who are most interested or to target products in ways that could exclude certain populations. The remainder of this report is intended to guide companies on some of the laws that may apply when using big data, raise awareness about the ethical implications of using big data, and to highlight potential biases that companies should consider as they use big data.

IV. Considerations for Companies in Using Big Data

The challenge for companies is not *whether* they should use big data; indeed, the reality of today's marketplace is that big data now fuels the creation of innovative products and systems that consumers and companies quickly are coming to rely upon and expect. Rather, the challenge is *how* companies can use big data in a way that benefits them and society, while minimizing legal and ethical risks.

In assessing risks, companies should first have an understanding of the laws that may apply to big data practices. Second, they should be aware of important research in the field of big data aimed at identifying potential biases and inaccuracies. This section provides a starting point for companies using big data analytics. It is not intended to provide an exhaustive list of considerations. Rather, companies using big data should consider the issues raised in this report as they engage in big data practices and build on the questions posed to examine the legal, privacy, and ethical implications of their work.

A. Potentially Applicable Laws

The following section describes some of the laws that may apply to big data practices.[61] Although the laws discussed do not address every potential misuse, as noted above, this report is not intended to identify legal or policy gaps; rather, it attempts to guide companies on laws, such as the Fair Credit Reporting Act, equal opportunity laws, and the Federal Trade Commission Act, that may apply to big data practices.[62]

1. The Fair Credit Reporting Act

The FTC has the authority to enforce compliance with the Fair Credit Reporting Act ("FCRA").[63] The FCRA applies to companies, known as consumer reporting agencies or CRAs, that compile and sell consumer reports, which contain consumer information that is used or expected to be used for credit, employment, insurance, housing, or other similar decisions about consumers' eligibility for certain benefits and transactions.[64] Among other things, CRAs must implement reasonable procedures to ensure maximum possible accuracy of consumer reports[65] and provide consumers with access to their own information, along with the ability to correct any errors.[66] CRAs can only provide consumer reports to those entities that will use them for certain specified permissible purposes, such as for credit, employment, insurance, or housing eligibility determinations.[67]

Traditionally, CRAs include credit bureaus, employment background screening companies, and other specialty companies that provide particularized services for making consumer eligibility decisions, such as check authorizations or tenant screenings. Some data brokers that compile non-traditional information, including social media information, may also be considered CRAs subject to the FCRA, as demonstrated by the Commission's enforcement actions. For example, the Commission entered into a consent decree with online data broker Spokeo to resolve allegations that the company violated the FCRA.[68] As set forth in the FTC's complaint, Spokeo assembled personal information from hundreds of online and offline data sources, including social networks, and merged that data to create detailed personal profiles, including name, address, age range, hobbies, ethnicity, and religion, and marketed these profiles for use by human resources departments in making hiring decisions.[69] Based on the allegations that the company marketed consumer profiles specifically for employment purposes, the Commission charged that Spokeo was subject to, but had failed to comply with, the FCRA. Accordingly, the FTC entered into a consent decree that required Spokeo to pay $800,000 in civil penalties.

In another matter, the Commission alleged that the data broker Instant Checkmate advertised potential uses of its consumer data for employment and tenant screening purposes, both through its website and through blog posts, but did not comply with the FCRA.[70] According to the complaint, the company used a Google AdWords campaign to display ads for its services that would appear in search results when consumers sought background checks on "nannies," "babysitters," "maids," and "housekeepers." Thus, the Commission alleged that the company was subject to the FCRA, entered into a consent order to ensure future compliance, and obtained $550,000 in civil penalties.[71] In both *Spokeo* and *Instant Checkmate*, the companies included a disclaimer on their websites stating that they were not CRAs and that users could not use their data for eligibility purposes. These disclaimers were not effective in insulating the companies from FTC enforcement. As these cases demonstrate, the scope of the FCRA extends beyond traditional credit bureaus.

Companies that use consumer reports also have obligations under the FCRA. They must, among other things, provide consumers with "adverse action" notices if the companies use the consumer report information to deny credit, insurance, employment, housing, or certain other covered benefits.[72] Similarly, companies that use consumer reports must provide "risk-based pricing" notices if they charge consumers more to obtain credit or insurance based on consumer report information.[73] The purpose of both types of notices is to enable consumers to check their consumer reports and correct any inaccuracies.[74] The Commission has brought actions against various companies for violation of these provisions.[75] For example, in 2013, the FTC brought an action against Time Warner Cable because it used a consumer report to determine whether to require deposits on consumers' cable bills.[76] The complaint alleged that consumers who were charged a deposit should have received a risk-based pricing notice informing them that the charge was based on information in their consumer report. The consent order barred Time Warner Cable from future violations of the Risk-Based Pricing Rule and required the company to pay $1.9 million in civil penalties.[77] In addition, in 2015, the Commission brought an action against Sprint alleging that the company failed to give proper risk-based pricing notices to consumers who were placed in a program for customers with lower credit scores and charged an extra monthly fee.[78] The consent order requires Sprint to pay a $2.95 million penalty and to give timely notice to consumers placed in such a program.[79]

The FCRA, however, does not apply to companies when they use data derived from their own relationship with their customers for purposes of making decisions about them.[80] But if an unaffiliated firm regularly evaluates companies' own data and provides the evaluations to the companies for eligibility determinations, the unaffiliated firm would likely be acting as a CRA, each company would likely be a user of consumer reports, and all of these entities would be subject to Commission enforcement under the FCRA.

Workshop panelists and commenters discussed a growing trend in big data, in which companies may be purchasing predictive analytics products for eligibility determinations.[81] Under traditional credit scoring models, companies compare known credit characteristics of a consumer—such as past late payments—with historical data that shows how people with the same credit characteristics performed over time in meeting their credit obligations. Similarly, predictive analytics products may compare a known characteristic of a consumer to other consumers with the same characteristic to predict whether that consumer will meet his or her credit obligations. The difference is that, rather than comparing a traditional credit characteristic, such as debt payment history, these products may use non-traditional characteristics—such as a consumer's zip code, social media usage, or shopping history—to create a report about the creditworthiness of consumers that share those non-traditional characteristics, which a company can then use to make decisions about whether that consumer is a good credit risk.[82] The standards applied to determine the applicability of the FCRA, however, are the same.

In exercising its enforcement authority, the Commission looks to the FCRA's definition of a "consumer report." The FCRA defines a consumer report as a communication from a CRA (1) bearing on a consumer's personal characteristics or mode of living[83] (2) that "is used or expected to be used. . . for the purpose of serving as a factor in establishing *the* consumer's eligibility."[84] Under this definition, the communication must be prepared or provided to others to make an eligibility determination about a particular consumer.

Suppose a company asks a consumer to provide her zip code and information about her social media and shopping behavior on a credit application, strips the consumer's identifying information, and sends the application to an analytics firm. The firm then analyzes the creditworthiness of people in the same zip code with similar social media and shopping behaviors as the consumer and provides that analysis—be it, for example, in the form of a score, a grade, or a recommendation—to the company, knowing that it is to be used for a credit decision. Because the company is using information about the consumer to generate an analysis of a group that shares some characteristics with the consumer and then is using that analysis to make a decision about the consumer, the Commission would likely regard the analysis to be a consumer report, and FCRA requirements and protections would likely apply.[85]

In contrast, if a company uses an analytics firm's report simply to inform its general policies, then the Commission would likely not regard the report to be a consumer report under the FCRA because such a general report does not relate to a particular consumer. For example, if an analytics firm's report simply provides an "aggregate credit score" for every zip code in the United States, a company finds the report through a search engine, and the company uses the report to inform its policies, the Commission would likely not consider the analytics firm's report to be a consumer report or the analytics firm to be a CRA.[86]

As noted above, it is well settled under the FCRA that when a company denies a consumer credit, or charges a higher price for credit, based on information from a CRA, the company must provide the consumer with an adverse action notice. But a creditor may still have obligations under the FCRA even in cases where the creditor obtains information from a company other than a CRA. Section 615(b) of the FCRA provides that, when a company denies a consumer credit, or charges a higher price for credit, based on information from a person *other than a CRA*, the consumer may request, in writing, that the company disclose to him or her the nature of the information leading to the denial or increase in charge.[87] Thus, continuing with the example above, even if a store finds a general analytics company report through a search engine and then uses the report to inform its credit granting policies, the store would have to disclose the nature of the report upon the consumer's request if the consumer's application for credit is denied or the charge for such credit is increased as a result of reliance on the report.

Only a fact-specific analysis will ultimately determine whether a practice is subject to or violates the FCRA, and as such, companies should be mindful of the law when using big data analytics to make FCRA-covered eligibility determinations.

2. Equal Opportunity Laws

When engaging in big data analytics, companies should also consider federal equal opportunity laws, including the Equal Credit Opportunity Act ("ECOA"),[88] Title VII of the Civil Rights Act of 1964,[89] the Americans with Disabilities Act,[90] the Age Discrimination in Employment Act ("ADEA"),[91] the Fair Housing Act ("FHA"),[92] and the Genetic Information Nondiscrimination Act ("GINA").[93] These laws prohibit discrimination based on protected characteristics such as race, color, sex or gender, religion, age, disability status, national origin, marital status, and genetic information.[94]

Companies should review these laws and take steps to ensure their use of big data analytics complies with the discrimination prohibitions that may apply. This section discusses some examples of relevant considerations under these laws related to employment and credit, as highlighted in the workshop.

To prove a violation of federal equal credit or employment opportunity laws, plaintiffs typically must show "disparate treatment" or "disparate impact."[95] Disparate treatment occurs when an entity, such as a creditor or employer, treats an applicant differently based on a protected characteristic such as race or national origin.[96] Systemic disparate treatment occurs when an entity engages in a pattern or practice of differential treatment on a prohibited basis.[97] In some cases, the unlawful differential treatment could be based on big data analytics.[98] For example, an employer may not disfavor a particular protected group because big data analytics show that members of this protected group are more likely to quit their jobs within a five-year period.[99] Similarly, a lender cannot refuse to lend to single persons or offer less favorable terms to them than married persons even if big data analytics show that single persons are less likely to repay loans than married persons. Evidence of such violations could include direct evidence of the reasons for the company's choices, or circumstantial evidence, such as significant statistical disparities in outcomes for protected groups that are unexplained by neutral factors.

Practices that have a "disparate impact" on protected classes may also violate equal credit or employment opportunity laws.[100] While specific disparate impact standards vary depending on the applicable law, in general, disparate impact occurs when a company employs facially neutral policies or practices that have a disproportionate adverse effect or impact on a protected class,[101] unless those practices or policies further a legitimate business need[102] that cannot reasonably be achieved by means that have less disparate an impact.[103]

Disparate impact analysis has important implications for big data.[104] Under such an analysis, a company that avoids, for example, expressly screening job applicants based on gender and instead uses big data analytics to screen job applicants in a way that has a disparate impact on women may still be subject to certain equal employment opportunity laws, if the screening does not serve a legitimate business need or if the need can reasonably be achieved by another means with a smaller disparate impact.[105] Likewise, if a company makes credit decisions based on zip codes, it may be violating ECOA if the decisions have a disparate impact on a protected class and are not justified by a legitimate business necessity.[106] Even if evidence shows the decisions are justified by a business necessity, if there is a less discriminatory alternative, the decisions may still violate ECOA.[107]

The FTC's enforcement actions include dozens of consent orders resolving alleged violations of ECOA. Some of these cases have been based on a disparate treatment theory. For example, ECOA prohibits discrimination against applicants who are receiving public assistance.[108] The Commission has brought cases against lenders that allegedly excluded public assistance income in deciding whether to extend credit.[109] Likewise, ECOA prohibits discounting or refusing to consider income on the basis of marital status.[110] The FTC has brought cases against lenders that allegedly failed to aggregate the income of unmarried joint applicants, while combining incomes for applicants who were married.[111]

The FTC also has alleged discrimination under a disparate impact legal standard under ECOA. For example, the FTC settled two cases alleging that lenders failed to appropriately monitor loan officers whose mortgage loans resulted in minority applicants' being charged higher prices than non-Latino white applicants.[112] The Commission alleged that the statistically significant pricing disparities could not be explained by any legitimate underwriting risk factors or credit characteristics of the applicants.

Workshop discussions focused in particular on whether advertising could implicate equal opportunity laws.[113] For example, suppose big data analytics show that single women are more likely to apply for subprime credit products. Would targeting advertisements for these products to single women violate ECOA?[114] Certainly, prohibiting single women from applying for a prime credit card based on their marital status would violate ECOA.[115] But what if a single woman would qualify for the prime product, but because of big data analytics, the subprime product with a higher interest rate is the only one advertised to her?

In most cases, a company's advertisement to a particular community for a credit offer that is open to all to apply is unlikely, by itself, to violate ECOA, absent disparate treatment or an unjustified disparate impact in subsequent lending.[116] Nevertheless, companies should proceed with caution in this area. In credit transactions,[117] Regulation B, which is the implementing regulation for ECOA, prohibits creditors[118] from making oral or written statements, in advertising or otherwise, to applicants or prospective applicants that would discourage on a prohibited basis a reasonable person from making or pursuing an application.[119] With respect to prescreened solicitations, Regulation B also requires creditors to maintain records of the solicitations and the criteria used to select potential recipients.[120] Advertising and marketing practices could impact a creditor's subsequent lending patterns and the terms and conditions of the credit received by borrowers, even if credit offers are open to all who apply. In some cases, the DOJ has cited a creditor's advertising choices as evidence of discrimination.[121]

Ultimately, as with the FCRA, the question of whether a practice is unlawful under equal opportunity laws is a case-specific inquiry. Accordingly, companies should proceed with caution if their practices could suggest disparate treatment or have a demonstrable disparate impact based on protected characteristics.

3. The Federal Trade Commission Act

Section 5 of the Federal Trade Commission Act ("Section 5") prohibits unfair or deceptive acts or practices in or affecting commerce.[122] Unlike the FCRA or equal opportunity laws, Section 5 is not confined to particular market sectors but is generally applicable to most companies acting in commerce.[123] Under Section 5, an act or practice is *deceptive* if it involves a material statement or omission that is likely to mislead a consumer acting reasonably under the circumstances.[124] For example, if a company violates a material promise—whether that promise is to refrain from sharing data with third parties,[125] to provide consumers choices about sharing,[126] or to safeguard consumers' personal information[127]—it will likely be engaged in a deceptive practice under Section 5.

Likewise, a failure to disclose material information may violate Section 5. In *CompuCredit*, for instance, the FTC included an allegation in the complaint that although a credit card marketing company touted the ability of consumers to use the card for cash advances, it deceptively failed to disclose that, based on a behavioral scoring model, consumers' credit lines would be reduced if they used their cards for such cash advances or if they used their cards for certain types of transactions, including marriage counseling, bars and nightclubs, pawn shops, and massage parlors.[128] Among other things, the settlement prohibits CompuCredit from making misrepresentations to consumers in the marketing of credit cards, including misrepresentations about the amount of available credit.[129]

In addition, under Section 5, an act or practice is *unfair* if it is likely to cause substantial consumer injury, the injury is not reasonably avoidable by consumers, and the injury is not outweighed by benefits to consumers or competition.[130] One example of a potentially unfair practice is the failure to reasonably secure consumers' data where that failure is likely to cause substantial injury.[131] Companies that maintain big data on consumers should take care to reasonably secure that data commensurate with the amount and sensitivity of the data at issue, the size and complexity of the company's operations, and the cost of available security measures.[132] For example, a company that maintains Social Security numbers or medical information about individual consumers should have particularly robust security measures as compared to a company that maintains consumers' names only.

Another example of a potentially unfair practice that the Commission has challenged is the sale of data to customers that a company knows or has reason to know will use the data for fraudulent purposes. The Commission's cases against Sequoia One and ChoicePoint are instructive in this regard. In *Sequoia One*, the FTC's complaint alleges that the company sold the personal information of financially distressed payday loan applicants—including Social Security numbers, financial account numbers, and bank routing numbers—to non-lender third-parties and one of these third parties used the information to withdraw millions of dollars from consumers' accounts without their authorization.[133]

In *ChoicePoint*, the Commission alleged that the company sold the personal information of more than 163,000 consumers to identity thieves posing as legitimate subscribers, despite obvious red flags that should have alerted the company to the potential fraud.[134] As these cases show, at a minimum, companies must not sell their big data analytics products to customers if they know or have reason to know that those customers will use the products for fraudulent purposes.

Section 5 may also apply under similar circumstances if products are sold to customers that use the products for discriminatory purposes.[135] The inquiry will be fact-specific, and in every case, the test will be whether the company is offering or using big data analytics in a deceptive or unfair way.

Questions for Legal Compliance

In light of these existing laws, companies already using or considering engaging in big data analytics should, among other things, consider the following:

- If you compile big data for others who will use it for eligibility decisions (such as credit, employment, insurance, housing, government benefits, and the like), are you complying with the accuracy and privacy provisions of the FCRA? FCRA requirements include requirements to (1) have reasonable procedures in place to ensure the maximum possible accuracy of the information you provide, (2) provide notices to users of your reports, (3) allow consumers to access information you have about them, and (4) allow consumers to correct inaccuracies.
- If you receive big data products from another entity that you will use for eligibility decisions, are you complying with the provisions applicable to users of consumer reports? For example, the FCRA requires that entities that use this information for employment purposes certify that they have a "permissible purpose" to obtain it, certify that they will not use it in a way that violates equal opportunity laws, provide pre-adverse action notice to consumers, and thereafter provide adverse action notices to those same consumers.

- If you are a creditor using big data analytics in a credit transaction, are you complying with the requirement to provide statements of specific reasons for adverse action under ECOA? Are you complying with ECOA requirements related to requests for information and record retention?
- If you use big data analytics in a way that might adversely affect people in their ability to obtain credit, housing, or employment:
  - Are you treating people differently based on a prohibited basis, such as race or national origin?
  - Do your policies, practices, or decisions have an adverse effect or impact on a member of a protected class, and if they do, are they justified by a legitimate business need that cannot reasonably be achieved by means that are less disparate in their impact?
- Are you honoring promises you make to consumers and providing consumers material information about your data practices?
- Are you maintaining reasonable security over consumer data?
- Are you undertaking reasonable measures to know the purposes for which your customers are using your data?
  - If you know that your customer will use your big data products to commit fraud, do not sell your products to that customer. If you have reason to believe that your data will be used to commit fraud, ask more specific questions about how your data will be used.
  - If you know that your customer will use your big data products for discriminatory purposes, do not sell your products to that customer. If you have reason to believe that your data will be used for discriminatory purposes, ask more specific questions about how your data will be used.

B. Special Policy Considerations Raised by Big Data Research

Workshop and seminar panelists, academics, and others have also engaged in important research in the field of big data.[136] Some of this research has focused on how big data analytics could negatively affect low-income and underserved populations.[137] Researchers note there is a potential for incorporating errors and biases at every stage, from choosing the data set used to make predictions, to defining the problem to be addressed through big data, to making decisions based on the results of big data analysis.[138] While having the ability to use more data can increase the power of the analysis, simply adding more data does not necessarily correct inaccuracies or remove biases. In addition, the complexity of the data and statistical models can make it difficult for analysts to fully understand and explain the underlying model or its results. Even when data analysts are very careful, the results of their analysis may affect particular sets of individuals differently because their models may use variables that turn out to operate no differently than proxies for protected classes.[139] Or researchers may simply lack information that would allow them to determine whether their results have such effects. Numerous researchers and commenters discuss how big data could be used in the future to the disadvantage of low-income and underserved communities and adversely affect consumers on the basis of legally protected characteristics in hiring, housing, lending, and other processes.[140]

On the other hand, several stakeholders argue that these concerns are overstated.[141] Some emphasize that, to the extent the various steps in data mining lead to disparate impact, these issues are not new—they are inherent in any statistical analysis.[142] Other writers note that, rather than disadvantaging minorities in the hiring process, big data can help to create "a labor market that's fairer to people at every stage of their careers."[143] For example, companies can use big data algorithms to find employees from within underrepresented segments of the population.[144] They can also use big data to identify biases so that they can choose candidates based on merit rather than using mechanisms that depend on the reviewers' biases.[145] Furthermore, as other stakeholders have noted, big data can help "reduce the rate of 'false positive' cases that potentially make disparate treatment a problem"[146] and can help identify whether correlations exist between prices and variables such as race, gender or ethnicity.[147] These stakeholders do not argue that we should ignore discrimination where it occurs; rather, they argue that we should recognize the potential benefits of big data to reduce discriminatory harm.

Collectively, this research suggests that big data offers both new potential discriminatory harms and new potential solutions to discriminatory harms. To maximize the benefits and limit the harms, companies should consider the questions raised by research in this area. These questions include the following:

1. How Representative Is Your Data Set?

Workshop participants and researchers note that the data sets, on which all big data analysis relies, may be missing information about certain populations, e.g., individuals who are more careful about revealing information about themselves, who are less involved in the formal economy, who have unequal access or less fluency in technology resulting in a digital divide[148] or data desert,[149] or whose behaviors are simply not observed because they are believed to be less profitable constituencies.[150]

Recent examples demonstrate the impact of missing information about particular populations on data analytics. For example, Hurricane Sandy generated more than twenty million tweets between October 27 and November 1, 2012.[151] If organizations were to use this data to determine where services should be deployed, the people who needed services the most may not have received them. The greatest number of tweets about Hurricane Sandy came from Manhattan, creating the illusion that Manhattan was the hub of the disaster. Very few messages originated from more severely affected locations, such as Breezy Point, Coney Island, and Rockaway—areas with lower levels of smartphone ownership and Twitter usage. As extended power blackouts drained batteries and limited cellular access, even fewer tweets came from the worst hit areas. As one researcher noted, "data are assumed to accurately reflect the social world, but there are significant gaps, with little or no signal coming from particular communities."[152]

Organizations have developed ways to overcome this issue. For example, the city of Boston developed an application called Street Bump that utilizes smartphone features such as GPS feeds to collect and report to the city information about road conditions, including potholes. However, after the release of the application, the Street Bump team recognized that because lower income individuals may be less likely to carry smartphones, the data was likely not fully representative of all road conditions. If the city had continued relying on the biased data, it might have skewed road services to higher income neighborhoods. The team addressed this problem by issuing its application to city workers who service the whole city and supplementing the data with that from the public.[153] This example demonstrates why it is important to consider the digital divide and other issues of underrepresentation and overrepresentation in data inputs before launching a product or service in order to avoid skewed and potentially unfair ramifications.

2. Does Your Data Model Account for Biases?

While large data sets can give insight into previously intractable challenges, hidden biases at both the collection and analytics stages of big data's life cycle could lead to disparate impact.[154] Researchers have noted that big data analytics "can reproduce existing patterns of discrimination, inherit the prejudice of prior decision-makers, or simply reflect the widespread biases that persist in society."[155] For example, if an employer uses big data analytics to synthesize information gathered on successful existing employees to define a "good employee candidate," the employer could risk incorporating previous discrimination in employment decisions into new employment decisions.[156] Even prior to the widespread use of big data, there is some evidence of the use of data leading to the reproduction of existing biases. For example, one researcher has noted that a hospital developed a computer model to help identify "good medical school applicants" based on performance levels of previous and existing students, but, in doing so, the model reproduced prejudices in prior admission decisions.[157]

Companies can also design big data algorithms that learn from human behavior; these algorithms may "learn" to generate biased results. For example, one academic found that Reuters and Google queries for names identified by researchers to be associated with African-Americans were more likely to return advertisements for arrest records than for names identified by researchers to be associated with white Americans.[158] The academic concluded that determining why this discrimination was occurring was beyond the scope of her research, but reasoned that search engines' algorithms may learn to prioritize arrest record ads for searches of names associated with African-Americans if people click on such ads more frequently than other ads.[159] This could reinforce the display of such ads and perpetuate the cycle.

Companies should therefore think carefully about how the data sets and the algorithms they use have been generated. Indeed, if they identify potential biases in the creation of these data sets or the algorithms, companies should develop strategies to overcome them. As noted above, Google changed its interview and hiring process to ask more behavioral questions and to focus less on academic grades after discovering that replicating its existing definitions of a "good employee" was resulting in a homogeneous tech workforce.[160] More broadly, companies are starting to recognize that if their big data algorithms only consider applicants from "top tier" colleges to help them make hiring decisions, they may be incorporating previous biases in college admission decisions.[161] As in the examples discussed above, companies should develop ways to use big data to expand the pool of qualified applicants they will consider.[162]

3. How Accurate Are Your Predictions Based on Big Data?

Some researchers have also found that big data analysis does not give sufficient attention to traditional applied statistics issues, thus leading to incorrect results and predictions.[163] They note that while big data is very good at detecting correlations, it does not explain which correlations are meaningful.[164]

A prime example that demonstrates the limitations of big data analytics is Google Flu Trends, a machine-learning algorithm for predicting the number of flu cases based on Google search terms. To predict the spread of influenza across the United States, the Google team analyzed the top fifty million search terms for indications that the flu had broken out in particular locations. While, at first, the algorithms appeared to create accurate predictions of where the flu was more prevalent, it generated highly inaccurate estimates over time.[165] This could be because the algorithm failed to take into account certain variables. For example, the algorithm may not have taken into account that people would be more likely to search for flu-related terms if the local news ran a story on a flu outbreak, even if the outbreak occurred halfway around the world. As one researcher has noted, Google Flu Trends demonstrates that a "theory-free analysis of mere correlations is inevitably fragile.

If you have no idea what is behind a correlation, you have no idea what might cause that correlation to break down."[166]

As another example, workshop participants discussed the fact that lenders can improve access to credit by using non-traditional indicators, e.g., rental or utility bill payment history.[167] Consumers, however, have the right to withhold rent if their landlord does not provide heat or basic sanitation services. In these instances, simply compiling rental payment history would not necessarily demonstrate whether the person is a good credit risk.[168]

In some cases, these sources of inaccuracies are unlikely to have significant negative effects on consumers. For example, it may be that big data analytics shows that 30 percent of consumers who buy diapers will respond to an ad for baby formula. That response rate may be enough for a marketer to find it worthwhile to send buyers of diapers an advertisement for baby formula. The 70 percent of consumers who buy diapers but are not interested in formula can disregard the ad or discard it at little cost. Similarly, consumers who are interested in formula and who do not buy diapers are unlikely to be substantially harmed because they did not get the ad.

On the other hand, if big data analytics are used as the basis for access to credit, housing, or other similar benefits, the potential effects on consumers from inaccuracies could be substantial.[169] For example, suppose big data analytics predict that people who do not participate in social media are 30 percent more likely to be identity thieves, leading a fraud detection tool to flag such people as "risky." Suppose further that a wireless company uses this tool and requires "risky" people to submit additional documentation before they can obtain a cell phone contract. These people may not be able to obtain the contract if they do not have the required documentation. And they may never know why they were denied the ability to complete the transaction or be able to correct the information used to flag them as "risky" even if the underlying information was inaccurate.[170]

In using big data to make decisions that affect consumers' ability to complete transactions, companies should consider the potential benefits and harms, especially where their policies could negatively affect certain populations.

4. Does Your Reliance on Big Data Raise Ethical or Fairness Concerns?

Companies should consider performing their own assessment of the factors that go into an analytics model and balancing the predictive value of the model with fairness considerations.[171] Indeed, overreliance on the predictions of big data analytics could potentially result in a company not thinking critically about the value, fairness, and other implications of their uses of big data.[172] For example, one company determined that employees who live closer to their jobs stay at these jobs longer than those who live farther away.[173] However, another company decided to exclude this factor from its hiring algorithm because of concerns about racial discrimination, particularly since different neighborhoods can have different racial compositions.[174]

Many companies are not only considering ethical concerns with using big data, but are actively using big data to advance the interests of minorities and fight discrimination. For example, there are now recruiting tools available that match companies in search of employees with candidates who hold the necessary qualifications, but also ensure that those candidates are not limited to particular gender, racial, and experiential backgrounds.[175] Individual companies are also changing their hiring techniques to promote diversity.[176] Xerox now uses an online evaluation tool developed by a data analytics firm to assess applicants, in addition to conducting interviews, to determine which applicants are most qualified for available jobs.[177] In developing this new assessment process, Xerox also learned that previous similar employment experience—one of the few criteria that Xerox had explicitly prioritized in the past—turns out to have no bearing on either productivity or retention.[178]

In addition, state and local government entities are using big data to help underrepresented communities obtain better municipal services. For example, states are using big data to identify the needs of lesbian, gay, bisexual, and transgender individuals and to create more tailored approaches to reduce health disparities impacting these individuals.[179] And big data was used to convince a city to redraw its boundaries to extend city services to historically African-American neighborhoods.[180] As these examples show, organizations can use big data in ways that provide opportunity to underrepresented and underserved communities.

Summary of Research Considerations

In light of this research, companies already using or considering engaging in big data analytics should:

- Consider whether your data sets are missing information from particular populations and, if they are, take appropriate steps to address this problem.
- Review your data sets and algorithms to ensure that hidden biases are not having an unintended impact on certain populations.
- Remember that just because big data found a correlation, it does not necessarily mean that the correlation is meaningful. As such, you should balance the risks of using those results, especially where your policies could negatively affect certain populations. It may be worthwhile to have human oversight of data and algorithms when big data tools are used to make important decisions, such as those implicating health, credit, and employment.
- Consider whether fairness and ethical considerations advise against using big data in certain circumstances. Consider further whether you can use big data in ways that advance opportunities for previously underrepresented populations.

V. Conclusion

Big data will continue to grow in importance, and it is undoubtedly improving the lives of underserved communities in areas such as education, health, local and state services, and employment. Our collective challenge is to make sure that big data analytics continue to provide benefits and opportunities to consumers while adhering to core consumer protection values and principles. For its part, the Commission will continue to monitor areas where big data practices could violate existing laws, including the FTC Act, the FCRA, and ECOA, and will bring enforcement actions where appropriate. In addition, the Commission will continue to examine and raise awareness about big data practices that could have a detrimental impact on low-income and underserved populations and promote the use of big data that has a positive impact on such populations. Given that big data analytics can have big consequences, it is imperative that we work together—government, academics, consumer advocates, and industry—to help ensure that we maximize big data's capacity for good while identifying and minimizing the risks it presents.

Appendix: Separate Statement of Commissioner Maureen K. Ohlhausen

Big Data: A Tool for Inclusion or Exclusion?

January 6, 2016

I support today's report on big data as a useful contribution to the ongoing policy discussion about the effect of big data analysis on low-income, disadvantaged, and vulnerable consumers. One part of the report summarizes the concerns of several privacy advocates and academics over the potential inaccuracies of big data analytics. I write separately to emphasize the importance of evaluating these opinions in the context of market and competitive forces that affect all companies using big data analytics.

The report details the use of big data as it affects low-income, disadvantaged, or vulnerable consumers. Importantly, the report describes some of the many ways companies are already using big data to benefit such consumers—and others. The report also recognizes big data's massive potential benefits. In addition, the report sketches the legal landscape implicated by big data and offers questions that companies may find useful as they apply big data techniques to solve their business challenges.

The report also describes certain concerns about big data tools raised by some consumer advocates and researchers. Specifically, some fear that big data analysis will produce inaccurate or incomplete results, and that actions based on such flawed analysis will harm low-income, disadvantaged, or vulnerable consumers.[1] For example, some worry that companies may use inaccurate big data analysis to deny opportunities to otherwise eligible low-income or disadvantaged consumers, or to fail to advertise high-quality lending products to eligible low-income customers.[2]

Concerns about the effects of inaccurate data are certainly legitimate, but policymakers must evaluate such concerns in the larger context of the market and economic forces companies face. Businesses have strong incentives to seek accurate information about consumers, whatever the tool. Indeed, businesses use big data specifically to increase accuracy. Our competition expertise tells us that if one company draws incorrect conclusions and misses opportunities, competitors with better analysis will strive to fill the gap.[3]

Therefore, to the extent that companies today misunderstand members of low-income, disadvantaged, or vulnerable populations, big data analytics combined with a competitive market may well *resolve* these misunderstandings rather than *perpetuate* them.[4] In particular, a company's failure to communicate premium offers to eligible consumers presents a prime business opportunity for a competitor with a better algorithm.[5]

To understand the benefits and risks of tools like big data analytics, we must also consider the powerful forces of economics and free-market competition. If we give undue credence to hypothetical harms, we risk distracting ourselves from genuine harms and discouraging the development of the very tools that promise new benefits to low income, disadvantaged, and vulnerable individuals.

Today's report enriches the conversation about big data. My hope is that future participants in this conversation will test hypothetical harms with economic reasoning and empirical evidence.[6]

End Notes

[1] *See, e.g.*, EXEC. OFFICE OF THE PRESIDENT, BIG DATA: SEIZING OPPORTUNITIES, PRESERVING VALUES 2–3 (2014) [hereinafter "WHITE HOUSE MAY 2014

REPORT"], http://www.whitehouse.gov/sites/default/files/docs/big_data_privacy_report_5.1.14_ final_print.pdf; Jim Thatcher, *Living on Fumes: Digital Footprints, Data Fumes, and the Limitations of Spatial Big Data*, 8 INT'L J. OF COMMC'N 1765, 1767–69 (2014), http://ijoc.org/index.php/ijoc/article/view/2174/1158. *See also* Comment #00018 from Persis Yu, Nat'l Consumer L. Ctr., to Fed. Trade Comm'n, attached report at 10 (Aug. 15, 2014), https://www.ftc.gov/ system/files/documents/public_comments/2014/08/00018-92374.pdf.

[2] *See, e.g.*, Transcript of Big Data: A Tool for Inclusion or Exclusion?, in Washington, D.C. (Sept. 15, 2014), at 15 (Solon Barocas), 32 (Joseph Turow), 40–41 (Joseph Turow), 261 (Christopher Wolf) [hereinafter Big Data Tr.], https://www.ftc.gov/ system/files/documents/public_events/313371/bigdata-transcript-9_15_14.pdf. *See also* WHITE HOUSE MAY 2014 REPORT, *supra* note 1, at 4–5; Comment #00067 from Mark MacCarthy, Software & Info. Indus. Assoc., to Fed. Trade Comm'n 2 (Oct. 31, 2014), https://www.ftc.gov/system/files/documents/public_comments/2014/10/00067-92918.pdf; Comment #00065 from Jules Polonetsky & Christopher Wolf, Future of Privacy Forum, to Fed. Trade Comm'n 2 (Oct. 31, 2014), https://www.ftc.gov/system/files/documents/public_comments/2014/10/00065-92921.pdf; Comment #00049 from Martin Abrams, Info. Accountability Found., to Fed. Trade Comm'n 3–4 & n.6, https://www.ftc.gov/system/files/documents/public_ comments/2014/10/00049-92780.pdf; Comment #00031 from M. Gary LaFever & Ted Myerson, anonos, to Fed. Trade Comm'n 1 (Aug. 21, 2014), https://www.ftc.gov/system/files/documents/public_comments/2014/08/00031-92442.pdf. Others suggest that there is a "fourth V," veracity, to denote the accuracy and integrity of data used. *See, e.g.*, Brian Gentile, *The New Factors of Production and the Rise of Data-Driven Applications*, FORBES (Oct. 31, 2011), http://www.forbes.com/sites/ ciocentral/2011/10/31/the-new-factors-of-production-and-the-rise-of-data-driven-applications/.

[3] WHITE HOUSE MAY 2014 REPORT, *supra* note 1, at 5.

[4] The materials from the workshop are available on the FTC website at http://www.ftc.gov/news-events/eventscalendar/2014/09/big-data-tool-inclusion-or-exclusion.

[5] On March 19, 2014, the Commission hosted a seminar on alternative scoring products and received nine public comments in connection with the seminar. *Spring Privacy Series: Alternative Scoring Products*, FED. TRADE COMM'N (Mar. 19, 2014), http://www.ftc.gov/news-events/events-calendar/2014/03/spring-privacy-series-alternative-scoring-products.

[6] The report does include some examples from non-commercial fields, but it is intended to guide companies as they use big data about consumers.

[7] *See, e.g.*, Nat'l Consumer L. Ctr. Comment #00018, *supra* note 1, attached report at 11–12. In May 2014, the Commission released a report studying data brokers, which focused on the first three phases of the life cycle of big data. FED. TRADE COMM'N, DATA BROKERS: A CALL FOR TRANSPARENCY AND ACCOUNTABILITY (2014) [hereinafter "DATA BROKERS REPORT"], https://www.ftc.gov/system/files/documents/reports/data-brokers-call-transparency-accountability-report-federal-tradecommission-may-2014/140527databrokerreport.pdf.

[8] *See generally* Comment #00055 from Daniel Castro, Ctr. for Data Innovation, to Fed. Trade Comm'n (Oct. 23, 2014), https://www.ftc.gov/system/files/documents/public_comments/2014/10/00055-92856.pdf; Comment #00026 from Daniel Castro, Ctr. for Data Innovation, to Fed. Trade Comm'n (Aug. 15, 2014), https://www.ftc.gov/system/files/documents/public_comments/2014/08/00026-92395.pdf; Comment #00024 from Alvaro Bedoya, Ctr. on Privacy & Tech. at Geo. L., to Fed. Trade Comm'n (Aug. 15, 2014),

https://www.ftc.gov/system/files/documents/public_ comments/2014/08/00024-92434.pdf; Nat'l Consumer L. Ctr. Comment #00018, *supra* note 1; Comment #00016 from James Steyer, Common Sense Media, to Fed. Trade Comm'n (Aug. 15, 2014), https://www.ftc.gov/system/files/documents/ public_comments/2014/08/00016-92371.pdf; Comment #00015 from Nathan Newman, N.Y.U. Info. L. Inst., to Fed. Trade Comm'n (Aug. 15, 2014), https://www.ftc.gov/system/files/documents/public_comments/2014/08/ 00015-92370. pdf; Comment #00010 from Thomas Lenard, Tech. Pol'y Inst., to Fed. Trade Comm'n (July 28, 2014), https://www.ftc.gov/ system/files/documents/public_comments/ 2014/07/00010-92280.pdf; Comment #00003 from Jeff Chester, Ctr. for Dig. Democracy, & Edmund Mierzwinski, U.S. PIRG Educ. Fund, to Fed. Trade Comm'n (May 9, 2014), https://www.ftc.gov/ system/files/documents/public_comments/2014/05/00003-90097.pdf.

[9] Tracking cookies are a specific type of cookie that is distributed, shared, and read across two or more unrelated websites for the purpose of gathering information or presenting customized data to a consumer. *See Tracking Cookie*, SYMANTEC, https:// www.symantec.com/ security_response/writeup.jsp?docid=2006-080217-3524-99 (last visited Dec. 29, 2015).

[10] "'Browser fingerprinting' is a method of tracking web browsers by the configuration and settings information they make visible to websites, rather than traditional tracking methods" such as cookies. *Panopticlick: Is Your Browser Safe Against Tracking?*, ELEC. FRONTIER FOUND., https://panopticlick.eff.org/about#browser-fingerprinting (last visited Dec. 29, 2015).

[11] History sniffing is the practice of tracking which sites a user has or has not visited. *See* Ben Schott, *History Sniffing*, N.Y. TIMES (Dec. 8, 2010), http://schott.blogs.nytimes.com/ 2010/12/08/history-sniffing/?_r=0. *See also* Brian Krebs, *What You Should Know About History Sniffing*, KREBS ON SEC. (Dec. 6, 2010), http://krebsonsecurity.com/ 2010/12/what-you-shouldknow-about-history-sniffing/.

[12] In November 2015, the Commission held a workshop to study the various alternative techniques used to track consumers across their devices. *See Cross-Device Tracking*, FED. TRADE COMM'N (Nov. 16, 2015), https://www.ftc.gov/news-events/ events-calendar/2015/11/cross-device-tracking.

[13] In January 2015, the Commission released a staff report entitled, INTERNET OF THINGS: PRIVACY & SECURITY IN A CONNECTED WORLD, recommending steps businesses can take to enhance and protect consumers' privacy and security as it relates to Internet-connected devices. FED. TRADE COMM'N, INTERNET OF THINGS: PRIVACY AND SECURITY IN A CONNECTED WORLD (2015), https://www.ftc.gov/system/files/ documents/reports/federal-trade-commission-staff-report-november-2013-workshop-entitled-internet-things-privacy/150127iotrpt.pdf.

[14] *See, e.g.*, DATA BROKERS REPORT, *supra* note 7, at 11–15.

[15] *See generally* Nat'l Consumer L. Ctr. Comment #00018, *supra* note 1; N.Y.U. Info. L. Inst. Comment #00015, *supra* note 8; Ctr. for Dig. Democracy & U.S. PIRG Educ. Fund Comment #00003, *supra* note 8.

[16] *See, e.g.*, DATA BROKERS REPORT, *supra* note 7, at 46–47.

[17] *See, e.g.*, Big Data Tr. 17 (Solon Barocas) ("[W]e can define data mining as the automated process of extracting useful patterns from large data sets, and in particular, patterns that can serve as a basis for subsequent decision making."). *See also* JURE LESKOVEC ET AL., MINING OF MASSIVE DATA SETS 1, 1 (2014), http://www.mmds.org/ (characterizing "data mining" as "the construction of a *statistical model*, that is, an underlying distribution from which the visible data is drawn") (emphasis in original).

[18] *See, e.g.*, Galit Shmueli, *To Explain or Predict?*, 25 STATiSTicAL Sci. 289, 291 (2010), http://www.stat.berkeley. edu/~aldous/157/Papers/shmueli.pdf. *See also* Mike Wu, *Big Data Reduction 2: Understanding Predictive Analytics*, Sci. oF SociAL BLoG (Mar. 26, 2013 9:41 AM), http://community.lithium.com/t5/Science-of-Social-blog/Big-Data-Reduction-2-Understanding-Predictive-Analytics/ba-p/79616 ("[P]redictive analytics is all about using *data you have* to predict *data that you don't have*.") (emphases in original).

[19] *Cf.* Comment #00014 from Pam Dixon & Robert Gellman, World Privacy Forum, to Fed. Trade Comm'n 8 (Aug. 14, 2014), https://www.ftc.gov/policy/public-comments/2014/08/14/comment-00014.

[20] *See generally* DATA BRoKERS REPoRT, *supra* note 7.

[21] *See, e.g.*, Big Data Tr. 31–32 (Gene Gsell), 32–33 (Joseph Turow), 34 (Mallory Duncan), 107–08 (Pamela Dixon).

[22] *See, e.g.*, Big Data Tr. 31–32 (Gene Gsell), 32–33 (Joseph Turow), 78 (danah boyd), 233 (Michael Spadea).

[23] *See, e.g.*, Big Data Tr. 83–85 (Mark MacCarthy), 250–51 (Christopher Wolf). *See generally* Comment #00076 from William Kovacs, U.S. Chamber of Commerce, to Fed. Trade Comm'n (Oct. 31, 2014), https://www.ftc.gov/system/files/documents/ public_comments/ 2014/10/00076-92936.pdf; Comment #00073 from Michael Beckerman, The Internet Assoc., to Fed. Trade Comm'n (Oct. 31, 2014), https://www.ftc.gov/system/files/ documents/public_comments/2014/10/00073-92923.pdf; Comment #00066 from Carl Szabo, NetChoice, to Fed. Trade Comm'n (Oct. 31, 2014), https://www.ftc.gov/system/ files/ documents/public_comments/2014/10/00066-92920.pdf; Comment #00063 from Peggy Hudson, Direct Mktg. Assoc., to Fed. Trade Comm'n (Oct. 31, 2014), https://www.ftc.gov/system/files/documents/public_comments/2014/10/00063-92909. pdf; Ctr. for Data Innovation Comment #00055, *supra* note 8; Comment #00027 from Jules Polonetsky, Future of Privacy Forum, to Fed. Trade Comm'n (Aug. 15, 2014), https://www.ftc.gov/system/files/documents/public_ comments/2014/08/00027-92420.pdf; Ctr. for Data Innovation Comment #00026, *supra* note 8; Comment #00017 from Mike Zaneis, Interactive Advert. Bureau, to Fed. Trade Comm'n (Aug. 15, 2014), https://www.ftc.gov/system/files/ documents/public_comments/2014/08/00017-92372.pdf; Tech. Pol'y Inst. Comment #00010, *supra* note 8.

[24] *See, e.g.*, Big Data Tr. 47–48 (Gene Gsell). *Cf.* Ctr. for Data Innovation Comment #00055, *supra* note 8, attached report entitled, THE RIsE oF DATA PoVERTY IN AMERIcA, at 4–6.

[25] *See, e.g.*, Big Data Tr. 84–85 (Mark MacCarthy). *See also* Software & Info. Indus. Assoc. Comment #00067, *supra* note 2, at 6–7; Ctr. for Data Innovation Comment #00026, *supra* note 8, at 2.

[26] *See, e.g.*, Big Data Tr. 250 (Christopher Wolf). *See also* Future of Privacy Forum Comment #00027, *supra* note 23, attached report entitled, BIG DATA: A TooL FoR FIGHTING DIscRIMINATIoN AND EMPoWERING GRoUPs, at 9.

[27] *See, e.g.*, Big Data Tr. 49–51 (Gene Gsell), 83–84 (Mark MacCarthy), 102–06 (Stuart Pratt), 231–32 (Michael Spadea). *See also* Software & Info. Indus. Assoc. Comment #00067, *supra* note 2, at 5–6; Tech. Pol'y Inst. Comment #00010, *supra* note 8, at 5–6 & attached report entitled, BIG DATA, PRIVAcY AND THE FAMILIAR SoLUTIoNs, at 7.

[28] *See, e.g.*, Software & Info. Indus. Assoc. Comment #00067, *supra* note 2, at 5–6.

[29] *See, e.g.*, *Rent Reporting for Credit Building Consulting*, CREDIT BUILDERs ALL., http://creditbuildersalliance.org/rent-reportingcredit-building-consulting (last visited Dec. 22, 2015).

[30] *See, e.g.*, Ctr. for Data Innovation Comment #00055, *supra* note 8, attached report entitled, THE RISE oF DATA PoVERTY IN AMERICA, at 9. *See generally* Fair Isaac Corp., *Can Alternative Data Expand Credit Access*, INSIGHTS WHITE PAPER No. 90 (2015), http://www.fico.com/en/latest-thinking/white-papers/can-alternative-data-expand-credit-access (finding that alternative scoring can help lenders safely and responsibly extend credit to many of the more than fifty million U.S. adults who do not currently have FICO scores).

[31] *See, e.g.*, Ctr. for Data Innovation Comment #00026, *supra* note 8, at 2. *See also* Shannon Pettypiece & Jordan Robertson, *Hospitals are Mining Patients' Credit Card Data to Predict Who Will Get Sick*, BLooMBERG (July 3, 2014), http://www. bloomberg.com/bw/articles/ 2014-07-03/hospitals-are-mining-patients-credit-card-data-to-predict-who-will-get-sick.

[32] *See, e.g.*, Ctr. for Data Innovation Comment #00055, *supra* note 8, attached report entitled, THE RISE oF DATA PoVERTY IN AMERICA, at 6–8; Future of Privacy Forum Comment #00027, *supra* note 23, attached report entitled, BIG DATA: A TooL FoR FIGHTING DISCRIMINATIoN AND EMPoWERING GRoUPS, at 4; Ctr. for Data Innovation Comment #00026, *supra* note 8, at 2. *Cf.* Software & Info. Indus. Assoc. Comment #00067, *supra* note 2, at 4–5.

[33] *See, e.g.*, David Shaywitz, *New Diabetes Study Shows How Big Data Might Drive Precision Medicine*, FoRBES (Oct. 30, 2015), http://www.forbes.com/sites/davidshaywitz/2015/10/ 30/new-diabetes-study-shows-how-big-data-might-drive-precisionmedicine/.

[34] *See, e.g.*, Big Data Tr. 84 (Mark MacCarthy). *See also* Software & Info. Indus. Assoc. Comment #00067, *supra* note 2, at 4.

[35] *See, e.g.*, Big Data Tr. 126 (Mark MacCarthy), 251 (Christopher Wolf); Software & Info. Indus. Assoc. Comment #00067, *supra* note 2, at 7; Future of Privacy Forum Comment #00027, *supra* note 23, attached report entitled, BIG DATA: A TooL FoR FIGHTING DISCRIMINATIoN AND EMPoWERING GRoUPS, at 1–2. *See also* Lauren Weber, *Can This Algorithm Find Hires of a Certain Race?*, WALL ST. J. (Apr. 30, 2014), http://blogs.wsj.com/atwork/2014/04/30/can-this-algorithm-find-hires-of-acertain-race/.

[36] *See, e.g.*, Big Data Tr. 251 (Christopher Wolf). *See also* Future of Privacy Forum Comment #00027, *supra* note 23, attached report entitled, BIG DATA: A TOOL FOR FIGHTING DISCRIMINATION AND EMPOWERING GROUPS, at 2; David Amerland, *3 Ways Big Data Changed Google's Hiring Process*, FORBES (Jan. 21, 2014), http://www.forbes.com/ sites/netapp/2014/01/21/big-datagoogle-hiring-process/; Adam Bryant, *In Head-Hunting, Big Data May Not Be Such a Big Deal*, N.Y. TIMES (June 19, 2013), http://www.nytimes.com/2013/06/20/business/in-head-hunting-big-data-may-not-be-such-a-big-deal.html?pagewanted=1&%2359&adxnnlx=1371813584-7rFFVvpSQsf/Nlnpu VABGQ&%2359;_r=3.

[37] *See, e.g.*, Big Data Tr. 21–22 (Solon Barocas), 29–31 (David Robinson), 100–02 (Dr. Nicol Turner-Lee); Transcript of Spring Privacy Series: Alternative Scoring Products, in Washington, D.C. (Mar. 19, 2014), at 44–45 (Pamela Dixon) [hereinafter Alternative Scoring Tr.], https://www.ftc.gov/system/files/documents/public_events/182261/alternative-scoring-products_ final-transcript.pdf. *See also* Ctr. for Data Innovation Comment #00055, *supra* note 8, attached report entitled, THE RISE OF DATA POVERTY IN AMERICA, at 2; Nat'l Consumer L. Ctr. Comment #00018, *supra* note 1, attached report entitled, BIG DATA: A BIG DISAPPOINTMENT FOR SCORING CONSUMER RISK, at 9, 27; Ctr. for Dig. Democracy & U.S. PIRG Educ. Fund Comment #00003, *supra* note 8, at 2. *See generally* Nir Grinberg et al., *Extracting Diurnal Patterns of Real World Activity from Social Media* (The 9th Int'l Conference on Web and Social Media, Working Paper 2013), http://sm.rutgers.edu/pubs/ Grinberg-SMPatterns-ICWSM2013.pdf.

[38] *See, e.g.*, Big Data Tr. 23–25 (Solon Barocas); Alternative Scoring Tr. 93 (Claudia Perlich). *See also* Cynthia Dwork & Deirdre Mulligan, *It's Not Privacy and It's Not Fair*, 66 STAN. L. REV. ONLINE 35, 36–37 (2013), http://www.stanfordlawreview.org/ sites/default/files/ online/topics/DworkMullliganSLR.pdf.

[39] Kate Crawford, *The Hidden Biases in Big Data*, HARV. BUS. REV. (2013), https://hbr.org/2013/04/the-hidden-biases-in-bigdata.

[40] *See generally* Helen F. Ladd, *Evidence on Discrimination in Mortgage Lending*, 12(2) J. OF ECON. PERSPECTIVES 41 (1998), https://www.aeaweb.org/atypon.php?return_to=/ doi/pdfplus/10.1257/jep.12.2.41.

[41] *See, e.g.*, Big Data Tr. 40–41 (Joseph Turow).

[42] *See generally* John Aldrich, *Correlations Genuine and Spurious in Pearson and Yule*, 10(4) STATiSTicAL Sci. 364 (1995), http:// www.jstor.org/stable/2246135. *See also Correlation*, XKcD, https://xkcd.com/552/ (last visited Dec. 29, 2015).

[43] *Winning Tradition*, SNoPES.coM, http://www.snopes.com/politics/ballot/redskins.asp (last visited Dec. 29, 2015).

[44] *See, e.g.*, *Spurious Correlations*, TYLERviGEN.coM, http://www.tylervigen.com/spurious-correlations (last visited Dec. 29, 2015) (showing a variety of spurious correlations, including, for example, a historical correlation between the annual number of people who have drowned by falling into a swimming pool and the annual number of films in which Nicolas Cage has appeared).

[45] *See, e.g.*, Big Data Tr. 222 (Jeremy Gillula). *See generally* Nat'l Consumer L. Ctr. Comment #00018, *supra* note 1; Common Sense Media Comment #00016, *supra* note 8; N.Y.U. Info. L. Inst. Comment #00015, *supra* note 8; Ctr. for Dig. Democracy & U.S. PIRG Educ. Fund Comment #00003, *supra* note 8.

[46] *See, e.g.*, Big Data Tr. 42–44 (danah boyd). *See also* Comment #00078 from Seeta Peña Gangadharan et al., New Am.'s Open Tech. Inst., to Fed. Trade Comm'n, attached report entitled, THE NETWoRKED NATURE oF ALGoRiTHMic DiScRiMiNATioN, at 53–57 (Oct. 31, 2014), https://www.ftc.gov/system/files/documents/public_comments/2014/ 10/00078-92938.pdf.

[47] *See, e.g.*, Nat'l Consumer L. Ctr. Comment #00018, *supra* note 1, at 27–28; N.Y.U. Info. L. Inst. Comment #00015, *supra* note 8, at 6.

[48] *See* FTC v. CompuCredit Corp., No. 1:08-cv-1976-BBM-RGV (N.D. Ga. June 10, 2008), https://www.ftc.gov/sites/default/ files/documents/cases/2008/12/081219compucreditstiporder.pdf. *See also* Danielle Keats Citron & Frank A. Pasquale III, *The Scored Society: Due Process for Automated Predictions*, 89 WASH. L. REv. 1, 4 (2014), http://ssrn.com/abstract=2376209.

[49] *See, e.g.*, Alternative Scoring Tr. 96 (Edmund Mierzwinski).

[50] *See, e.g.*, Big Data Tr. 228–30 (Christopher Calabrese); Alternative Scoring Tr. 64–67 (Ashkan Soltani). *See also* Ctr. for Dig. Democracy & U.S. PIRG Educ. Fund Comment #00003, *supra* note 8, at 10–11, 18–29.

[51] *See, e.g.*, Big Data Tr. 89–90 (Pamela Dixon), 71–72 (Kristin Amerling); Alternative Scoring Tr. 76 (Pamela Dixon), 92 (Ashkan Soltani). *See also* Am.'s Open Tech. Inst. Comment #00078, *supra* note 46, attached report entitled, HEALTH PRIVACY ONLINE: PATIENTS AT RISK, at 11–16; Ctr. on Privacy & Tech. at Geo. L. Comment #00024, *supra* note 8, at 9; DATA BROKERS REPORT, *supra* note 7, at 19–21, 47.

[52] *See* Michal Kosinski et al., *Private Traits and Attributes Are Predictable From Digital Records of Human Behavior*, 110 PROCEEDINGS OF THE NAT'L ACAD. OF SCIS. 5802, 5803–04 (2013), http://www.pnas.org/content/110/15/5802.abstract. *See also* Jon Green,

Facebook Knows You're Gay Before You Do, Aii. BLOG (Mar. 20, 2013), http://americablog.com/2013/03/ facebook-might-know-youre-gay-before-you-do.html.

[53] *See, e.g.*, Comment #00080 from David Robinson, Robinson + Yu, to Fed. Trade Comm'n 8–9 (Oct. 31, 2014), https://www. ftc.gov/system/files/documents/public_comments/2014/10/ 00080-92939.pdf; N.Y.U. Info. L. Inst. Comment #00015, *supra* note 8, at 6–7. *See also* FTC v. LeapLab, LLC, No. 2:14-cv-02750 (D. Ariz. filed Dec. 22, 2014), https://www.ftc.gov/ system/files/documents/cases/141223leaplabcmpt.pdf.

[54] *See, e.g.*, N.Y.U. Info. L. Inst. Comment #00015, *supra* note 8, at 6–7.

[55] *See, e.g.*, Mark Andrejevic, *The Big Data Divide*, 8 INT'L J. OF COMMC'N 1673, 1681 (2014), http://ijoc.org/index.php/ijoc/article/download/2161/1163. *See also Robot Recruiters*, ECONOMIST (Apr. 6, 2013), http://www.economist.com/news/ business/21575820-how-software-helps-firms-hire-workers-more-efficiently-robot-recruiters.

[56] *See, e.g.*, Lauren Kirchner, *When Big Data Becomes Bad Data*, PROPUBLICA (Sept. 2, 2015), https://www.propublica.org/ article/when-big-data-becomes-bad-data (finding that areas with high density of Asian residents are often charged more for the Princeton Review's online SAT tutoring). *But see* EXEC. OFFICE OF THE PRESIDENT, BIG DATA AND DIFFERENTIAL PRICING 17 (2015), [hereinafter WHITE HOUSE FEB. 2015 REPORT], http://www.whitehouse.gov/sites/default/files/whitehouse_files/ docs/Big_Data_Report_Nonembargo_v2.pdf ("[I]f historically disadvantaged groups are more price-sensitive than the average consumer, profit-maximizing differential pricing should work to their benefit" in competitive markets.). This holds true for relatively competitive markets. However, the report also points out that disadvantaged groups may face less competitive markets and be penalized by differential pricing. *Id.* Economists have shown that price discrimination can improve or reduce consumer welfare, depending on how price discrimination is implemented. *See generally* Dirk Bergemann et al., *The Limits of Price Discrimination*, 105(3), AM. ECON. REv. 921 (2015), https://www.aeaweb.org/ articles.php?doi=10.1257/aer.20130848. Economists have also shown that greater price discrimination could raise or reduce the intensity of competition. *See generally* Kenneth S. Corts, *Third-Degree Price Discrimination in Oligopoly: All-Out Competition and Strategic Commitment*, RAND J. OF ECONS. 306 (1998), http://www.jstor.org/stable/2555890? seq=1#page_scan_tab_contents.

[57] *See, e.g.*, Alternative Scoring Tr. 62–64 (Askhan Soltani). *See also* Jennifer Valentino-Devries et al., *Websites Vary Prices, Deals Based on Users' Information*, WALL ST. J. (Dec. 24, 2012), http://www.wsj.com/articles/SB1000142412788732377720457818 9391813881534.

[58] *See, e.g.*, Nat'l Consumer L. Ctr Comment #00018, *supra* note 1, at 27; N.Y.U. Info. L. Inst. Comment #00015, *supra* note 8, at 4–5. *See also* Alternative Scoring Tr. 62–64 (Ashkan Soltani). For an example of differential pricing using IP addresses, see Valentino-Devries et al., *supra* note 57. For an example of steering based on the type of operating system, see Martha C. White, *Orbitz Shows Higher Prices to Mac Users*, TIME (June 26, 2012), http://business.time.com/2012/06/26/orbitz-showshigher-prices-to-mac-users/.

[59] Solon Barocas & Helen Nissenbaum, *Big Data's End Run Around Anonymity and Consent*, *in* PRIvACY, BIG DATA, AND THE PUBLIC GOOD: FRAMEWORKS FOR ENGAGEMENT 44, 61–63 (Julia Lane et al. eds., 2014).

[60] *Id.*

[61] *See, e.g.*, Big Data Tr. 38 (Kristin Amerling), 45–47, 69–70 (David Robinson), 95, 120–22 (Stuart Pratt), 99, 108 (Pamela Dixon), 268 (Christopher Calabrese), 163–213 (Leonard Chanin, Carol Miaskoff, Montserrat Miller, C. Lee Peeler, and Peter Swire in conversation);

Alternative Scoring Tr. 36–37, 71 (Stuart Pratt). *See generally* Comment #00075 from Michelle De Mooy, Ctr. for Democracy & Tech., to Fed. Trade Comm'n (Oct. 31, 2014), https://www.ftc.gov/system/ files/documents/public_comments/2014/10/00075-92928.pdf; Comment #00068 from Julie Kearney & Alexander Reynolds, Consumer Elecs. Assoc., to Fed. Trade Comm'n (Oct. 31, 2014), https://www.ftc.gov/system/files/documents/ public_comments/2014/10/00068-92917.pdf; Software & Info. Indus. Assoc. Comment #00067, *supra* note 2; Future of Privacy Forum Comment #00065, *supra* note 2; Direct Mktg. Assoc. Comment #00063, *supra* note 23; Comment #00062 from David Hoffman, Intel Corp., to Fed. Trade Comm'n (Oct. 31, 2014), https://www.ftc.gov/system/files/ documents/public_comments/2014/10/00062-92887.pdf; Comment #00061 from Jeff Chester, Ctr. for Dig. Democracy, & Edmund Mierzwinski, U.S. PIRG Educ. Fund, to Fed. Trade Comm'n (Oct. 29, 2014), https://www.ftc.gov/system/files/ documents/public_ comments/2014/10/00061-92886.pdf; Comment #00059 from Laura Murphy & Rachel Goodman, Am. Civil Liberties Union, to Fed. Trade Comm'n (Oct. 27, 2014), https://www.ftc.gov/system/files/documents/public_ comments/2014/10/00059-92874.pdf; Ctr. for Data Innovation Comment #00026, *supra* note 8; Comment #00025 from Dennis Hirsch, Cap. Univ. L. Sch., to Fed. Trade Comm'n (Aug. 15, 2014), https://www.ftc.gov/ system/files/documents/ public_comments/2014/08/00025-92435.pdf; Comment #00021 from U.S. Chamber of Commerce, to Fed. Trade Comm'n (Aug. 15, 2014), https://www.ftc.gov/system/files/documents/public_comments/2014/08/00021-92389.pdf; Comment #00020 from Jim Halpert, Internet Commerce Coal., to Fed. Trade Comm'n (Aug. 15, 2014), https://www.ftc.gov/system/files/documents/public_comments/ 2014/08/00020-92376.pdf; Comment #00019 from Michael Beckerman, Internet Ass'n, to Fed. Trade Comm'n (Aug. 15, 2014), https://www.ftc.gov/system/files/documents/public_ comments/2014/08/00019-92375.pdf; Nat'l Consumer L. Ctr. Comment #00018, *supra* note 1; Interactive Advert. Bureau Comment #00017, *supra* note 23; World Privacy Forum Comment #00014, *supra* note 19; Ctr. for Dig. Democracy & U.S. PIRG Educ. Fund Comment #00003, *supra* note 8.

[62] This discussion articulates considerations relevant to the Commission's exercise of its enforcement authority. Though this section discusses certain federal laws, companies should also be aware that other federal laws, as well as state and local laws, may apply to their big data practices. They should review these laws in jurisdictions where they operate.

[63] 15 U.S.C. §§ 1681–1681x (2014).

[64] *Id.* § 1681a(f) & (d). As discussed further below, the FCRA also applies to users of consumer reports and those who furnish consumer reports to CRAs.

[65] *Id.* § 1681e(b).

[66] *Id.* § 1681g–1681j.

[67] *Id.* §1681b(a).

[68] United States v. Spokeo, Inc., No. 2-12-cv-05001-MMM-SH (C.D. Cal. June 12, 2012), https://www.ftc.gov/sites/default/ files/documents/cases/2012/06/120612spokeoorder.pdf. *See also* Press Release, Fed. Trade Comm'n, Spokeo to Pay $800,000 to Settle FTC Charges Company Allegedly Marketed Information to Employers and Recruiters in Violation of FCRA (June 12, 2012), http://www.ftc.gov/news-events/press-releases/2012/06/spokeo-pay-800000-settle-ftccharges-company-allegedlymarketed.

[69] Complaint at 3–4, *Spokeo*, No. 2-12-cv-05001-MMM-SH (C.D. Cal. filed June 7, 2012), https://www.ftc.gov/sites/default/ files/documents/cases/2012/06/120612spokeocmpt.pdf.

[70] Complaint, United States v. Instant Checkmate, Inc., No. 3:14-cv-00675-H-JMA (S.D. Cal. filed Mar. 24, 2014), https:// www.ftc.gov/system/files/documents/cases/140409instant

checkmatecmpt.pdf. *See also* Press Release, Fed. Trade Comm'n, Two Data Brokers Settle FTC Charges That They Sold Consumer Data without Complying with Protections Required under the Fair Credit Reporting Act (Apr. 9, 2014), https://www.ftc.gov/news-events/press-releases/2014/04/two-data-brokerssettle-ftc-charges-they-sold-consumer-data.

[71] *Instant Checkmate*, No. 3:14-cv-00675-H-JMA (S.D. Cal. Apr. 1, 2014), https://www.ftc.gov/system/files/documents/cases/1 40409instantcheckmateorder.pdf.

[72] *See* 15 U.S.C. § 1681m(a). When using consumer reports for employment purposes, companies must also provide consumers with "pre-adverse action notices" before taking any adverse action. *See id.* § 1681b(b)(3).

[73] *See id.* § 1681m(h); 12 C.F.R. §§ 1022.70–1022.75 (2015); FTC Duties of Creditors Regarding Risk-Based Pricing Rule, 16 C.F.R. § 640 (2015).

[74] *See Using Consumer Reports for Credit Decisions: What to Know About Adverse Action and Risk-Based Pricing Notices*, FED. TraDE COMM'N (Dec. 2013), https://www.ftc.gov/tips-advice/business-center/guidance/using-consumer-reports-credit-decisionswhat-know-about-adverse.

[75] *See, e.g.*, Complaint, United States. v. Rail Terminal Servs., LLC, No. 09-cv-1111(MJP) (W.D. Wash. filed Aug.11, 2009), https://www.ftc.gov/sites/default/files/documents/cases/ 2013/08/090806rtscmpt.pdf; Complaint, United States. v. Quality Terminal Servs., LLC, No. 09-cv-01853-CMA-BNB (D. Colo. filed Aug. 11, 2009), https://www.ftc.gov/sites/ default/files/documents/cases/2009/08/090806ptscmpt.pdf.

[76] Complaint, United States v. Time Warner Cable, Inc., No. 13-cv-8998 (S.D.N.Y. filed Dec. 19, 2013), https://www.ftc.gov/sites/default/files/documents/cases/131219time warnercmpt.pdf. *See also* Press Release, Fed. Trade Comm'n, Time Warner Cable to Pay $1.9 Million Penalty for Violating Risk-Based Pricing Rule (Dec. 19, 2013), https://www.ftc.gov/news-events/ press-releases/2013/12/time-warner-cable-pay-19-million-penalty-violating-risk-based.

[77] *Time Warner Cable*, No. 13-cv-8998 (S.D.N.Y. Dec. 20, 2013), https://www.ftc.gov/ sites/default/files/documents/ cases/131219timewarnerstip.pdf.

[78] Complaint at 7–8, United States v. Sprint Corp., No. 2:15-cv-9340 (D. Kan. filed Oct. 21, 2015), https://www.ftc.gov/ system/files/documents/cases/151021sprintcmpt.pdf. *See also* Press Release, Fed. Trade Comm'n, Sprint Will Pay $2.95 Million Penalty to Settle FTC Charges It Violated Fair Credit Reporting Act (Oct. 21, 2015), https://www.ftc.gov/news-events/press-releases/2015/10/sprint-will-pay-295-million-penalty-settle-ftc-charges-it.

[79] The settlement also requires Sprint to send corrected risk-based pricing notices to consumers who received incomplete notices from the company. *See Sprint*, No. 2:15-cv-9340 (D. Kan. Oct. 21, 2015), https://www.ftc.gov/system/files/documents/ cases/151021sprintstip.pdf.

[80] 15 U.S.C. § 1681a(d)(2)(A)(i). *See also* FED. TRADE COMM'N, 40 YEARS OF EXPERIENCE WITH THE FAIR CREDIT REPORTING ACT: AN FTC STAFF REPORT WITH SUMMARY OF INTERPRETATIONS 1, 23–24 (2011) [hereinafter 40 YEARS FCRA REPORT], https://www.ftc.gov/sites/default/files/documents/reports/40-years-experience-fair-credit-reporting-act-ftc-staff-reportsummary-interpretations/110720fcrareport.pdf ("Reports limited to transactions or experiences between the consumer and the entity making the report are not consumer reports. An opinion that is based only on transactions or experiences between the consumer and the reporting entity is also within the exception.").

[81] *See, e.g.*, Big Data Tr. 38 (Kristin Amerling), 69–70 (David Robinson), 99–100 (Pamela Dixon); Alternative Scoring Tr. 100–101 (Pamela Dixon). *See also* Nat'l Consumer L. Ctr. Comment #00018, *supra* note 1, at 20–23; World Privacy Forum Comment #00014, *supra*

note 19, at 19–21; Ctr. for Dig. Democracy & U.S. PIRG Educ. Fund Comment #00003, *supra* note 8, at 13–15; Comment #00006 from Jeff Chester, Ctr. for Dig. Democracy, & Edmund Mierzwinski, U.S. PIRG Educ. Fund, to Fed. Trade Comm'n (Mar. 18, 2014), https://www.ftc.gov/system/files/documents/public_ comments/2014/03/00006-89085.pdf.

[82] *See, e.g.*, Big Data Tr. 69–70 (David Robinson) (noting that these "thinly aggregated scores . . . may be used to lower [consumers'] credit limits"); 99–100 (Pamela Dixon) (noting that these scores are "problematic for ensuring privacy and fairness" because they rely on "[un]regulated data"); Alternative Scoring Tr. 94 (Pamela Dixon) (describing "cohort scoring," which is a type of score based on a consumer's social media friends). *See also* World Privacy Forum Comment #00014, *supra* note 19, at 32–38. *But see supra* text accompanying notes 27–30 (explaining how big data analytics can be used to expand credit availability).

[83] As noted in *Trans Union Corp. v. FTC*, this part of the test is not a very demanding one, for almost any information about consumers arguably bears on their personal characteristics or mode of living. 81 F.3d 228, 231 (D.C. Cir. 1996).

[84] 15 U.S.C. § 1681a(d)(1) (emphasis added).

[85] In 2011, FTC staff issued the 40 YEARS FCRA REPORT. In that report, staff stated that "[i]nformation that does not identify a specific consumer does not constitute a consumer report even if the communication is used in part to determine eligibility." 40 YEARS FCRA REPORT, *supra* note 80, at 20. The Commission does not believe that this statement is accurate. If a report is crafted for eligibility purposes with reference to a particular consumer or set of particular consumers (e.g., those that have applied for credit), the Commission will consider the report a consumer report even if the identifying information of the consumer has been stripped.

[86] Companies that determine eligibility based on zip codes should exercise caution. Such a practice could still implicate equal opportunity laws, if that policy has a disproportionate adverse effect or impact on a protected class, unless those practices or policies further a legitimate business need that cannot reasonably be achieved by means that are less disproportionate in their impact. See discussion *infra* Part IV.A.2.

[87] *See* 15 U.S.C. § 1681m(b).

[88] 15 U.S.C. §§ 1691 *et seq.* (2014). In addition to prohibiting discrimination, ECOA and Regulation B include other requirements that may be implicated by business practices that utilize big data analytics. Informing credit applicants about adverse actions related to applications for credit and identifying the specific reasons an adverse action was taken may be challenging when those reasons implicate big data analytics. *See* 12 C.F.R. § 1002.9. Lenders may also need to review Regulation B requirements on how information is obtained and retained in the credit application process. *See* 12 C.F.R. § 1002.5(b)–(d), 1002.12(a)(2).

[89] 42 U.S.C. §§ 2000e *et seq.* (2014). The Civil Rights Act of 1964 also applies to education, voting, and public accommodations.

[90] 42 U.S.C. §§ 12101 *et seq.* (2014).

[91] 29 U.S.C. §§ 621 *et seq.* (2014).

[92] 42 U.S.C. §§ 3601 *et seq.* (2014).

[93] 42 U.S.C. §§ 2000ff *et seq.* (2014). GINA also applies to health insurance.

[94] A number of different agencies have the authority to enforce the various equal opportunity laws. The Equal Employment Opportunity Commission, for example, is responsible for enforcing Title VII of the Civil Rights Act of 1964 (along with the Department of Justice ("DOJ")), the Age Discrimination in Employment Act of 1967, and GINA. The Department

of Housing and Urban Development and the DOJ enforce the FHA. The FTC, DOJ, and the Consumer Financial Protection Bureau ("CFPB"), among other agencies, enforce ECOA and its implementing Regulation B.

[95] *See, e.g.*, Big Data Tr. 168–170 (Carol Miaskoff). Disparate impact claims are not permitted under Title II of GINA. *Background Information for EEOC Notice of Proposed Rulemaking on Title II of the Genetic Information Nondiscrimination Act of 2008*, U.S. EQUAl EMP'T OPPORTUNITY COMM'N, http://www.eeoc.gov/policy/docs/qanda_geneticinfo.html (last modified May 12, 2009).

[96] *See, e.g.*, 29 U.S.C. § 623(a)(1); 42 U. S. C. § 2000e–2(k)(1)(A)(i); 42 U.S.C. § 12112(b)(1); 12 C.F.R. Part 1002 Supp. I § 1002.4(a)–1.

[97] *See, e.g.*, Int'l Bhd. of Teamsters v. United States, 431 U.S. 324, 334–35 (1977).

[98] *See, e.g.*, Big Data Tr. 168–170 (Carol Miaskoff).

[99] *Cf. id.* (explaining how the various equal opportunity laws may apply to big data analytics).

[100] *See, e.g.*, 29 U.S.C. § 631(a); 42 U.S.C. § 2000e–2 (k); 42 U.S.C. § 12112(b)(6); 24 C.F.R. § 100.500; 12 C.F.R. Part 1002 Supp. I § 1002.6(a)–2. On June 25, 2015, the Supreme Court in *Texas Department of Housing and Community Affairs v. Inclusive Communities Project, Inc.*, 135 S.Ct. 2507 (2015), held that the disparate impact theory is valid under the FHA.

[101] *See, e.g.*, 12 C.F.R. § 1002.6 (citing Griggs v. Duke Power Co., 401 U.S. 424 (1971), and Albemarle Paper Co. v. Moody, 422 U.S. 405, 430–31 (1975)); 12 C.F.R. Part 1002 Supp. I § 1002.6(a)–2; Policy Statement on Discrimination in Lending, 59 Fed. Reg. 18,266, 18,268 (Apr. 14, 1994).

[102] *See, e.g.*, Tex. Dep't of Cmty. Affairs v. Burdine, 450 U.S. 248, 256–58 (1981); N.Y. City Transit Auth. v. Beazer, 440 U.S. 568, 587 (1979); Zamlen v. City of Cleveland, 906 F.2d 209, 218–20 (6th Cir. 1990); Evans v. City of Evanston, 881 F.2d 382, 383 (7th Cir. 1989); Aguilera v. Cook County Police & Corr. Merit Bd., 760 F.2d 844, 846–47 (7th Cir. 1985). *See also* 12 C.F.R. § 1002.6(a). However, with respect to ADEA cases, the formulation applied by courts is slightly different. *See, e.g.*, Smith v. City of Jackson, 544 U.S. 228, 243 (2005) (holding that the "reasonable factor other than age" test, rather than the business necessity test, is the appropriate standard for determining lawfulness of a practice that disproportionally affects older workers under the ADEA). *See also Questions and Answers on EEOC Final Rule on Disparate Impact and "Reasonable Factors Other Than Age" Under the Age Discrimination Employment Act of 1967*, U.S. EQUAL EMP'T OPPORTUNITY COMM'N, http://www.eeoc.gov/laws/regulations/adea_rfoa_qa_final_rule.cfm (last visited on Dec. 28, 2015).

[103] *See, e.g.*, *Albermarle Paper*, 422 U.S. at 425; Int'l Bhd. of Elec. Workers, AFL-CIO, Local Unions Nos. 605 & 985 v. Miss. Power & Light Co., 442 F.3d 313, 318–19 (5th Cir. 2006); Smith v. City of Des Moines, Iowa, 99 F.3d 1466, 1473 (8th Cir. 1996); Contreras v. City of Los Angeles, 656 F.2d 1267, 1285 (9th Cir. 1981); El v. Se. Pa. Transp. Auth., 418 F. Supp. 2d 659, 672 (E.D. Pa. 2005) *aff'd*, 479 F.3d 232 (3d Cir. 2007).

[104] Big data can also facilitate the identification of disparate impact. *See infra* notes 145–47 and accompanying text.

[105] *See, e.g.*, Big Data Tr. 170 (Carol Miaskoff).

[106] The use of zip codes can also raise concerns of redlining, a form of discrimination involving differential treatment on the basis of the race, color, national origin, or other protected characteristic of residents of those areas in which the credit seeker resides, or will reside, or in which residential property to be mortgaged is located. The CFPB and DOJ recently concluded a redlining enforcement action against Hudson City Savings Bank. *See* Complaint, CFPB v. Hudson City Sav. Bank, No. 15- 07056 (D.N.J. Sept. 24, 2015),

http://files.consumerfinance.gov/f/201509_cfpb_hudson-city-joint-complaint.pdf. *See also* CONSUMER FIN. PROTECTION BUREAU, CFPB EXAMINATION PROCEDURES: ECOA BASELINE REVIEW MODULES 16–18 (2013), http://files.consumerfinance.gov/f/201307_cfpb_ecoa_baseline-review-module-fair-lending.pdf.

[107] The examples above are illustrative and do not necessarily provide an exhaustive list of all ways that big data could have a disparate impact on consumers.

[108] 15 U.S.C. § 1691(a)(2).

[109] *See, e.g.*, Complaint, United States v. Franklin Acceptance Corp., No. 99-cv-2435 (E.D. Penn. filed May 13, 1999), https:// www.ftc.gov/sites/default/files/documents/cases/1999/05/franklincmp.htm.

[110] 15 U.S.C. § 1691(a)(1).

[111] *See, e.g.*, Complaint, United States v. Ford Motor Credit Co., No. 99-cv-57887 (GEW) (E.D. Mich. filed Dec. 9, 1999), https://www.ftc.gov/sites/default/files/documents/cases/1999/12/fordmotorcompanyfederalcourtcomplaint.pdf.

[112] *See* Complaint, FTC v. Gateway Diversified Funding Mortg. Servs., No. 08-5805 (E.D. Pa. filed Dec. 16, 2008), https:// www.ftc.gov/sites/default/files/documents/cases/2008/12/081216gatewaycmpt.pdf; Complaint, FTC v. Golden Empire Mortgage, Inc., No. 09-03227 CAS(SHx) (C.D. Cal. filed May 7, 2009), https://www.ftc.gov/sites/default/files/documents/cases/2009/05/090511gemcmpt.pdf.

[113] *See, e.g.*, Big Data Tr. 179–83 (Peter Swire), 187–90 (Peter Swire, Leonard Chanin, and C. Lee Peeler in conversation), 204–05 (Peter Swire), 268–69 (Christopher Calabrese).

[114] In the context of mortgage advertising, creditors should also consider the FHA. 42 U.S.C. §§ 3601–3631; 24 C.F.R. Parts 100, 103, and 104. Regulations that implement the FHA prohibit "[f]ailing or refusing to provide to any person information regarding the availability of loans or other financial assistance, application requirements, procedures or standards for the review and approval of loans or financial assistance, or providing information which is inaccurate or different from that provided others, because of race, color, religion, sex, handicap, familial status, or national origin." 24 C.F.R. § 100.120(b)(1).

[115] 15 U.S.C. § 1691(a)(1).

[116] *See, e.g.*, Big Data Tr. 178–191 (Peter Swire, C. Lee Peeler, and Leonard Chanin in conversation).

[117] Under Regulation B, credit transaction means "every aspect of an applicant's dealings with a creditor regarding an application for credit or an existing extension of credit (including, but not limited to, information requirements; investigation procedures; standards of creditworthiness; terms of credit; furnishing of credit information; revocation, alteration, or termination of credit; and collection procedures)." 12 C.F.R. § 1002.2(m).

[118] Under Regulation B, a creditor "does not include a person whose only participation in a credit transaction involves honoring a credit card." *Id.* § 1002.2(l).

[119] *Id.* § 1002.4(b).

[120] *Id.* § 1002.12(b)(7).

[121] *See, e.g.*, Complaint, United States v. First United Sec. Bank, No. 1 09-cv-00644 (S.D. Ala. filed Sept. 30, 2009), http://www. justice.gov/sites/default/files/crt/legacy/2010/12/14/fusbcomp.pdf.

[122] 15 U.S.C. § 45(a)(1) (2012).

[123] The FTC's consumer protection mandate is broad. Under Section 5 of the FTC Act, 15 U.S.C. § 45, the Commission has the power to prevent "persons, partnerships, and corporations" from using unfair or deceptive acts or practices in or affecting commerce, with certain limited exceptions. Those exceptions include: (1) banks and savings and loan institutions as

described in 15 U.S.C. § 57a(f)(2) and (3); (2) federal credit unions as described in 15 U.S.C. § 57a(f)(4); (3) common carrier activities subject to subtitle IY of title 49 and the Communications Act of 1934; and (4) air carriers and foreign air carriers.

[124] FTC Policy Statement on Deception, 103 F.T.C. 110, 174 (1984) (appended to Cliffdale Assocs., Inc., 103 F.T.C. 110, 174 (1984)). *See also* POM Wonderful LLC, No. C-9344, 2013 WL 268926, at *18 (F.T.C. Jan. 16, 2013).

[125] *See, e.g.*, Goldenshores Techs., LLC, No. C-4446 (F.T.C. Mar. 31, 2014), https://www.ftc.gov/system/files/documents/cases/140409goldenshoresdo.pdf; FTC v. Myspace LLC, No. C-4369 (F.T.C. Aug. 30, 2012), https://www.ftc.gov/sites/default/files/documents/cases/2012/09/120911myspacedo.pdf.

[126] *See, e.g.*, Compete, Inc., No. D-4384 (F.T.C. Feb. 20, 2013), https://www.ftc.gov/sites/default/files/documents/cases/2013/02/130222competedo.pdf; United States v. Path, Inc., No. C-13-0448 (N.D. Cal. Feb. 8, 2013), https://www. ftc.gov/sites/default/files/documents/cases/2013/02/130201pathincdo.pdf; Google Inc., No. C-4336 (F.T.C. Oct. 13, 2011), https://www.ftc.gov/sites/default/files/documents/cases/2011/10/111024googlebuzzdo.pdf; Facebook, Inc., No. C-4365 (F.T.C. July 27, 2012), https://www.ftc.gov/sites/default/files/documents/cases/2012/08/120810facebookdo.pdf; Chitika, Inc., No. C-4324 (F.T.C. June 7, 2011), https://www.ftc.gov/sites/default/files/documents/cases/2011/06/110617chitikado.pdf.

[127] *See, e.g.*, Snapchat, Inc., C-4501 (F.T.C. Dec. 23, 2014), https://www.ftc.gov/system/files/documents/cases/141231snapchatdo.pdf; Fandango, LLC, No. C-4481 (F.T.C. Aug. 13, 2014), https://www.ftc.gov/system/files/ documents/cases/140819fandangodo.pdf; Credit Karma, Inc., C-4480 (F.T.C. Aug. 13, 2014), https://www.ftc.gov/system/ files/documents/cases/1408creditkarmado.pdf; Twitter, Inc., No. C-4316 (F.T.C. Mar. 2, 2011), https://www.ftc.gov/sites/default/files/documents/cases/2011/03/110311twitterdo. pdf; Reed Elsevier Inc., No. C-4226 (F.T.C. July 29, 2008), https://www.ftc.gov/sites/default/files/documents/cases/2008/08/080801reeddo.pdf.

[128] Complaint, *CompuCredit*, No. 1:08-cv-1976-BBM-RGV (N.D. Ga. filed June 10, 2008), https://www.ftc.gov/sites/default/files/documents/cases/2008/06/080610compucredit cmplt.pdf.

[129] *Id.*

[130] 15 U.S.C. § 45(n) (2012). *See also* FTC Policy Statement on Unfairness (appended to Int'l Harvester Co., 104 F.T.C. 949, 1070 (1984)).

[131] *See, e.g.*, GMR Transcription Servs., Inc., No. C-4482 (F.T.C. Aug. 14, 2014), https://www.ftc.gov/system/files/documents/ cases/140821gmrdo.pdf; GeneWize Life Scis., Inc., No. C-4457 (F.T.C. May 8, 2014), https://www.ftc.gov/system/files/documents/cases/140512foruintdo.pdf; HTC Am., Inc., No. C-4406 (F.T.C. June 25, 2013), https://www.ftc.gov/sites/default/files/documents/cases/2013/07/130702htcdo.pdf; *Compete*, No. C-4384 (F.T.C. Feb. 20, 2013), https://www.ftc.gov/ sites/default/files/documents/cases/2013/02/130222competedo.pdf; Upromise, Inc., No. C-4351 (F.T.C. Mar. 27, 2012), https://www.ftc.gov/sites/default/files/documents/cases/2012/04/120403 upromisedo.pdf.

[132] *See generally* FED. TRADE COMM'N, START WiTh SECURiTY: A GUiDE FOR BUSiNESS (2015), https://www.ftc.gov/system/files/ documents/plain-language/pdf0205-startwithsecurity.pdf.

[133] FTC v. Sequoia One, LLC, No. 2:15-cv-01512 (D. Nev. Aug. 10, 2015), https://www.ftc.gov/system/files/documents/case s/150812sequoiaonemcdonnellstip.pdf; Complaint, *Sequoia One*, No. 2-15-cv-01512 (D. Nev. filed Aug. 7, 2015), https://

www.ftc.gov/system/files/documents/cases/150812sequoiaonecmpt.pdf. *See also* Press Release, Fed. Trade Comm'n, FTC Charges Data Broker with Facilitating the Theft of Millions of Dollars from Consumers' Accounts (Dec. 23, 2014), https:// www.ftc.gov/news-events/press-releases/2014/12/ftc-charges-data-broker-facilitating-theft-millions-dollars. In *LeapLab*, the Commission's complaint alleges that the company bought payday loan applications of financially strapped consumers, and then sold that information—including Social Security numbers and financial account numbers—to marketers whom it knew had no legitimate need for it. Complaint at 5–10, LeapLab, LLC, No. 2:14-cv-02750 (D. Ariz. filed Dec. 22, 2014), https:// www.ftc.gov/system/files/documents/cases/141223 leaplabcmpt.pdf. One of these marketers allegedly used the information to withdraw millions of dollars from consumers' accounts without their authorization. *Id.* at 9–10.

[134] United States v. ChoicePoint, Inc., No. 1:06-cv-0198-JTC (N.D. Ga. Feb. 15, 2006), https://www.ftc.gov/sites/default/files/ documents/cases/2006/01/stipfinaljudgement.pdf.

[135] *Cf.* DATA BROKERS REPORT, *supra* note 7, at 56.

[136] *See generally* Robinson + Yu Comment #00080, *supra* note 53; Ctr. for Data Innovation Comment #00055, *supra* note 8; Comment #00042 from Peter Swire, Ga. Inst. of Tech. & Future of Privacy Forum, to Fed. Trade Comm'n (Sept. 15, 2014), https://www.ftc.gov/system/files/documents/public_comments/2014/09/00042-92638.pdf; Future of Privacy Forum Comment #00027, *supra* note 23; Ctr. on Privacy & Tech. at Geo. L. Comment #00024, *supra* note 8; Nat'l Consumer L. Ctr. Comment #00018, *supra* note 1; N.Y.U. Info. L. Inst. Comment #00015, *supra* note 8; World Privacy Forum Comment #00014, *supra* note 19; Tech. Pol'y Inst. Comment #00010, *supra* note 8; Ctr. for Dig. Democracy & U.S. PIRG Educ. Fund Comment #00003, *supra* note 8.

[137] *See, e.g.*, Solon Barocas & Andrew Selbst, *Big Data's Disparate Impact*, 104 CAL. LAw R. _ (forthcoming 2016), http://papers. ssrn.com/sol3/papers.cfm?abstract_id=2477899##; Alex Rosenblat et al., *Networked Employment Discrimination*, (Data & Society Research Inst.,Working Paper Oct. 8, 2014), http://www.datasociety.net/ pubs/fow/ EmploymentDiscrimination.pdf; Gary Marcus & Ernest Davis, *Eight (No, Nine!) Problems With Big Data*, N.Y. TIMEs (Apr. 6, 2014), http://www.nytimes. com/2014/04/07/ opinion/eight-no-nine-problems-with-big-data.html?_r=0; Tim Harford, *Big Data: Are We Making a Big Mistake?*, FT MAGAZINE (Mar. 28, 2014), http://www.ft.com/ intl/cms/s/2/21a6e7d8-b479-11e3-a09a-00144feabdc0.html. *See generally* JosEPH TuRow, THE DAILY You: How THE NEw ADVERTIsING INDusTRY Is DEFINING YouR IDENTITY AND YouR WoRTH (2012).

[138] *See, e.g.*, Big Data Tr. 19–25 (Solon Barocas). *See also* Nat'l Consumer L. Ctr. Comment #00018, *supra* note 1, at 14–15; World Privacy Forum Comment #00014, *supra* note 19, at 6–17. *See generally* Barocas & Selbst, *supra* note 137.

[139] Barocas & Selbst, *supra* note 137, at 20–22. Researchers note that data mining poses the additional problem of giving data miners the ability to disguise intentional discrimination as unintentional. *Id.* at 22–23. *See also* Paul Ohm, *Changing the Rules: General Principles for Data Use and Analysis*, *in* PRIVACY, BIG DATA, AND THE PuBLIC GooD: FRAMEwoRKs FoR ENGAGEMENT 100–02 (Julia Lane et al. eds., 2014). For examples of the kinds of analyses that can be conducted to detect whether model variables are proxies for protected characteristics, see generally FED. TRADE CoMM'N, CREDIT-BAsED INsuRANCE SCoREs: IMPACTs oN CoNsuMERs oF AuToMoBILE INsuRANCE (2007), http://www.ftc.gov/sites/default/files/ documents/reports/credit-based-insurance-scores-impacts-consumers-automobile-insurance-report-congress-federal-trade/ p044804facta_report_credit-based_insurance_scores.pdf, and BD. oF GoVERNoRs oF

THE FED. RESERVE SYS., REPORT TO CONGRESS ON CREDIT SCORING AND ITS EFFECTS ON THE AVAILABILITY AND AFFORDABILITY OF CREDIT (2007), http://www. federalreserve.gov/boarddocs/rptcongress/creditscore/creditscore.pdf.

140 *See generally* Robinson + Yu Comment #00080, *supra* note 53; Am.'s Open Tech. Inst. Comment #00078, *supra* note 46; Ctr. for Democracy & Tech. Comment #00075, *supra* note 61; Am. Civil Liberties Union Comment #00059, *supra* note 61; Ctr. on Privacy & Tech. at Geo. L. Comment #00024, *supra* note 8; Nat'l Consumer L. Ctr. Comment #00018, *supra* note 1; Common Sense Media Comment #00016, *supra* note 8; N.Y.U. Info. L. Inst. Comment #00015, *supra* note 8; World Privacy Forum Comment #00014, *supra* note 19; Ctr. for Dig. Democracy & U.S. PIRG Educ. Fund Comment #00003, *supra* note 8. *See also* Barocas & Selbst, *supra* note 137; Crawford, *supra* note 39.

141 *See, e.g.*, Big Data Tr. 75 (Gene Gsell). *See generally* Comment #00081 from Berin Szoka & Tom Struble, TechFreedom, & Geoffrey Manne & Ben Sperry, Int'l Ctr. for L. & Econ., to Fed. Trade Comm'n (Nov. 3, 2014), https://www.ftc. gov/system/files/documents/ public_comments/2014/11/00081-92956.pdf; Comment #00074 from Howard Fienberg, Mktg. Research Assoc., to Fed. Trade Comm'n (Oct. 31, 2014), https://www.ftc.gov/ system/files/documents/public_ comments/2014/10/00074-92927.pdf; Comment #00070 from Bijan Madhani, Computer & Commc'ns Indus. Assoc., to Fed. Trade Comm'n (Oct. 31, 2014), https://www.ftc.gov/system/files/documents/public_comments/2014/10/00070-92912. pdf; NetChoice Comment #00066, *supra* note 23; Ctr. for Data Innovation Comment #00055, *supra* note 8; Ctr. for Data Innovation Comment #00026, *supra* note 8; Tech. Pol'y Inst. Comment #00010, *supra* note 8; VIKTOR MAYER-SCHONBERGER & KENNETH CUKIER, BIG DATA: A REVOLUTION THAT WILL TRANSFORM HOW WE LIVE, WORK, AND THINK (2013).

142 *See, e.g.*, Dan Gray, *Ethics, Privacy and Discrimination in the Age of Big Data*, DATACONOMY (Dec. 3, 2014), http:// dataconomy.com/ethics-privacy-and-discrimination-in-the-age-of-big-data/. *But see* Jeff Leek, *Why Big Data Is in Trouble: They Forgot About Applied Statistics*, SIMPLYSTATS (May 7, 2014), http://simplystatistics.org/2014/05/07/ why-big-data-isin-trouble-they-forgot-about-applied-statistics/ (noting that big data users have not given sufficient attention to issues that statisticians have been thinking about for a long time: sampling populations, multiple testing, bias, and overfitting).

143 *See, e.g.*, Don Peck, *They're Watching You at Work*, ATLANTIC (Dec. 2013), http://www.theatlantic.com/magazine/archive/2013/12/theyre-watching-you-at-work/354681/.

144 *See, e.g.*, Big Data Tr. 126 (Mark MacCarthy), 251 (Christopher Wolf). *See also* Software & Info. Indus. Assoc. Comment #00067, *supra* note 2, at 7; Future of Privacy Forum Comment #00027, *supra* note 23, attached report entitled, BIG DATA: A TOOL FOR FIGHTING DISCRIMINATION AND EMPOWERING GROUPS, at 1–2.

145 *See, e.g.*, Anne Loehr, *Big Data for HR: Can Predictive Analytics Help Decrease Discrimination in the Workplace?*, HUFFINGTON POST (Mar. 23, 2015), http://www.huffingtonpost.com/anne-loehr/big-data-for-hr-can-predi_b_6905754.html.

146 WHITE HOUSE FEB. 2015 REPORT, *supra* note 56, at 16.

147 *Id.* at 17. Economists have documented ways that data can help identify discrimination against protected groups in a wide variety of settings. For example, a randomized experiment changed the names on resumes sent to employers from white-sounding names to African-American sounding names; resumes with white-sounding names were 50 percent more likely to be called back for an interview. Marianne Bertrand & Sendhil Mullainathan, *Are Emily and Greg More Employable Than Lakisha and Jamal? A Field Experiment on Labor*

Market Discrimination, 94 AM. ECoN. REv. 991, 991–1013 (2004). Research from the early days of the Internet found that African-Americans and Latinos paid about 2 percent more for used cars purchased offline, but paid similar prices for those purchased online; the proffered reason was that individuals were anonymous online. Fiona Scott Morton et al., *Consumer Information and Discrimination: Does the Internet Affect the Pricing of New Cars to Women and Minorities?*, 1 QUANTITATIvE MKTG. & ECoNS. 65, 65–92 (2003). *See also* Devin Pope & Justin Sydnor, *Implementing Anti-Discrimination Policies in Statistical Profiling Models*, 3 AM. ECoN. J.: ECoN. PoL'Y 206, 206–231 (2011), http://faculty.chicagobooth.edu/devin.pope/research/pdf/Website_Antidiscrimination %20Models.pdf.

[148] A digital divide refers to the fact that certain populations may not have access to the Internet. *See, e.g.*, Ctr. for Data Innovation Comment #00055, *supra* note 8, at 2; Nat'l Consumer L. Ctr. Comment #00018, *supra* note 1, at 9, 27; Ctr. for Dig. Democracy & U.S. PIRG Educ. Fund Comment #00003, *supra* note 8, at 2.

[149] Data deserts are geographic "areas characterized by a lack of access to high-quality data that may be used to generate social and economic benefits." Ctr. for Data Innovation, Comment #00055, *supra* note 8, at 3. "[I]f some communities are not represented in the data, decisions may overlook members of these communities and their unique needs." *Id.*, attached report entitled, WIKIPEDIA EDITS REVEAL AMERIcA'S DATA DESERTS, at 1.

[150] *See, e.g.*, Big Data Tr. 100–02 (Dr. Nicol Turner-Lee), 256–58 (Daniel Castro). *See also* Ctr. for Dig. Democracy & U.S. PIRG Educ. Fund Comment #00003, *supra* note 8, at 2; Quentin Hardy, *Why Big Data Is Not Truth*, N.Y. TIMES (June 1, 2013), http://bits.blogs.nytimes.com/2013/06/01/why-big-data-is-not-truth/?_php=true&_type=blogs&_r=1 (reviewing a speech provided by Kate Crawford); danah boyd & Kate Crawford, *Critical Questions for Big Data*, 15 INFo., CoMM'N & Soc'y 662, 668–70 (2012), http://dx.doi.org/10.1080/1369118X.2012.678878.

[151] *See, e.g.*, Crawford, *supra* note 39. *See also* Grinberg et al., *supra* note 37.

[152] Crawford, *supra* note 39.

[153] *See, e.g.*, Big Data Tr. 21–22 (Solon Barocas), 259–60 (Michael Spadea). *See also* Tech. Pol'y Inst. Comment #00010, *supra* note 8, at 4 & attached report at 15; WHITE HOUSE MAY 2014 REPORT, *supra* note 1, at 51–52.

[154] *See, e.g.*, Big Data Tr. 19–25 (Solon Barocas), 40–41 (Joseph Turow).

[155] Barocas & Selbst, *supra* note 137, at 3–4.

[156] *See, e.g.*, Big Data Tr. 168–70 (Carol Miaskoff). *Cf.* Barocas & Selbst, *supra* note 137, at 9–11.

[157] *See generally* Stella Lowry & Gordon Macpherson, *A Blot on the Profession*, 296 BRITISH MED. J., 657, 657–58 (1988), http://www.ncbi.nlm.nih.gov/pmc/articles/PMC 2545288/pdf/bmj00275-0003.pdf.

[158] *See generally* Latanya Sweeney, *Discrimination in Online Ad Delivery*, 56 COMMC'NS OF THE ACM 44 (2013), http://papers. ssrn.com/sol3/papers.cfm?abstract_id=22082 40&download=yes. *See also* Big Data Tr. 64–65 (David Robinson); Robinson + Yu Comment #00080, *supra* note 53, at 16–17; N.Y.U. Info. L. Inst. Comment #00015, *supra* note 8, at 6.

[159] Sweeney, *supra* note 158, at 34. *See also* Bianca Bosker, *Google's Online Ad Results Guilty of Racial Profiling, According to New Study*, HUFFINGTON POST (Feb. 5, 2013), http://www.huffingtonpost.com/2013/02/05/online-racial-profiling_n_2622556.html ("[O]ver time, as certain templates are clicked more frequently than others, Google will

attempt to optimize its customer's ad by more frequently showing the ad that garners the most clicks.").

[160] *See supra* notes 35–36 and accompanying text. *See also* Am.'s Open Tech. Inst. Comment #00078, *supra* note 46, at 60–61.

[161] *Cf.* Matt Richtel, *How Big Data Is Playing Recruiter for Specialized Workers*, N.Y. TIMES (Apr. 27, 2013), http://www.nytimes. com/2013/04/28/technology/how-big-data-is-playing-recruiter-for-specialized-workers.html (noting that some companies are using technology to find candidates based on their ability to succeed on the job rather than traditional markers, such as a degree from a top college).

[162] The Commission recognizes that, to address data sets that incorporate previous prejudices, companies may need to collect demographic information about consumers that they would not otherwise collect. If they do collect this information, they should provide disclosures and choices to consumers where appropriate.

[163] *See, e.g.*, David Lazer et al., *The Parable of Google Flu: Traps in Big Data Analysis*, 343 SdI. 1203, 1203–05 (2014), http:// gking.harvard.edu/files/gking/files/0314 policyforumff.pdf; Marcus & Davis, *supra* note 137; Steve Lohr, *Google Flu Trends: The Limits of Big Data*, N.Y. TIMES (Mar. 28, 2014), http://bits.blogs.nytimes.com/ 2014/03/28/google-flu-trends-the-limitsof-big-data/?_r=0.

[164] *See, e.g.*, Marcus & Davis, *supra* note 137. Likewise, these researchers note that whenever the source of information for a big data analysis is itself a product of big data, opportunities for reinforcing errors exist. *See id.*

[165] *See supra* note 163 and accompanying text. *Cf.* Tech. Pol'y Inst. Comment #00010, *supra* note 8, attached report at 5–6.

[166] Harford, *supra* note 137, at 133.

[167] *See, e.g.*, Big Data Tr. 51–52 (David Robinson), 83–84 (Mark MacCarthy), 102–06 (Stuart Pratt), 231–32 (Michael Spadea). *See also* Software & Info. Indus. Assoc. Comment #00067, *supra* note 2, at 5–6 and attached report at 7; Tech. Pol'y Inst. Comment #00010, *supra* note 8, at 5–6.

[168] Some workshop participants and commenters note other challenges of using utility payments as a non-traditional indicator. *See, e.g.*, Big Data Tr. 51–53 (David Robinson). *See also* Robinson + Yu Comment #00080, *supra* note 53, at 10–11; Nat'l Consumer L. Ctr. Comment #00018, *supra* note 1, at 13–14; Ctr. for Dig. Democracy & U.S. PIRG Educ. Fund Comment #00003, *supra* note 8, at 17.

[169] *See, e.g.*, Frank Pasquale, *The Dark Market for Personal Data*, N.Y. TIMES (Oct. 16, 2014), http://www.nytimes.com/2014/10/17/opinion/the-dark-market-for-personal-data.html?module=Search&mabReward=relbias%3Aw; Danielle Keats Citron, *Big Data Should Be Regulated By 'Technological Due Process,'* N.Y. TIMES (Aug. 6, 2014), http://www.nytimes. com/roomfordebate/2014/08/06/is-big-data-spreading-inequality/big-data-should-be-regulated-by-technological-due-process; Cathy O'Neil, *The Dark Matter of Big Data*, MATHBABE (June 25, 2014), http://mathbabe.org/2014/06/25/the-darkmatter-of-big-data/; boyd & Crawford, *supra* note 150, at 670–73; Ylan Q. Mui, *Little Known Firms Tracking Data Used in Credit Scores*, WASH. POST (July 16, 2011), http://www.washingtonpost.com/business/economy/little-known-firms-trackingdata-used-in-credit-scores/2011/05/24/gIQAXHcWII_story.html. For the reasons set forth in her separate statement, Commissioner Ohlhausen believes that to assess properly any risks of harm from big data inaccuracies, such risks must be evaluated in the context of the competitive process.

[170] *See* DATA BRoKERS REPoRT, *supra* note 7, at 53–54.

[171] *See, e.g.*, Big Data Tr. 238–40 (Jeanette Fitzgerald). *See generally* The Internet Assoc. Comment #00073, *supra* note 23; Comment #00071 from Pam Dixon, World Privacy Forum, to Fed. Trade Comm'n (Oct. 31, 2014), https://www.ftc.gov/system/files/documents/public_comments/2014/10/00071-92911.pdf; Computer & Commc'ns Indus. Assoc. Comment #00070, *supra* note 141; Consumer Elecs. Assoc. Comment #00068, *supra* note 61; Intel Corp. Comment #00062, *supra* note 61; Comment #00060 from Yael Weinman, Info. Tech. Indus. Council, to Fed. Trade Comm'n (Oct. 27, 2014), https:// www.ftc.gov/system/files/documents/public_comments/2014/10/00060-92877.pdf; Info. Accountability Found. Comment #00049, *supra* note 2; Comment #00048 from Bojana Bellamy & Markus Heyder, Ctr. for Info. Pol'y Leadership, to Fed. Trade Comm'n (Oct. 8, 2014), https://www.ftc.gov/system/files/documents/ public_ comments/2014/10/00048-92775.pdf; Future of Privacy Forum Comment #00027, *supra* note 23.

[172] *See, e.g.*, Michael Schrage, *Big Data's Dangerous New Era of Discrimination*, HARv. BUS. REv. (Jan. 29, 2014), https://hbr. org/2014/01/big-datas-dangerous-new-era-of-discrimination/. *Cf.* Alessandro Acquisti et al., *Face Recognition and Privacy in the Age of Augmented Reality*, 6 J. oF PRIvACY & CoNFIDENTIAiITY 1–20 (2014), http://repository.cmu.edu/cgi/viewcontent. cgi?article=1122&context=jpc (showing that big data analytics can now identify strangers online (on a dating site where individuals protect their identities by using pseudonyms) and offline (in a public space), based on photos made publicly available on a social network site, and then infer additional and sensitive information about those consumers with relative ease).

[173] *See, e.g.*, Robinson + Yu Comment #00080, *supra* note 53, at 15. *See also* Joseph Walker, *Meet The New Boss: Big Data*, WAii ST. J. (Sept. 20, 2012), http://online.wsj.com/news/articles/SB10000872396390443890304578006252019616768.

[174] *See supra* note 173.

[175] *See, e.g.*, Future of Privacy Forum Comment #00027, *supra* note 23, attached report entitled, BIG DATA: A Tooi FoR FIGHTING DISCRIMINATIoN AND EMPoWERING GRoUPS, at 1.

[176] *See, e.g.*, Tim Smedley, *Forget the CV, Data Decide Careers*, FIN. TIMES (July 9, 2014), http://www.ft.com/cms/s/2/e3561cd0-dd11-11e3-8546-00144feabdc0.html#axzz373 wnekp7.

[177] *See, e.g.*, Peck, *supra* note 143.

[178] *Id.*

[179] *See, e.g.*, Future of Privacy Forum Comment #00027, *supra* note 23, attached report entitled, BIG DATA: A Tool FoR FIGHTING DISCRIMINATIoN AND EMPoWERING GRoUPS, at 4; Computer & Commc'ns Indus. Assoc. Comment #00070, *supra* note 141, at 6–7. *See also* Laura Nahmias, *State Agencies Launch LGBT Data-Collection Effort*, PolITICo N.Y. (July 24, 2014), http://www.capitalnewyork.com/article/albany/2014/07/8549536/state-agencies-launch-lgbt-data-collection-effort.

[180] *See, e.g.*, Future of Privacy Forum Comment #00027, *supra* note 23, attached report entitled, BIG DATA: A Tool FoR FIGHTING DISCRIMINATIoN AND EMPoWERING GRoUPS, at 3.

End Notes for Appendix

[1] FED. TRADE COMM'N, BIG DATA: A TOOL FOR INCLUSION OR EXCLUSION? UNDERSTANDING THE ISSUES 8–11, 25–27 (2016). The report also references other concerns that big data analysis will be *too* accurate: companies will understand their consumers too well and misuse that data to the consumer's detriment. Market forces also constrain many such potential harms, but other such harms could actually undermine market forces. For example, the report describes concerns that unscrupulous businesses will use big data techniques to develop "sucker lists" of consumers particularly vulnerable to scams and misleading offers. The report does a good job laying out the existing legal framework that applies to such harmful uses.

[2] *Id.* at 9–11.

[3] A real world example of the competitive advantages of novel but accurate application of data analytics was famously chronicled in the book (and movie) *Moneyball*. *See* MICHAEL LEWIS, MONEYBALL: THE ART OF WINNING AN UNFAIR GAME (2004). Oakland's strategy succeeded precisely because it "liberated" baseball players from "unthinking prejudice rooted in baseball's traditions . . . allowing them to demonstrate their true worth." *Id.* at iiv. Each baseball franchise continually faces marketplace pressures to improve player quality predictions. Similarly, companies using big data analytics face competitive forces that punish inaccuracy and reward accuracy.

[4] Indeed, there is strong theoretical and empirical economic evidence that low income and other disadvantaged households stand to gain more than the wealthy from many applications of big data analytics. *See* JAMES C. CooPER, SEPARATIoN, PooLING, AND PREDIcTIvE PRIvAcY HARMS FRoM BIG DATA: CoNFUSING BENEFITS FoR CoSTS 38–49 (2015), http:// ssrn.com/abstract=2655794 (describing theoretical and empirical studies on the effects of big data in credit markets, price discrimination, and labor markets for low income individuals). One simple example: lenders do not need big data analytics to identify creditworthy high-income persons, as nearly all have credit files and most are lower-risk. However, lower-income groups contain both high- and low-risk borrowers. Big data analysis can help bring credit to the lower-risk low income borrowers with thin or no credit files. *See id.* at 38–39.

[5] Transcript of Big Data: A Tool for Inclusion or Exclusion?, in Washington, D.C. (Sept. 15, 2014), at 231–32 (Daniel Castro and Michael Spaeda in conversation), https://www.ftc.gov/system/files/documents/public_events/313371/bigdatatranscript-9_15_14.pdf (highlighting the business opportunities in improved accuracy of credit scoring for low-income individuals). Indeed, our workshop on lead generation showed that lenders and other businesses are highly motivated to reach potential customers and spend a lot of money and effort to do so. *See generally Follow the Lead: An FTC Workshop on Lead Generation*, FED. TRADE CoMM'N (Oct. 30, 2015), https://www.ftc.gov/news-events/events-calendar/2015/10/followlead-ftc-workshop-lead-generation.

[6] For example, Cooper describes a useful framework to help identify under which conditions the presumption should be for or against big data uses. *See* CooPER, *supra* note 4, at 33–38.

In: The Use of Big Data
Editor: Diana Simpson
ISBN: 978-1-63485-318-7

Chapter 2

COMMENTS OF THOMAS M. LENARD, PRESIDENT AND SENIOR FELLOW, TECHNOLOGY POLICY INSTITUTE. WORKSHOP ON "BIG DATA: A TOOL FOR INCLUSION OR EXCLUSION?"*

These comments respond to the Federal Trade Commission's June 25 request for comments in preparation for its September 15 public workshop, "Big Data: A Tool for Inclusion or Exclusion?" In its announcement, the Commission observes that "tremendous benefits flow from the insights of big data," but notes that "concerns have been raised about whether big data may be used to categorize consumers in ways that may affect them unfairly, or even unlawfully." The purpose of the workshop is to "examine the potentially positive and negative effects of big data on low income and underserved populations."

The Commission's plan for this workshop reflects two themes prevalent in recent privacy-centric big data literature, in statements from FTC Commissioners[1], and in a major White House report on big data (the Big Data Report). [2] First, that the use of big data to develop predictive models may be harmful to consumers; and, second, that the use of big data for marketing and other purposes may favor the rich over the poor or in other ways be

* This is an edited, reformatted and augmented version of comments offered July 28, 2014 in response to a request from the Federal Trade Commission in preparation of a public workshop on September 15, 2014.

discriminatory. I address each of these concerns in turn, drawing from a 2014 Technology Policy Institute paper.[3]

IS THE USE OF BIG DATA TO DEVELOP PREDICTIVE MODELS HARMFUL TO CONSUMERS?[4]

The systematic use of individuals' data for a wide range of purposes is not new. The direct marketing industry for decades has assembled mailing lists of consumers interested in specific products and services. Credit bureaus use formulas that determine individuals' eligibility for loans and the rates they may be offered. Similarly, the insurance industry uses key variables that indicate risk to determine whether and at what rates to offer insurance policies.

The use of credentials and test scores is also ubiquitous in American life. For example, the educational testing industry is based on the use of such correlations.[5] The Federal Government, including the FTC, uses class rank in hiring lawyers. These decisions are based on "small data"—sometimes, one test score or one data point.

The claim that predictive models harm consumers, if valid, would apply to quantitative analysis used for decision-making throughout the economy. Much of the concern seems to be that the predictive models may not be totally accurate. Big data, however, can be expected to improve accuracy. The use of more data points makes it less likely that any single data point will be determinative, and more likely that a correct decision will be reached.

Companies that devote resources to gathering data and undertaking complex analysis do so in order to reduce errors. The data and models have limited value unless they improve accuracy. Thus, big data should lead to less mis-categorization of consumers and less arbitrary decision making.

The use of more variables made possible by big data should lead to more accurate decisions that also might be perceived as "fairer." For example, more data are now being used by state parole boards to help inform parole decisions.[6] Proponents believe the use of big data in this manner provides more accurate predictions of the risk of recidivism and can help determine which prisoners should be released, improving public safety and perhaps also reducing prison costs. Other examples involve the use of data to help underwrite loans to individuals who otherwise would not qualify and to help consumers compare prices. These are discussed in more detail below.

IS THE USE OF BIG DATA DISCRIMINATORY?[7]

Writers who argue that data collection and analytics favor the rich over the poor rely on hypothetical rather than actual examples.[8] The White House Big Data Report argues that "big data analytics have the potential to eclipse longstanding civil rights protections in how personal information is used in housing, credit, employment, health, education, and the marketplace,"[9] but again the supporting evidence is weak. Indeed, the two specific examples of discrimination cited in the Big Data Report turn out to be essentially non-examples. Also, both examples involve government—not private sector—use of data.

The first example involves StreetBump, a mobile application developed to collect information about potholes and other road conditions in Boston. Even before its launch, the city recognized that this app, by itself, would be biased toward identifying problems in wealthier neighborhoods, because wealthier individuals would be more likely to own smartphones and make use of the app. As a result, the city adjusted accordingly to assure reporting of road conditions was accurate and consistent throughout the city.[10]

The second example involves the E-verify program used by employers to check the eligibility of employees to work legally in the United States. The report cites a study that "found the rate at which U.S. citizen (sic) have their authorization to work be initially erroneously unconfirmed by the system was 0.3 percent, compared to 2.1 percent for non-citizens. However, after a few days many of these workers' status was confirmed."[11] It seems almost inevitable that the error rate for citizens would be lower, because citizens are automatically eligible to work, whereas additional information is needed to confirm eligibility for non-citizens (i.e., evidence of some sort of work permit). Hence, it is not clear this is an example of discrimination.

If the concern is about the use of big data to facilitate price discrimination, it is more likely that price discrimination will favor lower-income individuals. Since price discrimination involves charging different prices to different consumers for the same product based on their willingness to pay, and since willingness to pay is generally positively related to ability to pay, price discrimination will, other things equal, result in lower prices to lower-income consumers.

Moreover, big data are being used to develop products that specifically benefit lower-income consumers. For example, companies, such as ZestFinance, LendUp and Better Finance Inc. are using models containing many more variables than traditional credit scoring to help lenders determine whether or not to offer small, short-term loans to people who are otherwise poor credit risks.[12] This provides a better alternative to people who otherwise might rely on payday lenders or even loan sharks. Other companies, such as Kabbage and On Deck Capital, provide lending services to very small businesses.[13]

Big data have the potential to provide cost savings to consumers through the analysis and comparison of the prices of goods sold over the internet. Two successful startups, Farecast and Decide.com, use big data to help consumers find the lowest prices.[14] Farecast uses billions of flight-price records to predict the movement of airfares, saving purchasers an average of $50 per ticket. Decide.com predicts price movements for millions of products with potential savings for consumers of around $100 per item.

CONCLUSION

The Commission asks whether big data is a tool for inclusion or exclusion and, of course, it is both. Any tool that categorizes individuals will necessarily include some and exclude others. There is, however, no evidence that big data unfairly favors or disfavors particular groups. The use of more information through big data lowers error rates and improves accuracy. Importantly, the analysis presented here suggests that the use of data is benefiting lower-income consumers in a variety of ways.

End Notes

1 See, for example, Edith Ramirez, "The Privacy Challenges of Big Data: A View from the Lifeguard's Chair," (speech, Technology Policy Institute's Aspen Forum, August, 2013) accessed at http://ftc.gov/speeches/ramirez.shtm; and Julie Brill, "Demanding transparency from data brokers," Washington Post, August 15, 2013, accessed at http://www.washingtonpost.com/opinions/demanding-transparency-from-databrokers/2013/08/15/00609680-0382-11e3-9259-e2aafe5a5f84 story.html.

2 Executive Office of the President, Big Data: Seizing Opportunities, Preserving Values, May, 2014 (Big Data Report).

3 Thomas M. Lenard and Paul H. Rubin, "Big Data, Privacy and the Familiar Solutions," May 13, 2014, available at https://www.techpolicyinstitute.org/files/lenard_big% 20dataprivacyandthefamiliarsolutions.pdf.

4 See Lenard and Rubin, pp. 11-14.

5 See, for example, William A. Mehrens, "Using Test Scores for Decision Making", Test Policy and Test Performance: Education, Language, and Culture, 1989, pp. 93-113.

[6] See Joseph Walker, "State Patrol Boards Use Software to Decide Which Inmates to Release", The Wall Street Journal Online, October 12, 2013, available at: http://online.wsj.com/news/article_email/SB10001424052702304626104579121251595240852-lMyQjAxMTAzMDEwMDExNDAyWj.

[7] See Lenard and Rubin, pp. 14-15.

[8] See, for example, Joseph Jerome, "Buying and Selling Privacy: Big Data's Different Burdens and Benefits," 66 Stanford Law Review Online 47, 2013 available at http://www.stanfordlawreview.org/sites/default/files/online/topics/66_StanLRevOnline_47_Jerome.pdf; and Omar Tene, "Privacy: For the Rich or for the Poor," July 2012, Concurring Opinions Blog Post, available at: http://www.concurringopinions.com/archives/2012/07/privacy-for-the-rich-or-for-the-poor.html.

[9] Executive Office of the President, Big Data: Seizing Opportunities, Preserving Values, May, 2014, Cover Letter.

[10] Big Data Report, pp. 51-52.

[11] Big Data Report, p. 52.

[12] ZestFinance see http://www.zestfinance.com/how-we-do-it.html. LendUp see https://www.lendup.com/about. Better Finance Inc. see http://www.smartpaylease.com/.

[13] Kabbage see https://www.kabbage.com/how-it-works. OnDeck see https://www. ondeck.com/company/

[14] Mayer-Schönberger, Victor and Kenneth Cukier. Big Data: a revolution that will transform how we live, work and think. Houghton Mifflin Harcourt, 2013, p. 124.

In: The Use of Big Data
Editor: Diana Simpson

ISBN: 978-1-63485-318-7

Chapter 3

COMMENTS OF MICHELLE DE MOOY, DEPUTY DIRECTOR, CONSUMER PRIVACY PROJECT, CENTER FOR DEMOCRACY AND TECHNOLOGY. WORKSHOP ON "BIG DATA: A TOOL FOR INCLUSION OR EXCLUSION?"*

October 31, 2014

Federal Trade Commission, Office of the Secretary
Room H-113 (Annex X)
600 Pennsylvania Avenue, NW
Washington, DC 20580

RE: Comments to the Federal Trade Commission on the "Big Data: A Tool for Inclusion or Exclusion?" Workshop, Project No. P145406

> "Too many information handlers seem to measure a man by the number of bits of storage capacity his dossier will occupy."

Arthur R. Miller, The Assault on Privacy: Computers, Data Banks, and Dossiers

---

* This is an edited, reformatted and augmented version of comments offered October 31, 2014 in response to a request from the Federal Trade Commission in preparation of a public workshop on September 15, 2014.

The Center for Democracy & Technology (CDT) is pleased to submit comments in response to the Federal Trade Commission's Request For Information (RFI) on the September 15th workshop entitled "Big Data: A Tool for Inclusion or Exclusion?"

At its core, big data is simply information about people that can be rapidly processed by powerful new analytic tools. The potential for big data to inform discussions on critical global issues like public health, climate change, and financial markets is exciting. But the primary application of big data, in a commercial context for marketing purposes, offers neither a solution nor a salve to the world's problems – it is but one of many technical tools that capitalize on advances in computer speed and improved memory capacity to further business interests. For big data to function, it must have a constant stream of personal information about consumers, often information that includes sensitive matters such as a person's health, location, and financial status.

Personal privacy, in contrast, is a deeply held belief and human right that is foundational to the concept of individual liberty, autonomy and freedom, one that has been validated by hundreds of years of philosophy and case law. The idea that a loss of control over one's personal privacy is a reasonable price tag for the potential of big data is a fallacy that seems only to give industries an excuse not to ask consumers for permission to use their information. Instead, it's clear that a fair trade in this context would naturally give consumers more leverage over companies who seek to continually feed their data machines. Rather than make a value proposition to consumers for their personal information, many in the business world have moved to a system of hidden pervasive surveillance and collection. Heightened data collection, processing, and retention capacity should indicate that consumers need stronger controls and protections, not weaker and less transparent.

The Fair Information Practice Principles (FIPPs) were originally articulated to address the first wave of big data driven by machine processing and credit scoring in the 1960s and 70s. These principles have guided policymakers in safeguarding privacy for forty years; we believe they are just as relevant today as they were when they were first articulated. We strongly urge the Commission to stress the need for the full range of FIPPs protections over personal data. While big data and algorithmic processing raises interesting and important questions about fairness, harmful uses, and accountability, ultimately consumers may not want to rely on the black box protections offered by companies, and deserve autonomy and agency over the collection and use of their personal information.

TRANSPARENCY

For all the societal benefits that can come with the availability of large data sets, big data has also given institutions a much greater capacity to monitor, process, and retain data about consumers, all with little to no transparency available to the data contributors themselves. Today, most people have no idea what exists about them in company databases, on digital dossiers collected by data brokers, or the data points that go into complex algorithms used to make determinations about the prices, terms, products, and services they are offered.

We believe that some traditional privacy-enhancing tools are still valuable in pursuing transparency. While few consumers are likely to read even improved privacy policies, they play an important role in public accountability for data processing activities. In theory, these policies make actionable information available to regulators and consumer advocates to assess actual behaviors. Too often, though, these policies do not specifically describe actual practices, and instead reserve broad, vague rights over the collection and use of personal information.

Privacy transparency needs to be improved. Companies should be required to make available within privacy policies specific information about what they're doing with personal information. Moreover, companies should provide contextual, just-in-time notices and other effective consumer notification for data collection or usage practices that would likely surprise users. Without adequate notice and consent provisions, customers who don't approve of what a particular business does won't be able to "vote with their feet" and choose another business with different practices.

For this reason, we strongly support the FTC's use of "material omission" to pursue companies that fail to disclose certain sensitive data practices or gain consent for their collection, such as in the case against Goldenshores Technologies Brightest Flashlight App which deceptively accessed information such as location without users' knowledge. The FTC should continue to aggressively pursue cases like this to promote transparency of practices and to unearth new categories and combinations of information that may require special disclosure and consent, whether in a stand-along privacy policy or, in some cases, in prominent notices during consent flows.

The FTC should also explore ways that companies could introduce transparency into algorithmic data processing as well. Investigating or holding accountable practices that might lead to discriminatory or disparate impact – such as price discrimination – is made extremely difficult without algorithmic transparency. Achieving transparency in this space has proved challenging. Most consumers also don't have the time, interest, or ability to technically parse their online data trail, and companies have little interest in exposing their proprietary algorithms or the underlying data. To move the discussion forward, we encourage the FTC to consider new ways of thinking about transparency.

The technical details of how a broker transforms "white, 28, female, bicycling, craft beer" into "urban hipster" are largely irrelevant to the regulatory question of whether or not the mechanisms behind the profile are perpetuating discriminatory practices. The FTC should establish conventions around acceptable and unacceptable data streams and data linkages in order to build a consistent regulatory framework that doesn't compromise business models or impede competition. For example, the FTC might consider whether certain streams of data (like Facebook friends and employment history) should be coupled at all.

This guidance would largely echo the core Fair Information Practice Principles. Author Paul Schwartz, for example, recommends that companies using big data analytics "develop reasonable mitigation processes and reasonable remedies as appropriate when analytics lead to decisions that harm individuals,"[1] a suggestion closely aligned with both the redress element of the individual participation and accountability FIPPs. Recognizing the data quality FIPP, Schwartz also recommends that companies "engage in decision-making based on analytic output that is reasonably accurate" and "only use information that is predictive."

Potential discriminatory impact assessments are also a promising transparency idea in order to prevent misuse of big data analytics; however, structuring such assessments and implementing oversight programs would require significant time and investment from the private sector. Moreover, without the voluntary release of such assessments and clarity regarding how companies audit their programs, it may difficult to ensure that they are being properly implemented and performed.

Laws such as the Fair Credit Reporting Act (FCRA) and the Equal Credit Opportunity Act (ECOA) offer more useful transparency tools that should be used aggressively by the FTC to enforce broader access and correction rights for consumers. The transparency and correction provisions in the FCRA, for example, provide individuals with a right to obtain a free copy of their consumer report once a year as well as the right to dispute or correct anything in the report, after which the FCRA has 30 days to do a "reasonable" investigation. It makes sense to apply these protections to the gigantic data sets on individuals that are mathematically bound to be incorrect or inaccurate some of the time. Like classifications, errors matter, particularly when they affect vulnerable populations and their ability to obtain credit with reasonable rates. Like traditional Credit Reporting Agencies (CRAs), most people have little to no contact with big data firms and have no remedy for correction or accountability.

PURPOSE SPECIFICATION AND USE LIMITATIONS

Purpose specification and use limitation are two closely related principles that are vital to protecting individual privacy. With respect to consumers, the Administration's Privacy Bill of Rights well describes the two principles when it says, "Consumers have a right to expect that companies will collect, use, and disclose personal data in ways that are consistent with the context in which consumers provide the data." Even in the era of big data, purpose specification remains a crucial first step in any system design, requiring entities to detail on what grounds they will collect data and the uses that they plan for it. The use limitation principle requires entities to follow through on the delineated uses and refrain from using the collected data for undisclosed purposes.

Certainly, it will not be possible for companies to spell out every single processing activity — or potential secondary use — even in a standalone privacy policy. However, companies should still endeavor to provide detailed information about the categories of ways it uses data and to provide representative examples. New applications of data that had not been previously disclosed may well be reasonable, so long as they are consistent with the purposes for which the information was taken in the first place. These applications will typically be first-party uses (or done through a dedicated service provider with no independent right to use the data), and should be of a nature such that an ordinary consumer would not find the uses surprising or objectionable. Respect for context must include the understanding that a big data scientist's notion of context may vary wildly from an ordinary consumer's viewpoint and nominal expectations.

While substantive limitations on data usage should play a role in any privacy protection framework, *overreliance* on reasonable commercial use requirements at the expense of individual autonomy and control would in most cases weaken — not strengthen — personal privacy protection.

Relying on responsible use will always be insufficient from a consumer's perspective because it addresses mostly internal accountability and liability, offering no meaningful way for consumers to evaluate practices in the context of their own lives. However, we agree that there should still be some specific constraints on uses that are clearly harmful, particularly to vulnerable populations. Use limitations are an important way to make sure entities to follow through on the delineated uses and refrain from using the collected data for undisclosed purposes. Companies must confine their uses of data to the purposes disclosed to consumers and if the company plans to share data collected with a third party, that sharing should be disclosed to consumers in advance, as should the third party's uses (e.g. analytics). Especially in the big data context, entities collecting personal information could very well develop new uses of data in future years that are loosely (if at all) related to the uses that the data was originally collected for. If that happens, entities must at the very least provide transparency about those new uses before they begin. Entities holding data should consider whether the new uses can be performed with de-identified data. They should carefully weigh the potential adverse consequences that may befall individuals from the use of such data and design their programs to avoid such consequences or ensure that they are reliable and justified. However, if data custodians conclude that the new uses can only be performed with identifiable data, and are not contextually related to the purposes for which the data was originally collected, they must seek new consent for those new uses. User expectations – and the potential for user *surprise* – are important indicia for whether a new purpose is contextually related to an older one.

Fundamentally, consumers have the right to control how and when they share information about themselves. This is especially true for consumers in disadvantaged communities, for whom being targeted and tracked can have adverse financial consequences. The United States has a long history of discrimination based on racial and economic profiling and fears of "digital redlining" are far from hypothetical. A report from policy researchers Robinson + Yu[2] details how even seemingly neutral data can reflect biases in favor of one group over another. In one example cited by the report, a car insurer decided to raise premiums on late-night drivers after remote tracking devices installed by the company determined that drivers on the road past a certain hour in the evening are more often impaired and thus a higher risk to insure. While the decision to bump up rates on these drivers might appear reasonable on the surface, a closer look shows that the greatest financial impact of the rate increase would land squarely on the shoulders of low-income persons of color, a population more likely to work night shifts and live further away from their jobs. The data has effectively created "disparate impact" by penalizing a group based on their socioeconomic status and location. In a report issued for the FTC's workshop, Peter Swire posits that the

ECOA, Fair Housing Act (FHA), and Title VII of the Civil Rights Act of 1964 cover both online and offline marketing activities[3]. Additionally, Swire suggests that these laws already apply disparate impact analysis to targeted marketing. He also brings up the concept of "steering," defined by the FHA as "deliberately guiding loan applicants or potential purchasers toward or away from certain types of loans or geographic areas because of race." In one example, Wells Fargo was found by the Justice Department to have used steering by several methods including its marketing activities and profiling mechanisms to target its subprime lending practices to poor communities and ultimately settled with the department for $175 million. The company developed software to generate marketing materials for its loan officers that offered a menu of language options. These employees routinely choose a language category entitled "African-American" in order to market subprime loans to poor neighborhoods[4]. Subsequent investigations done by the Justice Department show that it was tactics like this that enabled Wells Fargo brokers to systematically steer thousands of minority borrowers towards higher rates and fees, as well as costlier subprime loans, than white borrowers with similar credit profiles.

Consumers need a greater ability to control the information that flows to third-party data brokers that fall outside the Fair Credit Reporting Act. In many if not most cases, sale of personal information to a data broker falls outside the realm of reasonable expectations, and is not consistent with the purpose for which the consumer provided the information. Certainly, merchants today do not do a very good job of explaining secondary transfers of personal information to consumers; even when consumers sign up for a loyalty program or register for a warranty, they are not meaningfully told that their information may be sold to third parties. Reports from the Federal Trade Commission[5] and the Senate Commerce Committee[6] reveal that these data broker records often contain highly prejudicial characterizations of people based on their ethnicity, economic status, and even English-speaking ability. As illustrated in the Wells Fargo example, designations like these are not benign for vulnerable consumers.

Using these classifications, the data broker industry facilitates the discriminatory targeting that can lead to groups being penalized based on the perceived risk of that population, whether the penalty is costly subprime loans or the denial of a job. Because the collection, categorization, scoring determinations, and the ways in which these scores are derived, are mostly concealed from consumers, they are powerless to refute, amend or correct information in their profiles. Though the consequences of their practices and products closely mirror those of the regulated consumer scoring industry, data brokers remain largely unregulated and unaccountable for the economic harm their industry engenders.

To address this, the FTC should consider investigating scoring practices to unearth circumstances when data is being used as a proxy for discrimination. The Commission should also require data brokers to make current scoring determinations and marketing lists available to the public to dispute, delete or alter if they so choose, and work collaboratively with the Consumer Financial Protection Bureau to investigate how the data used by data brokers might contribute to financial and other impactful determinations such as employment eligibility.

Providing a centralized resource for consumers to find the various companies that are selling profiles about them would be greatly beneficial. In addition, the FTC should require companies to make reasonable default determinations about what data will be collected, how data will be used, how long data will be retained, and with whom data will be shared. Reasonable defaults including making the collection of marketing information opt-out as long as there is an easy and clearly visible way to turn the collection off.

Collection Limitations and Data Minimization

One of the key policy debates around Big Data has been around whether collection limitations and data minimization remain relevant, as getting rid of old data (or not collecting data in the first place) could potentially limit serendipitous uses or insights based on that data. We recognize the valuable societal benefits that could come from secondary research into large data sets, and as we note above, we support secondary uses of previously-collected data that are consistent with ordinary consumer understanding and the purposes for which data was originally given.

On the other hand, mere collection and retention of personal information also presents significant costs and potential for abuse. The mere possession of consumer data puts the information at risk and the longer a company holds onto to personal data, the higher the risk becomes. These risks include the increasingly common data breach; internal misuses such as the case of an engineer at a prominent company using his access to spy on user accounts of minors or the recent case in which an AT&T employee obtained customer social security numbers and driver's license numbers; uses that change as company policies change and become inimical to a consumer's best interest;

and illegitimate government access.[7] As such, data minimization is closely related to data security. *Collecting data without a clear (and disclosed) purpose in mind, or the failure to purge old data in accordance with reasonable minimization procedures, should be factors in evaluating whether an entity's data security practices were reasonable.*

As part of their security programs, companies, government agencies and other entities should implement specific, publicly-stated retention periods for data, rather than retaining that information indefinitely in all cases (certainly for some cases, like cloud-stored email, users naturally expect personal data to be stored indefinitely). If entities implement minimization procedures and delete unnecessary, outdated, or irrelevant entries, fewer records will be accessible to unauthorized parties if and when a data breach occurs. By removing identifying information and deleting data after it is no longer needed, companies will both protect their customers' security and promote consumer trust.

CONTROL

Consumers should in many (if not most) cases have the ability to make decisions about how their personal information will be collected, used, and retained, with contextual factors including the sensitivity of the data, the circumstance in which it is collected, and the necessity of it to the core functions of a product, In particular, they should be able to restrict access or use of certain sensitive data or provide permission through affirmative consent, with companies retaining the reciprocal ability to deny service if they are unwilling to adhere to a user's stated privacy preferences.

As data flows increase in complexity, it's unrealistic and overly burdensome to force consumers to set data collection, use, and retention preferences on a company-by-company basis. Users should have access to technical mechanisms that allow them to set global controls that express their own personal privacy policies (an idea noted in the White House Big Data report[8]), such as the FTC-endorsed Do Not Track technical standard. Furthermore, efforts to trick user agents in order to evade privacy settings are inherently deceptive and should be enforced as such by the FTC. We believe that technical controls will become increasingly important in the modern age and the FTC must be very clear to companies that using hidden mechanisms to subvert user settings is a deceptive practice.

As mentioned above, giving consumers control is a trade off. Apple's recent launch of its HealthKit platform offers an example of the intrinsic exchange that occurs between consumers and companies when customer control is commercialized. Apple rightly gives its customers complete control over what sensitive health information gets shared with what apps and prohibits those apps from selling to restricted data brokers. The decision to recognize the sensitivity of health data and provide true control options, however, necessarily limits Apple's revenue stream from data brokers and means that users of HealthKit will pay directly (as opposed to indirectly through the scooping up of their data) for the service. This exchange creates an imbalance in which privacy is made an expensive commodity, afforded only for the richest and credit-enabled. As the creation of paid-for alternatives to data sharing is likely to be the next phase in the tech marketplace, it's worth considering how restrictions on ad revenue might negatively affect consumers.

ACCOUNTABILITY, REGULATION AND LEGISLATION

As we have seen over the last ten years, purely self-regulatory models for governing data privacy (bounded only by FTC Section 5 enforcement authority) are inadequate. The inability of the industry to create and enforce meaningful privacy self-regulatory schemes is well documented, none quite as illustrative as in the case of online behavioral advertising. In the early 2000s, with the threat of legislation from Congress looming, industry representatives fought hard for self-regulation and began releasing a series of public initiatives. From the original failure of the Network Advertising Initiative in the early 2000s, to current fragile and, confusing opt-outs that are largely unused by the public and do not fundamentally limit data collection, to the AdChoices icon which is poorly understood by consumers, to the failure to adhere to browser Do Not Track signals, industry self-regulation schemes have been too weak placeholders for fundamental rights-based legislation.[9] On the other hand, prescriptive legislative approaches offer neither enough flexibility nor realistic counters to legitimate constraints to Internet innovation.

We believe that the FTC should back a principles-based legislative model enforced by the Commission, state attorneys general, and a private right of action. This would provide a framework with flexibility in the fast-changing tech environment. In fact, we believe that the FTC's use of its existing unfairness authority to pursue companies that fail to provide reasonable security, one of the key Fair Information Practice Principles, has been successful. By targeting bad security practices and delineating rules of the road for other companies to follow, the agency has effectively created legal precedent for this FIPP in US law. The FTC should continue on this regulatory path by reviewing all of the FIPPs when evaluating practices. In addition, the FTC should rigorously investigate current data collection and use practices for new fact patterns and do extensive legal research on how existing law might be invoked to stop data practices that (intentionally or unintentionally) double as proxies for discrimination, such as the ECOA. In one example of the unintended consequences of routine practices online, researchers found that the personal profiles of guests and hosts on lodging website *Airbnb.com*, which include photos, were providing a mechanism for racial discrimination[10]. The study found that hosts identified as white received 12% more for their listings than black hosts despite similar offerings. It also found that black hosts paid a larger penalty for a less desirable location than non-black hosts.

CDT also supports as part of privacy legislation allowing the FTC to endorse industry codes of conduct that are compliant with privacy law, as a mechanism to provide guidance and adaptability to the privacy regulation landscape. Giving the FTC the authority to certify certain practices as a statutory safe harbor from privacy enforcement, in conjunction with legislation, would incentivize industries to develop flexible codes that reflect real-world practices. However, legislation should be quite clear that the FTC's approval authority, while given broad discretion, is still contingent upon a code addressing all elements of the Fair Information Practice Principles — including data collection limits, data minimization, and individual control. Regulatory and co-regulatory oversight — as well as express commitments from companies — will in the short term likely be more effective in preventing big data analytics from being used for discriminatory ends.

The FTC should highlight the importance of individual control and autonomy while signaling out practices that run counter to an open and fair Internet, such as price discrimination, the collection and use of sensitive categories improperly, and opacity of industry practices and algorithms that prohibit effective accountability and responsible innovation.

Sincerely,

Michelle De Mooy
Deputy Director,
Consumer Privacy Project Center for Democracy and Technology

End Notes

[1] See Paul Schwartz, Data Protection Law and the Ethical Use of Analytics, Privacy & Security Law (Jan. 10, 2011), and Paul Schwartz, Property, Privacy, and Personal Data, 117 HARV. L. REV.2055, 2096 (2004).

[2] Rieke, Aaron; Robinson, David; Yu, Harlan. Civil Rights, Big Data, and Our Algorithmic Future (2014). http://bigdata.fairness.io/wp-content/uploads/2014/09/Civil_Rights_ Big_ Data_and_Our_Algorithmic- Future_2014-09-12.pdf.

[3] Swire, Peter. Lessons from Fair Lending Law for Fair Marketing and Big Data (Sept. 20140). http://www.futureofprivacy.org/wp-content/uploads/FairMarketingLessonsWhitePaper FTC.pdf

[4] Deposition of Tony Paschal, City of Maryland v. Wells Fargo, N.A. https://www.nclc. org/images/pdf/unreported/paschal-decl-balt.pdf.

[5] Federal Trade Commission, Data Brokers: A Call for Transparency and Accountability (2014), http://www.ftc.gov/system/files/documents/reports/data-brokers-call-transparency-accountability-reportfederal-trade-commission-may-2014/140527databrokerreport.pdf.

[6] United States Senate Committee on Commerce, Science, and Transportation, A Review of the Data Broker Industry: Collection, Use, and Sale of Consumer Data for Marketing Purposes (2013).

[7] Brookman, Justin; Hans, G.S., Why Collection Matters: Surveillance as a De Facto Privacy Harm, http://www.futureofprivacy.org/wpcontent/uploads/BrookmanWhyCollectionMatters.pdf.

[8] Big Data: Seizing Opportunities, Preserving Values (May 2014). http://www.whitehouse.gov/ sites/default/files/microsites/ostp/PCAST/pcast_big_data_and_privacy_may_2014.pdf.

[9] Brookman, Justin, Testimony before the Senate Committee on Commerce, Science, and Transportation, "A Status Update on the Development of Voluntary Do-Not-Track Standards," April 24, 2013, https://cdt.org/files/pdfs/Brookman-DNT-Testimony.pdf.

[10] Edelman, Benjamin G. and Luca, Michael. Digital Discrimination: The Case of Airbnb.com (Jan. 10, 2014). Harvard Business School NOM Unit Working Paper, No. 14-054. http://journalistsresource.org/studies/society/internet/possibilities-online-racial-discriminationresearch-airbnb#sthash.LQKNGwqT.dpuf.

In: The Use of Big Data
Editor: Diana Simpson
ISBN: 978-1-63485-318-7

Chapter 4

COMMENTS OF DANIEL CASTRO, DIRECTOR, CENTER FOR DATA INNOVATION. WORKSHOP ON "BIG DATA: A TOOL FOR INCLUSION OR EXCLUSION?"*

August 15, 2014

Mr. Donald S. Clark Federal Trade Commission Office of the Secretary Room H-113 (Annex J) 600 Pennsylvania Avenue, NW

Washington, DC 20580

Re: Big Data: A Tool for Inclusion or Exclusion? Workshop, Project No. P145406 Dear Mr. Clark,

On behalf of the Center for Data Innovation (www.datainnovation.org), I am pleased to submit these comments in response to the Federal Trade Commission's (FTC) request for public comment on big data and inclusivity in advance of its upcoming workshop.[1]

The Center for Data Innovation is a non-profit, non-partisan, Washington, D.C.-based think tank focusing on the impact of the increased use of information on the economy and society. In addition, the Center formulates and promotes pragmatic public policies designed to enable data-driven innovation in the public and private sectors, create new economic

---

* This is an edited, reformatted and augmented version of comments offered August 15, 2014 in response to a request from the Federal Trade Commission in preparation of a public workshop on September 15, 2014.

opportunities, and improve quality of life. The Center is affiliated with the Information Technology and Innovation Foundation (ITIF).

As we explain in these comments, organizations have always used predictive models; however, until recently these models were often quite rudimentary or relied on limited data sets.[2] These limitations result in inefficiencies for businesses, higher costs for consumers, and lower overall consumer experiences. While no predictive model is perfect and models vary in the levels of accuracy, precision, bias, and confidence they offer, big data offers many opportunities to create much improved predictive models that allow organizations to better tailor their products and services to meet individual needs.

HOW ARE ORGANIZATIONS USING BIG DATA TO CATEGORIZE CONSUMERS?

Organizations have always used methods to categorize consumers (e.g. "new customer" versus "returning customer"); however, the advent of big data allows them to do this on a much greater scale. Organizations may use analytical models to predict either categorical values (e.g. "qualifies for a loan") or continuous values (e.g. "credit score of 650"). Although the statistical methods behind classification algorithms differ from predictive algorithms, organizations across almost every industry—including health care, financial services, and insurance—use both types of analytical tools to customize their interactions with consumers and offer personalized products and services.

In health care, predictive models are used routinely. For example, there are well-established predictive models for life expectancy, as well as more modern inventions such as an individual's genetic predisposition to disease, likelihood of hospital readmission, and likelihood of adhering to a treatment plan.[3] These predictions allow doctors to tailor interventions according to individual patients' characteristics, improving outcomes by dispensing with one-size-fits-all treatments and lowering overall health care costs by reducing readmissions.

In education, standardized test scores are often used by schools as a predictor of students' likelihood of performing well in subsequent grades or education levels.[4] These scores allow educators to prioritize the scarce resources of supplementary tutoring or other remedial programs to the students who most need help. In recent years, higher education officials have begun to use predictive models for students' likelihood of succeeding in particular courses or graduating college. For example, Wichita State University implemented a predictive analytics program to reduce the dropout rate for its students and better identify high-quality applicants. The university found that predictive scores were a significantly more reliable indicator of student success than recommendations made by human reviewers.[5] This means that by using classification algorithms, a university might be able to not only create a fairer admissions system that is firmly rooted in merit, but also improve the quality of its student body.

Insurance providers quantify risk for an extremely broad array of events, including the likelihood that a homeowner will sell, the likelihood a farmer's crop will be wiped out by flood, and the likelihood that a particular stock will increase in price.[6] Predictive models in the insurance industry can ensure that safer drivers really do get lower rates and that potential home buyers do not get denied a loan for the wrong reasons. The Climate Corporation, a crop insurance company, creates such precise models based on the likelihood of extreme weather events that it can offer payouts automatically to farmers without requiring them to prove losses. This high level of efficiency allows farmers who grow crops with narrow planting windows to replant before it is too late for that season.[7]

Finally, predictive scores are used in a variety of online recommendation systems, with dating sites modeling how likely it is that two people are romantically compatible, Amazon determining which books a user might like to read, and LinkedIn determining what jobs a user might be interested in.[8] These scores allow companies to offer personalized services, saving consumers' time by obviating the need to slog through enormous numbers of listings to find relevant information and compare alternatives.[9]

What Benefits Do Consumers Gain from These Practices? Do These Practices Raise Consumer Protection Concerns? What Are the Social and Economic Impacts, Both Positive and Negative, from the Use of Big Data to Categorize Consumers?

Predictive models can be used to improve consumer welfare by personalizing products and services, including many applications in fields like health care where these predictive techniques are saving lives. For example, using public data, including news reports, social media, and government sources, a group of researchers from Children's Hospital Boston and Harvard Medical School predicted the current Ebola outbreak more than a week before it was recognized by the World Health Organization.[10] At Carnegie Mellon University, researchers have created a machine-learning algorithm that uses detailed patient data to predict up to four hours in advance patients who are likely to have a heart attack.[11] In addition, predictive models can often benefit consumers in other ways, such as by increasing privacy, freeing up resources to handle exceptional situations, and rewarding positive behaviors.

First, predictive scores can be used to trigger automated responses, preventing the need to disclose an individual's information to another person. For example, an online store may generate personalized product suggestions automatically, enabling shoppers to avoid discussing their preferences with a storekeeper. Or a health insurance company may send automated reminders to help patients adhere to their doctor's orders, thereby reducing the need for future medical exams. In general, predictive models reduce the need to communicate sensitive information to people who might divulge it later.

Second, using automated classification techniques can help make businesses more productive by reducing the need to manually review data about customers. For example, instead of a loan officer or admissions officer manually processing thousands of applications where the decision is clear, they can instead spend more time reviewing applications for individuals whose characteristics make them statistical outliers. Higher productivity results in savings that are generally passed on to consumers in competitive markets. This shift should also move workers into higher-paying, higher-productivity jobs. In addition, by automating many tasks, organizations can free up limited resources to help individuals most in need. For example, doctors can use a predictive model to learn which of their patients are most likely to benefit from a follow-up call.

Third, predictive modeling makes it easier to reward positive behavior. Individuals may alter their behavior if they know a company is using predictive modeling. While this is sometimes cited as a public policy concern, it is worth noting that many of these changes may be desirable.[12] For example, drivers may better adhere to the speed limit if they know their roadway habits will affect their insurance premiums, or consumers may make more responsible financial decisions in order not to negatively affect their credit rating.

Finally, data-driven automated systems can and should be used to reduce discrimination. For example, a properly tuned home loan evaluation algorithm could be made much fairer than a human loan officer; by definition, a successful loan evaluation algorithm should award loans to the most deserving and ignore unrelated factors like race, religion, or sexual orientation that cloud human judgment. Even in areas where automated decisions are the norm today, such as demographic assessment in insurance pricing, data-driven systems could offer improvement; pricing insurance based on the output of a car-bound sensor that measures driving ability is undeniably less discriminatory than pricing it based on the risk associated with a particular demographic profile.

As we discussed in a recent article, the pre-"big data" algorithms used to decide people's fate can often be improved with big data.[13] For example, some organ donation programs are based on how long individuals have been on a waiting list, a problem for disadvantaged populations who receive inadequate information about transplants may not be added to the waitlist until long after their diagnosis. These individuals are at a disadvantage when organs are allocated on a first-come, first-served basis. A better approach might use more data to more fairly allocate organs to individuals based on a number of factors, including their viability.

How Do Existing Laws Apply to Such Practices? Are There Gaps in the Legal Framework?

Numerous existing laws address discrimination of individuals based on various characteristics, and these laws should be applied to discrimination of those characteristics as represented in data. Title VII of the Civil Rights Act of 1964, the Equal Pay Act, the Fair Credit Reporting Act, the Age Discrimination Employment Act, the Americans with Disabilities Act, and the Genetic Information Nondiscrimination Act are just a few examples of laws that contain antidiscrimination provisions. These laws are, in essence, use restrictions on information, so they are naturally applicable to discrimination based on data analytics. They also extend naturally to algorithmically generated models; if a particular variable is prohibited from informing a human's employment decision, it should also be excluded from models that do the same job. To prevent algorithms from using variables that may be proxies for a prohibited variable, such as using an individual's zip code as a proxy for race, enforcement agencies could ensure that organizations not use models that make predictions or recommendations correlating above a certain threshold with membership in a protected class. To the extent that new types of discrimination are identified that are not covered under existing laws, they can be addressed through use restrictions modeled after the earlier legislative efforts.

This is not to say that every problem should be addressed with anti-discrimination laws. A frequently cited example of discrimination from big data comes from a 2013 study by researcher Latanya Sweeney that found the search engine ads for the background check website Instantcheckmate.com were disproportionately shown to users searching for "black-sounding names" than "white-sounding names."[14] The recent White House report on big data describes the problem as follows:

> Unfortunately, "perfect personalization" also leaves room for subtle and not-so-subtle forms of discrimination in pricing, services, and opportunities. For example, one study found web searches involving black-identifying names (e.g., "Jermaine") were more likely to display ads with the word "arrest" in them than searches with white-identifying names (e.g., "Geoffrey"). Outcomes like these, by serving up different kinds of information to different groups, have the potential to cause real harm to individuals.[15]

Clearly, it is harmful for advertisements to reinforce negative stereotypes about marginalized groups. But given that advertisers frequently come under criticism for accusations of racism, sexism, and ageism, this concern may have less to do with big data than it does with the conduct of advertisers.[16] In addition, changes in privacy laws would not address this harm since the root of the problem in this example was negative stereotypes in advertisements being linked to certain search terms. In this case, the issue was really about the ethics of the advertiser. Although it is unlikely that Congress would pass a law banning this type of activity (since, for better or worse, the 1st Amendment gives advertisers wide latitude in crafting public messages), the advertising industry, as well as individual advertisers and ad platforms, can adopt their own self-regulatory guidelines and company policies banning the negative portrayal of a particular race or ethnicity.

ARE COMPANIES APPROPRIATELY ASSESSING THE IMPACT OF BIG DATA PRACTICES ON LOW INCOME AND UNDERSERVED POPULATIONS? SHOULD ADDITIONAL MEASURES BE CONSIDERED?

Organizations should consider the potential discriminatory impact that the use of predictive tools has on protected classes. In some cases, such provisions may already exist. For example, the Equal Opportunity Employment Commission's (EEOC) Uniform Guidelines on Employee Selection Procedures state that employers should maintain information on whether their employee selection procedures for a particular job has an adverse impact on any protected class and update this information at least annually for groups that represent a significant portion of the workforce.[17] This can be straightforwardly applied to employee selection procedures that use data. If an employer takes online influence metrics—such as those offered by social media analytics company Klout—into account, and this process has an adverse impact on certain groups because it is correlated with access to the Internet and is not otherwise central to the job requirements, the employer would need to reassess its use of this method.

Industry groups, such as the Digital Advertising Alliance, have begun to develop self-regulatory guidelines specifying how data should be used in advertising, and these types of efforts can serve as a model for future initiatives to establish self-regulatory guidelines in other industries.[18] Self-regulation is generally more responsive to technological innovation than government regulation, thereby better serving rapidly evolving industries.[19] In addition, industry groups can often produce and update codes of conduct faster than government, thereby protecting consumers sooner. For example, the Network Advertising Initiative's code of conduct states that online advertising companies should disclose their data collection, purchase, and use practices in an understandable and prominent manner. In cases where self-regulatory guidelines govern data usage, it is critical to hold companies accountable when they violate their commitments or deceive consumers. Government oversight and enforcement by agencies such as the FTC can supplement these efforts to ensure their effectiveness and accountability.

Policymakers should ensure that predictive models based on positive consumer behaviors do not result in negative feedback to consumers. For example, since it is socially desirable to have people seek treatment for mental health issues, regulators should make sure this type of information is not used to deny someone housing, employment, or life insurance. Fortunately, many laws, including the Civil Rights Act, Americans with Disabilities Act, the Fair Housing Act, the Fair Credit Reporting, and the Genetic Information Nondiscrimination Act, already include restrictions on how data can be used for precisely this reason. To the extent that policymakers find gaps in these laws, they should work to ensure individuals are treated fairly.

Ultimately, predictive models offer substantial benefits to consumers in a broad range of fields, and using predictive analytics is superior to other, less-precise, non-computational forms of prediction commonly used today. To ensure consumers continue to benefit from this technology, the FTC should work with the private sector to encourage more widespread use of predictive analytics and highlight best practices that protect disadvantaged populations. It should also work to promote laws and regulations that support the use and reuse of data, which is a fundamental enabler of these types of tools. Finally, policymakers should promote the development of tools and techniques to de-identify data, as well as support research on topics like privacy-preserving data mining, so that these tools can be applied to a broader set of data while protecting consumer privacy.

CONCLUSION

In short, as organizations increasingly use advanced data analytics to make decisions, we should remember two things. First, prediction is not something to fear—we have always done it, it will always be imperfect, but technology can help us do it more accurately and in ways that greatly benefits consumers. Second, data analytics should not be a black box—we need to examine its underlying assumptions and values to ensure that protected groups are not treated unfairly. Doing so will enable us to gain the benefits of data while avoiding the tyranny of the algorithm.

Sincerely, Daniel Castro

Director,
Center for Data Innovation 1101 K Street NW,
Suite 610 Washington, DC 20005

End Notes

[1] "Big Data: A Tool for Inclusion or Exclusion," Federal Trade Commission, Accessed August 14, 2014, http://www.ftc.gov/es/node/313371.

[2] Daniel Castro, "Predictive Analytics and How to Decide Who Should Receive Organ Transplants," Center for Data Innovation, July 8, 2013, http://www.datainnovation.org/2013/07/predictive-analytics-and-how-todecide-who-should-receive-organ-transplants/.

[3] Alex Guazzelli, "Predictive analytics in healthcare," IBM DeveloperWorks, November 29, 2011, https://www.ibm.com/developerworks/library/ba-ind-PMML3/.

[4] Nathan Kuncel and Sarah Hezlett, "Standardized Tests Predict Graduate Students' Success." Science 315 (2007): 1080, http://www.unc.edu/~nielsen/soci708/cdocs/Kuncel_ Hezlett_ 2007_1080.pdf.

[5] Neal Ungerlieder, "Colleges Are Using Big Data To Predict Which Students Will Do Well--Before They Accept Them," Fast Company, October 21, 2013, http://www.fastcoexist.com/3019859/futurist-forum/colleges-areusing-big-data-to-predict-which-students-will-do-well-before-the.

[6] Susanne Sclafane. "Use of Predictive Models Widespread in P/C Insurance: Survey," Insurance Journal, November 7, 2013, http://www.insurancejournal.com/news/national/2013/11/07/310601.htm.

[7] "Agriculture and algorithms," The Economist, November 19, 2012, http://www.economist.com/blogs/schumpeter/2012/11/weather-insurance.

[8] Janet Wagner, "Machine Learning and Predictive Analytics Foster Growth," ProgrammableWeb. February 21, 2014, http://www.programmableweb.com/news/machine-learning-and-predictive-analytics-fostergrowth/2014/02/21 and Ryan Neal, "What Is Bright.com? Why LinkedIn Purchased The Job-Matching Website For $120 Million," International Business Times, February 6, 2014, http://www.ibtimes.com/what-brightcom-why-linkedin-purchased-job-matching-website-120-million-1553869.

[9] JP Mangalindan, "Amazon's recommendation secret," CNN Money, July 30, 2012, http://tech.fortune.cnn.com/2012/07/30/amazon-5/.

[10] "Online Tool Nailed Ebola Epidemic," Politico, August 9, 2014, http://www.politico.com/story/2014/08/healthmap-ebola-outbreak-109881.html

[11] Aviva Rutkin, "Machine predicts heart attacks 4 hours before doctors," New Scientist, August 11, 2014, ww.newscientist.com/article/mg22329814.400-machine-predicts-heart-attacks-4-hours-before-doctors.html.

[12] Daniel Solove, "'I've Got Nothing to Hide' and other Misunderstandings of Privacy," San Diego Law Review 44 (2007): 745.

[13] Daniel Castro, "Predictive Analytics and How to Decide Who Should Receive Organ Transplants," Center for Data Innovation, July 8, 2013, http://www.datainnovation.org/2013/07/predictive-analytics-and-how-todecide-who-should-receive-organ-transplants/.

[14] Latanya Sweeney, 'Discrimination in Online Ad Delivery,' Communications of the ACM, May 2013, http://privacytools.seas.harvard.edu/files/privacytools/files/p44-sweeney.pdf.

[15] John Podesta et al., 'Big Data: Seizing Opportunities, Preserving Values,' Executive Office of the President, May 2014, http://www.whitehouse.gov/sites/default/files/docs/big data privacy report may 1 2014.pdf.

[16] Emily Tess Katz, 'Feed A Child Apologizes For Allegedly Racist Ad,' Huffington Post, July 10, 2014, http://www.huffingtonpost.com/2014/07/10/feed-a-child-ad n 5573892.html, Stephanie Hayes, '#Letshoesbeshoes Encourages Sexist Clarks Shoe Ads to Enter This Century' June 2014, http://www.bustle.com/articles/28277-letshoesbeshoes-encourages-

sexist-clarks-shoe-ads-to-enter-thiscentury, and Brent Green, 'Taco Bell: Serving Up Ageism for Super Bowl Sunday?' Huffington Post, February 4, 2013, http://www.huffingtonpost.com/brent-green/taco-bell-super-bowl-ad b 2602647.html.

[17] Uniform Guidelines on Employee Selection Procedure, Section 15-A, EEOC, 1978, http://www.uniformguidelines.com/uniformguidelines.html.

[18] "Application of Self-Regulatory Principles to the Mobile Environment," Digital Advertising Alliance, July 2013, http://ww.aboutads.info/DAA_Mobile_Guidance.pdf.

[19] Daniel Castro, "Benefits and Limits of Industry Self-Regulation for Online Behavioral Advertising," Information Technology and Innovation Foundation, December 2011, http://www.itif.org/files/2011-selfregulation-online-behavioral-advertising.pdf.

In: The Use of Big Data
Editor: Diana Simpson
ISBN: 978-1-63485-318-7

Chapter 5

COMMENTS OF WILLIAM L. KOVACS, SENIOR VICE PRESIDENT, ENVIRONMENT, TECHNOLOGY & REGULATORY AFFAIRS, U.S. CHAMBER OF COMMERCE. WORKSHOP ON "BIG DATA: A TOOL FOR INCLUSION OR EXCLUSION?"*

August 15, 2014

VIA ELECTRONIC FILING
Mr. Donald S. Clark
Secretary
Federal Trade Commission
600 Pennsylvania Ave., NW, Room H-113 (Annex X)
Washington, DC 20580

Re: Big Data: A Tool for Inclusion or Exclusion? Workshop, Project No. P145406

* This is an edited, reformatted and augmented version of comments offered August 15, 2014 in response to a request from the Federal Trade Commission in preparation of a public workshop on September 15, 2014.

Dear Mr. Clark:

The U.S. Chamber of Commerce ("Chamber")[1] is pleased to submit these comments to the Federal Trade Commission ("Commission") in response to the agency's request for comments on issues to be discussed at its upcoming September 15, 2014, workshop on "Big Data: A Tool for Inclusion or Exclusion?"[2] The workshop "will examine the potentially positive and negative effects of big data on low income and underserved populations."[3] These comments incorporate by reference the Chamber's comments on big data filed with the White House Office of Science and Technology Policy ("OSTP") and the National Telecommunications and Information Administration ("NTIA") on March 31, 2014, and August 5, 2014, respectively.[4]

Entities using big data still must comply with the numerous U.S. laws and regulations that prohibit unfair discrimination. Therefore, given the benefits of big data to consumers and the U.S. economy, the Commission should restrain from acting in this area unless there are specific, identified harms that cannot be addressed adequately by the current legal framework.

I. Data is a Key Driver of U.S. Innovation and Economic Growth

To help our economy continue to recover, the Chamber believes that big data will be a key component in the creation of jobs and innovation. Data is used in many beneficial ways in our economy and by our society, including but certainly not limited to: improving healthcare, enabling businesses to better understand and serve their customers, increasing access to credit, detecting and preventing fraud as well as authenticating individual identities, and refining the manufacturing of products.[5] As White House Counselor John Podesta said at the March 3, 2014, White House/Massachusetts Institute of Technology (MIT) big data workshop:

> The value that can be generated by the use of big data is not hypothetical. The availability of large data sets, and the computing power to derive value from them, is creating new business models, enabling innovations to improve efficiency and performance in a variety of public and private sector settings, and making possible valuable data-driven

insights that are measurably improving outcomes in areas from education to healthcare.[6]

As it examines big data, the Commission should fully study the benefits of data and focus on how to enable more and better use of data.[7] Without fully understanding the capabilities and benefits of data, it will be impossible to understand the opportunity costs associated with limiting the use of data.[8] Beyond harnessing big data to answer specific questions, big data analysis allows "insights that could not be anticipated empirically or theoretically before the analysis took place....Instead, the data 'speak' and tell scientists something they did not know before."[9] Therefore, in addition to looking at data use, the Commission should also examine the implications to innovation and economic growth if this data is not allowed to be used. It is also worth noting that many of the benefits derived from data will come from business and scientific applications that do not involve the use of personal information.[10]

II. DATA CAN EMPOWER UNDERSERVED AND LOW INCOME POPULATIONS

Technology and data can increase safety, opportunity, and convenience—especially for underserved and low income populations.[11] In particular, data can be used to empower these populations. Using a greater number of data points reduces the chance that any single data point will be determinative.[12] By analyzing more factors, the use of big data reduces errors, improves accuracy, increases the probability of a correct decision, and hopefully obtains a result that may be perceived as "fairer."[13]

As the Commission acknowledges in its announcement of the workshop, big data can enhance the "ability of certain populations to find and access credit and other services."[14] For example, financial institutions may be able to better assess the creditworthiness of consumers and potentially grant credit to those who have been unable to obtain it (including those who have not yet established credit) by using big data analytics and not relying solely on credit scores.[15]

Additionally, data can identify unfair and discriminatory practices. However, methods to use data in this manner are not well understood outside the civil and voting rights communities. Therefore, to enable greater and better detection of unfair and discriminatory practices, groups with expertise in identifying these types of practices should share this knowledge with others, including the business community.

III. Existing Laws, Regulations, and Self-Regulatory Programs Protect Consumers While Enabling Innovation

In the United States, numerous laws and regulations as well as self-regulatory programs are aimed at protecting consumers and preventing unfair discrimination. Recognizing that the use of some sensitive types of data have a unique risk of harm, there are a variety of sector-specific federal laws (e.g., the Gramm-Leach-Bliley Act (GLBA), the Fair Credit Reporting Act (FCRA), and the Health Insurance Portability and Accountability Act (HIPAA)) designed to protect certain types of information that if misused or accessed without authorization could result in real harm to consumers. Additionally, the Commission has been aggressively asserting its authority under Section 5 of the FTC Act to prohibit unfair or deceptive acts or practices related to privacy. To address unfair discrimination, a multitude of laws also exist including: Title VII of the Civil Rights Act of 1964, the Fair Housing Act, the Equal Credit Opportunity Act, and the Generic Information Nondiscrimination Act. As a complement to these consumer protection and unfair discrimination laws, a variety of effective self-regulatory initiatives exist.

Discrimination is not a technology or data problem, but a long-standing societal issue. The laws that prohibit unfair discrimination for credit, employment, housing and education are not subverted or rendered void by a person or an organization using its own big data or the big data of a third party to unfairly discriminate against a protected class. These anti-discrimination laws are still in effect and all covered entities are still required to follow them. The use of big data does not change any of this.[16] Similarly, data used for marketing purposes should remain unregulated because any harm from this data is merely "irrelevant and uninteresting advertising and marketing."[17]

Concern has been expressed by some that big data could result in price differentiation leading to underserved and low income populations paying higher prices for goods and services.[18] However, as Thomas Lenard, Ph.D., President and Senior Fellow of the Technology Policy Institute, said in his recent comments to the Commission in this proceeding:

> [I]t is more likely that price discrimination will favor lower-income individuals. Since price discrimination involves charging different prices to different consumers for the same product based on their willingness to pay, and since willingness to pay is generally positively related to ability to pay, price discrimination will, other things equal, result in lower prices to lower-income consumers.[19]

Pricing is a complex economic decision based on a variety of factors including the cost of doing business in different areas of counties and states. It is worth highlighting that in a country as diverse and large—economically and geographically—as the United States, the price of an item in New York City, NY and the price of the same item in Phoenix, AZ may be different based on supply, demand (e.g., relative proximity of competitors' stores), and varying costs including rent, supply chain logistics, labor, overhead, etc. The same is true between U.S. cities, counties, states, and regions.

Businesses comply with the myriad of existing laws and regulations governing the use of information collected about consumers. Therefore, policymakers should restrain from acting unless there are specific, identified harms that cannot be addressed adequately by the current multi-layered approach for ensuring consumer protection and preventing unfair discrimination.

IV. Focusing on Improper Uses of Big Data and the Harms Created, Rather than Focusing Heavily on Collection, Provides a Balanced and Scalable Approach toward Big Data

Federal policy should recognize that differing risks of harm are caused by different types of data collection and usage. For example, there are fewer risks associated with non-personally identifiable data, especially when anonymized or aggregated, than with data that identifies a user. Similarly, encrypted data also results in reduced risk. Therefore, any federal policies in this area need to be flexible and adaptive to accommodate different uses of data along with rapidly developing technology.

The Chamber agrees with the recommendation in the President's Council of Advisors on Science and Technology's (PCAST) recent report on big data that "policy attention should focus more on the actual uses of big data and less on its collection and analysis."[20] Specifically, PCAST goes on to say:

> By actual uses, we mean the specific events where something happens that can cause an adverse consequence or harm to an individual or class of individuals....By contrast, PCAST judges that policies focused on the regulation of data collection, storage, retention, a priori limitations on applications, and analysis...are unlikely to yield effective strategies for improving privacy. Such policies would be unlikely to be scalable over time, or to be enforceable by other than severe and economically damaging measures.[21]

Additionally, societal benefits should be taken into account and certain uses, such as fraud prevention, may warrant fewer restrictions. Data can be analyzed in real time to identity anomalies in transactions, historical data can be used to predict and help prevent future fraud, and the use of data can also help to enhance verification and authentication techniques. For example, using big data to detect and prevent fraudulent activity has helped protect financial institutions and their customers.[22] In 2012, attempted fraud against bank deposit accounts reached $14.8 billion; however, through the use of data analytics and other loss prevention measures, banks stopped $13 billion in fraudulent transactions.[23]

Conclusion

As the Commission acknowledges in the announcement of this workshop, "tremendous benefits [to consumers and our economy] flow from the insights of big data."[24] Entities using this data still must comply with all existing laws and regulations as well as relevant self-regulatory practices. Therefore, as the Commission examines big data, the Chamber urges the agency to restrain from acting in this area unless there are specific, identified harms that cannot be addressed adequately by the myriad of means available today to ensure consumer protection and prevent unfair discrimination. Thank you for the opportunity to provide comments on this important matter.

Sincerely,
William L. Kovacs

End Notes

[1] The U.S. Chamber of Commerce is the world's largest business federation, representing the interests of more than three million businesses of all sizes, sectors, and regions, as well as state and local chambers and industry associations, and dedicated to promoting, protecting, and defending America's free enterprise system.

[2] Federal Trade Commission, Big Data: A Tool for Inclusion or Exclusion? (last accessed August 14, 2014), available at http://www.ftc.gov/news-events/events-calendar/2014/09/ big-data-tool-inclusion-or-exclusion. ("Big Data: A Tool for Inclusion or Exclusion? Workshop Announcement").

[3] Id.

[4] See, U.S. Chamber Comment Letter to the White House Office of Science and Technology Regarding its Big Data Study (filed Mar. 31, 2014), available at https://www.uschamber.com/comment/comment-letter-big-data-study; and U.S. Chamber Comments to NTIA on Big Data and Consumer Privacy in the Internet Economy (filed August 5, 2014), available at https://www.uschamber.com/comment/comments-ntia-big-data-and-consumer-privacy-interneteconomy.

[5] See also, Jeff Lundy, PhD, Data for Good (Jan. 17, 2014), available at http://www.uschamber foundation.org/blog/post/data-good/31581; Rich Cooper, Safer Cities through Data-Driven Crime Prevention (Mar. 25, 2014), available at http://www. uschamberfoundation.org/ blog/post/safer-citiesthrough-data-driven-crime-prevention/34326; and Rich Cooper, The Promise and Challenges of Data-Driven Healthcare (May 6, 2014), available at http://www.uschamberfoundation.org/blog/post/promise-and-challengesdata-driven-healthcare/34398.

[6] Remarks as Delivered by Counselor John Podesta at The White House/MIT "Big Data" Privacy Workshop at 2 (Mar. 3, 2014), available at http://www.whitehouse.gov/sites/default/files/ docs/030414_remarks_john_podesta_big_data.pdf.

[7] See, Comments of the Center for Data Innovation to OSTP Regarding Big Data at 2 (filed Mar. 31, 2014), available at http://www2.datainnovation.org/2014-ostp-big-data-cdi.pdf; and Comments of the Information Technology Industry Council to OSTP Regarding Big Data at 4 (filed Mar. 27, 2014), available at http://www.itic.org/dotAsset/bcae1b74-eb8e-4f01-a02d-7e8aa8bdaf0f.pdf.

[8] Id.

[9] Software & Information Industry Association Comments to OSTP Regarding Big Data at 2 (filed Mar. 31, 2014), available at http://www.siia.net/index.php?option=com_docman&task=doc_view&gid=5062&Itemid=318.

[10] See, Center for Data Innovation Comments at 2 and Information Technology Industry Council Comments at 4.

[11] For example, it is worth noting that according to a recent Pew Research Internet Project survey, African Americans and whites have identical rates of smartphone ownership. Aaron Smith, African Americans and Technology Use: A Demographic Portrait, Pew Research Internet Project, Jan. 6, 2014, available at http://www.pewinternet.org/2014/01/06/african-americans-and-technology-use.

[12] See, Comments of Thomas L. Lenard, Ph.D., President and Senior Fellow, Technology Policy Institute to the Commission Regarding "Effects of Big Data on Low Income and Underserved Consumers at 3 (filed July 28, 2014), available at http://www.ftc.gov/policy/ public-comments/2014/07/28/comment-00010. ("Technology Policy Institute Comments").

[13] Id.

[14] Big Data: A Tool for Inclusion or Exclusion? Workshop Announcement.

[15] Comments of the Financial Services Roundtable to OSTP regarding Big Data at 3 (filed Mar. 31, 2014), available at http://fsroundtable.org/letter-re-big-data-request-information.

[16] See also, Michael Hendrix, Does Big Data Discriminate? (June 26, 2014), available at http://www.uschamberfoundation.org/blog/post/does-big-data-discriminate/41553.

[17] Comments of the Software & Information Association on the FTC Workshop on Alternative Scoring Products at 9 (filed Apr. 17, 2014), available at http://www.ftc.gov/policy/public-comments/2014/04/17/comment-00010.

[18] See, for example, Executive Office of the President, Big Data: Seizing Opportunities, Preserving Values at 46-47, May 2014, available at http://www.whitehouse.gov/sites/default/files/docs/big_data_privacy_report_may_1_2014.pdf.

[19] Technology Policy Institute Comments at 4.

[20] President's Council of Advisors on Science and Technology, Report to the President, Big Data and Privacy: A Technological Perspective at xiii (May 2014), available at http://www.whitehouse.gov/sites/default/files/microsites/ostp/PCAST/pcast_big_data_and_privacy_-_may_2014.pdf.

[21] Id.

[22] See, Financial Services Roundtable Comments at 2.

[23] American Bankers Association, Banks Stop $13 Billion in Fraud Attempts in 2012, available at http://www.aba.com/Press/Pages/121213DepositAccountFraud.aspx.

[24] Big Data: A Tool for Inclusion or Exclusion? Workshop Announcement.

In: The Use of Big Data
Editor: Diana Simpson

ISBN: 978-1-63485-318-7

Chapter 6

COMMENTS OF ALVARO BEDOYA, EXECUTIVE DIRECTOR, CENTER ON PRIVACY & TECHNOLOGY, GEORGETOWN UNIVERSITY LAW CENTER. WORKSHOP ON "BIG DATA: A TOOL FOR INCLUSION OR EXCLUSION?"*

Federal Trade Commission, Office of the Secretary
Room H-113 (Annex X)
600 Pennsylvania Avenue, NW
Washington, DC 20580
VIA ELECTRONIC FILING

Re: Comments of Alvaro Bedoya,[1] Center on Privacy & Technology at Georgetown Law, on "Big Data: A Tool for Inclusion or Exclusion? Workshop, Project No. P145406."

This comment focuses on two legal issues surrounding Big Data. First, Big Data's is "big" in large part because companies are increasingly collecting personal data without users' active involvement — or in some cases, consent. Yet while existing privacy law protects user-generated content, it fails to protect these new streams of so-called "passive" data. Perversely, this means

* This is an edited, reformatted and augmented version of comments offered August 15, 2014 in response to a request from the Federal Trade Commission in preparation of a public workshop on September 15, 2014.

that the less you know about your data, the fewer protections it gets. This is wrong.

Second, industry advocates are promoting the idea that Big Data is essentially too big for consumer control: that consumer controls on the collection of data are impractical and undesirable, and that instead of empowering consumers with a better ability to control the *collection* of their data, the law should instead focus on implementing limits on how that data is *used*.

This strategy is ill-advised. What's more, a movement away from individual controls on collection may be especially harmful for groups that society has at some point deemed undesirable — the poor, the infirm, immigrants, racial and ethnic minorities, and LGBT communities. Privacy is in many ways a shield for the weak. An *exclusive* focus on use limitations would take away that shield and replace it with promises.[2]

I. The Less You Know About Your Data, the Fewer Protections It Receives

Kind of Data	Data Actively Created by Users	Data Passively Created *About* Users
Geolocation	GPS data from use of a mapping app or a "check-in"	Cell tower, Wi-Fi and/or GPS data collected by operating system providers in the background (e.g. Apple, Google) Cell tower data automatically collected by wireless carriers from phone calls Cell tower data automatically collected by wireless carriers from Internet use Cell tower, Wi-Fi and/or GPS data collected by a non-location-oriented app
Photo	Photo image	Faceprint derived from image
Email	Email content	Email metadata

Figure 1. Comparison of Actively and Passively Collected Data.

Geolocation confirms the Big Data report: passively generated geolocation is more plentiful than actively generated geolocation. A user may check herself into a location or use a mapping app three or four times a day. Unless location services are disabled, Android devices and iPhones automatically collect location data throughout the day and transmit it back to Google and Apple, respectively. One Android phone examined by the *Wall Street Journal* collected Wi-Fi location information every few seconds and transmitted it back to Google several times an hour.[4]

But the chart also highlights two problems. First, companies are often generating (or retaining) passive data entirely without a user's knowledge. Users are aware that their location information is being generated when they use Google Maps. But will they remember that Google collects their location information even when they do not use location-aware apps?[5] Similarly, Facebook users know when their friends post photos of them on Facebook. Do they know that Facebook has used those photos to enroll them in a facial recognition database?[6]

Second, in general, the law doesn't protect passively generated data in the same way it protects the actively generated data. This is a result of outdated distinctions between communications *contents* (which get high protections) and *non-contents* (which get low protections) in the Stored Communications Act (SCA).

Under the SCA, Internet companies cannot share the contents of communications without user consent — including, of course, emails. But they have the explicit right to sell or share non-content customer records with "any person other than a government entity" — i.e. any company.[7] Likewise, a photo image clearly constitutes the "contents" of a communication; it could only be shared with consumer consent. It's a little harder to say that for faceprints, meaning that they could potentially be shared freely without user consent.[8]

Finally, when you affirmatively open an app to share or determine your location, your location information is arguably the core "content" of your communication. If so, it couldn't be shared without your permission.[9] But in general, location information is considered non-content customer records under the Stored Communications Act, and can thus be shared freely with any nongovernmental entity.[10] The only passively generated location data afforded any meaningful protection is that held by wireless carriers as a result of *telephone* calls. The Telecommunications Act prohibits carriers from sharing that data without your consent.[11] But the moment you use that same smartphone to surf the Internet, your wireless carrier can likely share your location data with any other company.[12]

Bountiful, passively generated information is a defining feature of Big Data. But that data is also likely to have been generated without consumers' involvement or even consent — and likely lacks meaningful legal protection. In the world of Big Data, the *less* you know about your data, the *fewer* privacy protections it receives.[13]

This lack of protection for non-content data is especially problematic for health and fitness apps and "wearables" like Fitbit, Nike FuelBand, Jawbone UP, and Samsung Gear Fit. Once activated, these apps and devices are designed to automatically track user activity, be it sleep patterns, a morning jog, or a user's heart rate. Unlike many of the examples of passively generated data cited above, this data is gathered *with* user awareness and consent. But unless it's the contents of a communication, the data can likely be shared with any third party company. Are your heartbeats "the contents of a communication"?[14]

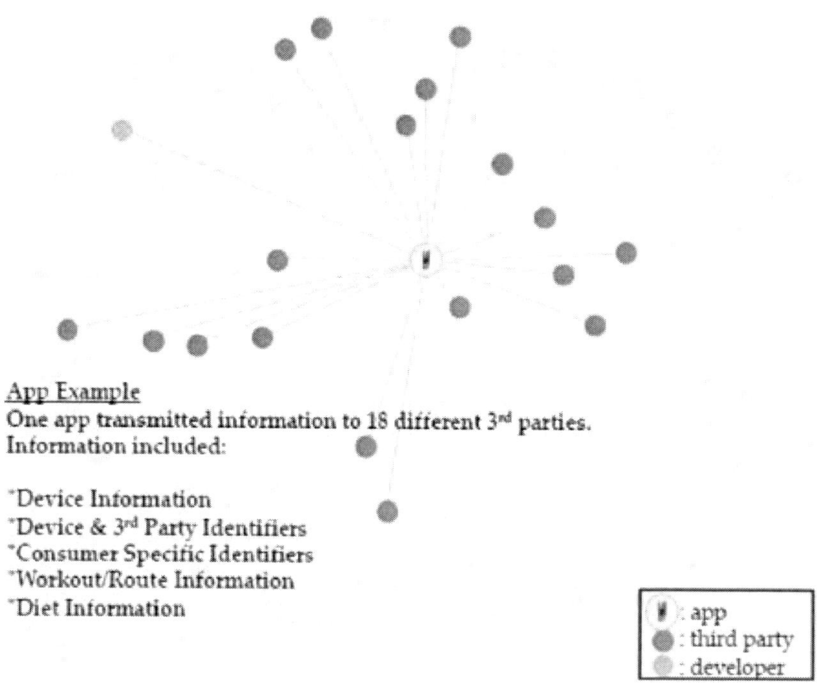

Figure 2. Commission Analysis of a Health & Fitness App.

App companies take advantage of this lax regulatory scheme. A 2013 audit of 43 health and fitness apps conducted by the Privacy Rights Clearinghouse found that about a third of the apps sent data to third parties who were *not* disclosed in-app or in a privacy policy.[15] A Commission audit of 12 health and fitness apps, including two apps associated with wearable devices, found that those dozen apps disclosed detailed user information — often including users' names, genders, emails, device identifiers, health and workout information — to 76 different third parties.

One app — pictured in Figure 2 above — sent information to 18 different third parties. One *third party* — an advertising services company — received detailed user data from *four of the twelve* apps that the Commission happened to study. The information included gender, workout data, and keywords like "ovulation," "fertilization," "pregnancy," and "baby." All of this data appears to have been tagged with certain identifiers that would make that data traceable to the same user.[16] This means that one ad company could track a specific user across four apps — *knowing it was tracking that one user across the different apps.*

The lack of protection for non-content data can also create end-runs around other, more powerful privacy laws. This is particularly true for geolocation. Health privacy laws generally prevent an OB/GYN from disclosing the names of his or her patients. But health privacy laws don't cover apps unaffiliated with medical service providers.[17] Investigations by the *New York Times*, the Commission, and the Senate Commerce Committee have found an acute interest in maternity information.[18] "Pregnant women and new parents, after all, are the holy grail of retail," writes the *Times*' Charles Duhigg.[19] It doesn't take much imagination to envision companies who infer pregnancies by geo-tracking users who repeatedly visit an OB/GYN branch. This tracking is already done through other methods.

In other settings, the Commission has recommended that Congress impose collection and sharing protections on certain sensitive data.[20] It has not limited that sensitive information to the *contents* of communications: for example, it has called for requirements that companies obtain users' express affirmative consent before collecting their geolocation data.[21]

I agree with the Commission. Consumers must be given greater control over all data collected about them — regardless of whether that data is "content," and regardless of the passive or automatic nature of that collection. The Commission should continue to support congressional efforts to create legal protections for that data. The Commission should also redouble its own enforcement efforts to protect users against the non-consensual collection of their sensitive data.

II. CONSUMER CONTROLS ARE CRITICAL FOR VULNERABLE POPULATIONS

There has been a concerted push to refocus privacy protections on *use* limitations, rather than controls empowering individuals to prevent collection in the first place. In February 2013, the World Economic Forum and the Boston Consulting Group released a report on Big Data. Based on a year of meetings culminating in a January session in Davos, the report set out a series of "new perspectives" on the use of personal data and highlighted "the need for a new approach" towards that data. Tellingly titled *Unlocking the Value of Personal Data: From Collection to Usage*, the report explained that "[t]he traditional data protection approach... was that the individual is involved in consenting to data use at the time of collection," and argued that this approach was "no longer fit for the purposes for which [it was] designed."[22]

This position is not limited to industry. This May, in paired reports from the Executive Office of the President and the President's Council of Advisors on Science and Technology (PCAST), senior White House officials indicated their own support for this new focus.[23] The Big Data Report actually suggested that it might be *impossible* to give consumers control over the data being collected about them. "[A] sea of ubiquitous sensors, each of which has legitimate uses, make the notion of limiting information collection challenging, if not impossible."[24]

I have argued with David Vladeck that this approach runs opposite to the White House's own Consumer Privacy Bill of Rights, which supported robust though flexible — individual controls on collection. We also explained that this belief in the inevitability of ubiquitous data collection is, frankly, inaccurate. Data collection sometimes happens by accident, but more often than not it's the result of careful and expensive policy and engineering decisions. Some companies choose to collect data ubiquitously and without consumer consent. Others do not.[25]

Here, I want to focus on a separate argument we made: that an exclusive focus on use limitations would likely hurt vulnerable communities.

Use limitations work well where the interests of companies and consumers align. For use limitations to be effective, they require that companies and consumers agree on which of those potentially harmful uses should be banned. There are a number of areas in which that is the case. But there are also many areas in which consumers' interests diverge significantly from those of the companies that serve them.

There is a growing body evidence that interests may diverge the most for the traditionally disadvantaged.[26] What is harder to recognize, however, is that uses of data that seem acceptable to us today may be found entirely unacceptable later: harmful uses are often deemed harmful only after the fact. Society is especially slow to condemn — or even acknowledge — uses of data that hurt marginalized communities. For example:

- In 1942, Congress repealed the confidentiality protections of the Census,27 letting the Census Bureau send block-by-block data on the locations of Japanese-Americans to the War Department. Many of them were subsequently rounded up and detained in internment camps.[28]
- After World War II, the U.S. military engaged in wiretapping and mail surveillance to identify and dishonorably discharge gay servicemembers.[29]
- In 1987, the U.S. Public Health Service instituted new mandatory AIDS tests for immigrants, subjecting 500,000 green card applicants to the blood tests annually and barring HIV-positive immigrants from permanent residence.[30]

Most of us now think that these cases of data use or collection were inappropriate, even repugnant. Yet the Census' role in the internment of Japanese Americans was only uncovered in the year 2000, after repeated denials by the Census Bureau.[31] The ban on gays in the military and the HIV travel ban were repealed *only in the last 5 years.*[32] Far too often, today's invidious discrimination was yesterday's national security or public health measure.

This moral lag persists today. And it isn't limited to government. Data brokers have been closely scrutinized for decades.[33] Yet recent investigations by the Commission, the Senate Commerce Committee, and privacy groups have revealed data broker uses of consumer data that are truly reprehensible.[34] A World Privacy Forum investigation, for example, identified consumer targeting lists titled "Aids and Hiv [*sic*] Infection Sufferers," "Rape Sufferers," "Dementia Sufferers" and "Hispanic Payday Loan Responders."[35]

Under what scenario would a victim of sexual assault find it beneficial to be on a marketing list of "rape sufferers?" Why would a company *acting in good faith* send a marketing offer to the mentally incapacitated?

It's just not realistic to think that Congress, companies, and consumers will agree on a set of use restrictions that they all find satisfactory. The American public may *never* make up its mind about women, gay people, immigrants, minorities, the mentally ill, and the poor — or how they and their data should be treated. Individual controls on data collection take that choice out of the hands of companies and the government, and into the hands of the individual.

To be clear, this is an argument in favor of individual controls; it is not an argument against use limitations. Use limitations are an essential backstop in a world where it is increasingly difficult for consumers to control the collection of their data. Certain privacy invasions can be stopped only through a strong use limitation regime. For example, strong, ex ante use limitations could have stopped Target from identifying pregnant women through their purchases.[36] Target would have of course collected the purchase data — the women would have still bought prenatal vitamins and maternity clothing — but a prohibition on medical profiling could have very much kept that genie in the bottle.

If someone truly wants to prevent the harmful use of his or her data, however, there is no better way to do that than to prevent its collection in the first place. As Chairwoman Ramirez has observed, "[i]nformation that is not collected in the first place can't be misused."[37]

III. Conclusion

Commissioner Ohlhausen said it well: Big Data is invaluable, but "data, even big data, isn't knowledge or wisdom. It can be misleading. Accurately understanding both the benefits and shortcomings of big data technology is critically important."[38] I urge the Commission to take actions that preserve the benefits of Big Data while protecting against potential privacy invasions and disparate impacts, particularly against the traditionally disadvantaged.

End Notes

[1] Executive Director, Center on Privacy & Technology, Georgetown University Law Center. The views expressed here are provided in a personal capacity and do not necessarily reflect those of the Center on Privacy & Technology or of Georgetown Law.

[2] This specific observation, like many others in this second argument, is drawn from a recent comment to the National Telecommunications & Information Administration. See Alvaro Bedoya and David Vladeck, Comments on "BiR Data and Consumer Privacy in the Internet Economy," NTIA Docket No. 140514424-01, August 5, 2014, at 6 (hereinafter "Bedoya and Vladeck").

[3] Executive Office of the President, BIG DATA: SEIZING OPPORTUNITIES, PRESERVING VALUES (2014)(hereinafter "Big Data Report") at 2 (emphasis added).

[4] See Julia Angwin and Jennifer Valentino-DeVries, Apple, Google Collect User Data, WALL STREET JOURNAL, April 22, 2011; Letter from Bruce Sewell, General Counsel, Apple, to Rep. Ed Markey (D. Mass.) and Rep. Joe Barton (R.-Tex.) re Apple Inc.'s Response to Request for Information Regarding Its Privacy Policy and Location-Based Services, July 12, 2010.

[5] Both Google and Apple notify users of this collection and take steps to anonymize the data. See Android "Location access" Screenshot, Android "Use Google location" Screenshot (presented during device setup), iOS 7 "Location Services & Privacy" Screenshot. But currently, the notifications are less salient than those provided for apps accessing location data, which are presented in a detailed app installation screen (Google) or a just-in-time notification (Apple). See iOS 7 App Location Permission Screenshot, Android App Installation Screenshot. It appears that Apple's new iOS 8 operating system will provide more detailed location notifications. See Apple refines location privacy in iOS 8 with new While Using' option, APPLEINSIDER, June 5, 2014.

[6] See, e.g., Letter from Sen. Franken (D.-Minn.) to National Telecommunications & Information Administration, April 2, 2012 at 12-14 (explaining Facebook's creation of a facial recognition database for its Tag Suggestions feature).

[7] 18 U.S.C. § 2702(b)(3),(c)(6).

[8] 18 U.S.C. § 2510(8) defines the "contents" of a communication as "any information concerning the substance, purport, or meaning of that communication," while § 2510(10) defines "communications" to include "any transfer of signs, signals, writing, images, sounds, data, or intelligence of any nature." An image sent via email or posted to a social networking site clearly constitutes the contents of a communication. It is a little harder to see how faceprints — literally metadata (i.e. data about data) measuring the facial characteristics of individuals in a photo — would concern "the substance, purport, or meaning" of a communication. In fairness, I am unaware of a court that has addressed this question.

[9] See Justin Brookman, Statement Before the Senate Judiciary Subcommittee on Privacy, Technology, and the Law, Hearing on "Protecting Mobile Privacy: Your Smartphones, Tablets, Cell Phones, and Your Privacy," May 10, 2011 (hereinafter "Brookman"), at 6 (explaining the potential protection of affirmatively provided or requested location data as "contents" under SCA).

[10] See ibid. See also Application of United States for an Order Directing a Provider of Electronic Communication Service to Disclose Records to Government, 620 F.3d 304, 307-308 (3rd Cir. 2010) ("[t]here is no dispute that historical CSLI is a 'record or other information pertaining to a subscriber...or customer,' and therefore falls within the scope of § 2703(c)(1).").

[11] See 47 U.S.C. § 222(f); 47 C.F.R. § 64.2001, et seq. (extending CPNI rules to cover IP-enabled VoIP services).

[12] Appropriate Regulatory Treatment for Broadband Access to the Internet Over Wireless Networks, Declaratory Ruling, WT Docket No. 07-53, FCC 07-30 (Mar. 23, 2007) (Concurring Statement of Commissioner Michael Copps) at 27, ¶ 3 (carriers offering Title I

[Internet] services "appear[] to be entirely free, under our present rules, to sell off aspects of the customer[s'] call or location information to the highest bidder.").

[13] See Brookman at 6 (describing "the perverse result that a consumer's information is afforded greater protections when she affirmatively shares sensitive data, as opposed to when her data is shared without her knowledge or consent").

[14] 18 U.S.C. § 2702(b)(prohibiting the disclosure of the "contents of a communication" absent consumer consent or other criteria).

[15] Linda Ackerman, MOBILE HEALTH AND FITNESS APPLICATIONS AND INFORMATION PRIVACY, REPORT TO CALIFORNIA CONSUMER PROTECTION FOUNDATION, Privacy Rights Clearinghouse, July 15, 2013, at 5.

[16] See Transcript, Consumer Generated and Controlled Health Data, Federal Trade Commission, Spring Privacy Series, May 7, 2014, at 25-27; Presentation Slides, Consumer Generated and Controlled Health Data, Federal Trade Commission, Spring Privacy Series, May 7, 2014 at 27-35.

[17] See generally, Department of Health and Human Services, Summary of HIPAA Privacy Rule, HHS.gov, accessed on August 15, 2014.

[18] Charles Duhigg, How Companies Learn Your Secrets, NEW YORK TIMES, Feb. 16, 2012 (describing Target's use of data mining to predict pregnancies among its shoppers)(hereinafter "Duhigg"); Federal Trade Commission, DATA BROKERS: A CALL FOR TRANSPARENCY AND ACCOUNTABILITY (2014) at 24 (listing data elements gathered by data brokers, including "Expectant or New Parent)(hereinafter "FTC Data Broker Report"); Senate Committee on Commerce, Science, and Transportation, A REVIEW OF THE DATA BROKER INDUSTRY: COLLECTION, USE, AND SALE OF CONSUMER DATA FOR MARKETING PURPOSES, MAJORITY STAFF REPORT, Dec.18, 2014, at 14 ("Equifax maintains approximately 75,000 individual data elements for its use in creating marketing products, including... OB/GYN doctor visits in the last 12 months")(hereinafter "Senate Commerce Report").

[19] Charles Duhigg, THE POWER OF HABIT (2014) at 184.

[20] See FTC Data Broker Report at 52.

[21] See Jessica Rich, Director, Bureau of Consumer Protection, Federal Trade Commission, Statement Before the Senate Judiciary Subcommittee on Privacy, Technology, and the Law, Hearing on the Location Privacy Protection Act of 2014, June 4, 2014 at 12-13 (supporting legislative measure requiring affirmative express consent before collecting or disclosing geolocation information).

[22] World Economic Forum, UNLOCKING THE VALUE OF PERSONAL DATA: FROM COLLECTION TO USAGE, Feb. 2013, at 11.

[23] Executive Office of the President, President's Council of Advisors on Science and Technology, BIG DATA AND PRIVACY: A TECHNOLOGICAL PERSPECTIVE (2014) at 49-50 ("Policy attention should focus more on the actual uses of big data and less on its collection and analysis. By actual uses, we mean the specific events where something happens that can cause an adverse consequences or harm to an individual or class of individuals.") (hereinafter "PCAST Report"); Big Data Report at 54.

[24] Ibid.

[25] See Bedoya and Vladeck at 1-4.

[26] See, e.g., Latanya Sweeney, Discrimination in Online Ad Delivery, Jan. 28, 2013 (study showing that a search engine treats first names associated with whites and blacks differently); Jennifer Valentino-Devries, Jeremy Singer, Ashkan Soltani, Websites Vary Prices, Deals Based on Users' Information, WALL STREET JOURNAL, Dec. 14, 2012

(investigation revealing that online retailers may quote higher prices to lower-income communities).

[27] Second War Powers Act, PUB. L. NO. 77-507, § 1402, 56 Stat. 186 (1942) (repealed). The measure passed the House on a near-unanimous voice vote. C.P. Trussell, Wider War Powers Win Vote of House, NEW YORK TIMES, March 1, 1942.

[28] See Steven A. Holmes, Report Says Census Bureau Helped Relocate Japanese, NEW YORK TIMES, March 17, 2000 (hereinafter "Holmes"); J.R. Minkel, Confirmed: The U.S. Census Bureau Gave Up Names of Japanese Americans in WWII, SCIENTIFIC AMERICAN, March 30, 2007.

[29] See, e.g., Randy Shilts, CONDUCT UNBECOMING: GAYS AND LESBIANS IN THE U.S. MILITARY (2014) at 304.

[30] Bernard Weintraub, Health Officials Seek AIDS Tests for Immigrants, May 16, 1987, NEW YORK TIMES.

[31] In 1983, a presidential commission concluded that the decisions surrounding the internment of Japanese-Americans were caused by "race prejudice, war hysteria and a failure of political leadership." REPORT OF THE COMMISSION ON WARTIME RELOCATION AND INTERNMENT OF CIVILIANS, PART 2: RECOMMENDATIONS (1983) at 5. Yet the role of the Census remained a secret until the year 2000 — 58 years after the fact. See Holmes at 17.

[32] President Obama ended the HIV ban in 2010, calling it "a decision rooted in fear rather than fact." By that time, the U.S. only one of a dozen countries that barred entry to the HIV-positive. See The White House, Remarks by the President at Signing of the Ryan White HIV/AIDS Treatment Extension Act of 2009, October 30, 2009 (ending the ban effective January 2010). President Clinton announced "Don't Ask, Don't Tell" in 1993. Yet homosexuality investigations continued long afterwards. See Roberto Suro, Navy Sends Agents into Gay Bars, WASHINGTON POST, June 17, 2000; Tim Weiner, Military Discharges of Homosexuals Soar, NEW YORK TIMES, April 7, 1998.

[33] See FTC Data Broker Report at 4 (discussing FTC's various investigations into data brokers since 1997).

[34] See generally, ibid, Senate Commerce Report.

[35] Pam Dixon, Statement before the Senate Committee on Commerce, Science and Transportation, Hearing on What Information Do Data Brokers Have on Consumers, and How Do They Use It?, December 18, 2013, at 9, 12, 13, 17.

[36] See generally Duhigg.

[37] Chairwoman Edith Ramirez, Federal Trade Commission, The Privacy Challenges of Big Data: A View from the Lifeguard's Chair, Keynote Address, Technology Policy Institute, Aspen Forum, Aug. 19, 2013 at 6.

[38] Commissioner Maureen K. Ohlhausen, Federal Trade Commission, Comments on "Big Data and Consumer Privacy in the Internet Economy," NTIA Docket No. 140514424-01, August 5, 2014.

In: The Use of Big Data
Editor: Diana Simpson
ISBN: 978-1-63485-318-7

Chapter 7

COMMENTS OF JAMES P. STEYER, CEO AND FOUNDER, COMMON SENSE MEDIA. WORKSHOP ON "BIG DATA: A TOOL FOR INCLUSION OR EXCLUSION?"*

I. INTRODUCTION & OVERVIEW

Common Sense Media, a nonpartisan, nonprofit organization dedicated to helping kids and families thrive in a world of media and technology, respectfully submits these comments in response to the Federal Trade Commission's request for comment in advance of its upcoming workshop, "Big Data: A Tool for Inclusion or Exclusion?" We applaud the Commission for examining big data and its impact on consumers.

As the FTC explores big data's ability to include or exclude, the public discourse ought to include one of our nation's most important and vulnerable groups: youth. The FTC has long been the leader in protecting kids' privacy. Now more than ever, the agency's expertise is needed to protect children and teens in a big data world.

Today's digital world offers young people limitless opportunities to create, communicate, connect, and learn in new and impactful ways. At the same time, our highly interconnected online ecosystem aggregates little bits of data into "big data" that may be used by unintended audiences in unexpected

* This is an edited, reformatted and augmented version of comments offered August 15, 2014 in response to a request from the Federal Trade Commission in preparation of a public workshop on September 15, 2014.

ways, and can deprive individuals of their right to self-determination. Data is amassed into extremely detailed profiles, which are used to label and steer individuals. Such ubiquitous data collection and profiling is disconcerting for everyone, but is particularly troubling for young people, who are growing up, developing, experimenting and learning in a digital world. Big data combines digital footprints into a full body scan, which can then be used to grant or deny their admission to future opportunities.

The FTC's recent Data Broker Report confirmed what many have suspected Ð that data brokers and other big data players are collecting, storing, mining, and sharing information about virtually every consumer Ð *including children and teens.*[1] As the FTC and others have recognized, children's and teens' personal information is particularly sensitive.[2] Accordingly, we need further investigation of data brokers' practices and the ramifications of big data on children and teens. While we understand the September workshop will appropriately focus on big data's inclusionary and exclusionary impact on low-income and underserved communities, any discussion of big data is not complete without considering our nation's youngest consumers. The FTC should investigate the impact of big data on kids in this or future proceedings. We also need clear rules that recognize that personal information about children and teens is a sensitive data category presenting unique risks and deserving special protections in a big data world. We respectfully urge the Commission to clarify this in its legislative recommendations for data brokers.

Simply Put, Big Data Should Not Label and Limit Kids

Imagine this:

- A student from a less affluent zip code, who can't afford a private tutor, struggles with a math-tutoring app and is labeled as "financially vulnerable."
- A child with an interest in extreme sports (discovered through web browser histories, YouTube searches, and book purchases) is categorized as a "risk-taker."
- A teenager, frequently home late (logged by the "smart" home monitoring system), who is friends with a popular crowd on social media and shares posts about parties, is categorized as an alcohol user and "socially influenced" (even if the teen doesn't drink).

Normal child and teen behavior can categorize, affecting educational options and admissions, employment opportunities, and product offers and pricing. Children and teens may suffer differential treatment, and be included or excluded, on the basis of collections of data points they do not understand and may not even know exist.

In its Data Broker Report, the Commission proposed legislation that would increase the transparency and accountability of data brokers. It recommended that consumer-facing companies obtain affirmative express consent before sharing sensitive information with data brokers for marketing products. The FTC also suggested as a "best practice" that data brokers "implement better measures to refrain from collecting information from children and teens, particularly in marketing products."[3] Given the special sensitivity of children's and teens' data (like financial and health information, and precise geolocation), collection and sharing of information from and about children and teens should—*as a matter of law*—require affirmative express consent either from parents (for children under 13) or from teens themselves.

Legislation should address the unique issues presented by young people's age and level of understanding to ensure transparency and individual control over their personal information, and to safeguard against the unexpected consequences of big data used beyond the context in which it was collected.

Common Sense Media has called for legislation that builds on the Children's Online Privacy Protection Act ("COPPA") protections for personal information collected from children under 13, extends parallel protections to teens, and broadens the FTC's legislative recommendation that companies obtain affirmative express consent before sharing sensitive information with data brokers.[4] Specifically, data brokers and their sources should provide the following heightened protections before profiling children and teens:

- Consumer-facing entities that share personal information about children or teens with third parties, such as data brokers, should provide notice to their customers and should obtain affirmative express consent from either a parent (for children under 13) or the teen before they collect or share their personal information.
- If a data broker knows or reasonably should know it is collecting information from or about a child under 13, it should stop collecting, until and unless it has affirmative express parental consent.
    - To the extent data brokers collect information from or about children, it should be used only to safeguard the child, such as prevention of fraud and identity theft.

- If a data broker knows or reasonably should know it is collecting information from or about a teen, it should stop collecting, until and unless it has the teen's affirmative express and informed consent.

These recommendations are consistent with Common Sense Media's long-standing belief that online companies should provide special protection for kids and teens, and get affirmative express consent from either parents (for children under 13) or teens before collecting their personal information or geolocation, or targeting them with behavioral ads.

Children and teens should be able to explore and express themselves freely, at home, in school, and everywhere in between. They should be given the space to discover and define themselves, before big data does it for them. Failure to safeguard their personal information, coupled with widespread concern about ubiquitous corporate and government surveillance, could jeopardize the collective trust in digital technology. Users may start to self-censor their thoughts, temper their online exploration, and withhold information. This could ultimately chill the right to free expression and squelch opportunities for youth.

Strong safeguards for personal information from and about children and teens would help create a more trusted online environment, where kids can enjoy the benefits of technological innovation without fear of jeopardizing their future.

II. The FTC Should Further Examine How Big Data Is Tracking

A. Children and Teens A. Children and Teens are Providing Increasing Amounts of Data

A number of factors put children and teens uniquely at risk in a big data world. More data will be collected from today's youth than from any generation before. They are the first to have a digital trail spanning the length of their entire lives, if not longer.[5] They are avid adopters of new technology. And they are particularly heavy users of mobile devices,[6] which can collect sensitive data (such as geolocation) anytime and anywhere. As the FTC has recognized, mobile apps on such devices collect a plethora of information—sometimes in compliance with current law, sometimes not.[7] In school, the proliferation of educational technology and digitization of school records and activities—from nurse visits to student keystrokes—means digital dossiers that are lengthier and stickier than any paper file.

Young people seem wired to share more information. Children may not appreciate the sensitivity of what they are sharing. And teens live in a culture that promotes sharing,[8] with no signs of abatement.[9] Teens also tend to act impulsively without fully thinking through the consequences.[10] Young people often do not understand what data they are sharing and with whom it will be shared afterwards.[11]

Moreover, young people are being monitored not only in their free time, but also in school and while completing their homework. Schools are integrating more laptops and tablets in the classroom and experimenting with educational learning platforms, fingerprint-purchased meals, and digitized student records stored in the cloud. Educational technology, used wisely, has the potential to positively transform America's schools, enhancing student learning and improving school efficiency. At the same time, it brings a host of privacy concerns. As the White House's recent Big Data Report recognizes, student data can be very personal.[12] Student data can reveal academic progress, health information, disciplinary records, and even eligibility for free or reduced price meals. Thus, "[t]he big data revolution in education É raises serious questions about how best to protect student privacy as technology reaches further into the classroom."[13] The relentless tracking of students exacerbates the privacy problems already faced by children and teens.

B. Data Brokers Are Collecting Data About Young People, Online and Offline

The FTC Data Broker Report has begun to shed some light on data brokers' treatment of information about kids and teens. The FTC Report confirmed that some data brokers include information about children and teens in products they sell to their clients.[14] Others "suppress" the information related to children and teens and do not include it in their products—but apparently make no effort to stop collecting, storing, and perhaps even mining, such data. And some data brokers simply rely on their sources to "suppress" information about children and teens, turning a blind-eye to whether or not they are collecting such information or including it in their products.[15]

Importantly, "suppression" does not mean deletion. Neither data brokers nor their sources have said what they do with the data when a teen turns 18.

But it seems likely that they start using it then (if they haven't already). Otherwise, why keep it at all?

One rationale given for collecting or providing information about children and teens is to prevent fraud. This in itself cannot justify unlimited collection or use of child and teen personal data. Indeed, data brokers acknowledge this implicitly in instances when they "suppress," or rely on their sources to "suppress," such information for a minor.[16]

Recent reports have explained how data brokers combine data from hundreds or thousands of data points, creating an incredibly detailed profile. Even the most innocuous seeming data can end up contributing to a rich and potentially incriminating individual profile. As the White House Report explains, "integrating diverse data can lead to what some analysts call the 'mosaic effect,' whereby personally identifiable information can be derived or inferred from datasets that do not even include personal identifiers, bringing into focus a picture of who an individual is and what he or she likes."[17]

This picture becomes even more focused when data brokers combine online data with offline data. Marketers admit to using "onboarding" to target consumers online based on their offline behavior. And they appear to be doing the reverse as well—targeting people offline based on browsing patterns online.[18] We can expect more of such data merging and marketing across online and offline platforms in the future.[19]

Offline data is expected to expand exponentially with the growth of wearables, facial recognition technology, and the internet of things. As offline data collection moves from the credit-card reader to the street camera or the smartwatch, more offline data will be collected from children and teens. This trove of offline data will be combined with ever-more online data[20] into even more detailed and potentially intrusive personal profiles at even younger ages.

The personal and sensitive data collected about young people may include everything from social media posts (anonymous or not) to geolocation, the content of emails and texts, the hours spent on various devices, online videos, newspapers, and books, school research interests, educational app progress, metadata, in-school grades, nurse visits, food choices, health and biometric information, in-store and online purchases, friends and family, and economic background.

Given the exponentially increasing amount of data created, collected, and combined, online and offline, coupled with the dwindling amounts it costs to store and mine such data, there are few practical constraints on big data brokers. Thus, legal, ethical and other constraints are needed to ensure that young people can grow up free of constant surveillance, free of digital labeling and related limitations. These topics are ripe for further FTC examination.

C. Big Data Is Labeling and Limiting Minors in Ways That Will Have Long-Term and Little-Understood Consequences

Big data has the power to determine and decide. In addition to the FTC Data Broker Report, recent scholarship demonstrates the extent to which individuals are being scored and categorized.[21] They are labeled as everything from allergy sufferers to sports enthusiasts to unlikely to pay the bills.[22] This ranking is not limited to adults. First-graders may be labeled as drop-out risks, elementary students are being counseled on certain careers, and teens are identified as pregnant.[23]

Labeling and predictions of future behavior can occur not just on the basis of past behavior, but on the basis of algorithmic inferences. As Chairwoman Ramirez has explained, big data can label people "not because of what they've done, or what they will do in the future, but because inferences or correlations drawn by algorithms suggest they may behave in certain ways that make them poor credit or insurance risks, unsuitable candidates for employment or admission to schools or other institutions, or unlikely to carry out certain functions." She terms this "data determinism," and has expressed concerns about "discrimination by algorithm" and "arbitrariness-by-algorithm."[24]

Other scholars have argued that algorithms are worse than arbitrary -- they are *biased*. This is because "human beings program predictive algorithms," so "their biases and values are embedded into the software's instructions."[25]

Arbitrary and biased labeling can be extremely limiting, and have both a social and economic impact on young people's current and future lives. Predictive algorithms may show only news articles from a certain point of view. Search results may provide medical information based on a computer's assessment of likely ability to afford treatment. College pamphlets or career guides might make their way into some postal and e-mail boxes, but not others. What's more, big data and scoring systems "have the potential to take a life of their own, contributing to or creating the situation they claim merely to predict."[26] Data collectors have the power to steer people's lives and drive individual decisions in ways that are opaque and not understood. Big data's most pronounced effect surely will involve kids and teens. Data may be collected during every moment of their lives, including key formative years during their childhood and adolescence, when exploration is encouraged and desirable. Data will also be collected as they research and develop in school. As students learn, big data will be learning about them. While this can have positive benefits in the individualized education context, it is difficult to ignore the risks. This data could be viewed by unintended audiences and may result in unexpected consequences.

Imagine if a grade school student struggles with a math app. She is also clocked at turning in every test at the very end of class, always taking the full time. She is labeled as a slow learner, and put in remedial classes the next year. The school's "career counselors" come to remedial classes to talk about trade schools, not college. The ads she sees online, and the informational materials she receives in her email box and at her house all trumpet the same message. She does not go to college. She does not end up in a high-paying job.[27]

Big data knows more and more about us with each passing day, and can channel our choices, our decisions, and even our emotions, without our knowledge. For example, earlier this year we learned that in January 2012, Facebook had intentionally altered news feeds of hundreds of thousands of its users (including teens) to make them happy or sad. Who knows what other secret experiments Facebook, or a data broker the public has never heard of, has conducted on users?

Young people need to be able to safely explore and express themselves without fear of being labeled or pigeonholed by invisible, automated decisionmakers. They need the freedom to make mistakes, try new things, and find their voices, unencumbered by the looming threat of a permanent digital record.

III. Legislative Recommendations Addressing "Big Data" Should Include Extra Safeguards for Sensitive Child and Teen Data

In order to reap the benefits of big data while also responding to its risks, we must enact laws that reflect the unique sensitivity of child and teen data and create a trusted environment for today's youth, with transparency and individual control over commercial tracking, targeting and profiling. The FTC has rightly recognized that children's and teens' personal information is sensitive and deserving of extra protections and precautions.[28] The FTC has also recognized that consumers need more transparency and control over commercial tracking, targeting, and profiling.[29] We are calling for legislation that explicitly provides more protection and control to children and teens, because of the inherent sensitivity of their personal information.

A. The Public Supports Safeguards to Rein in Corporate Tracking of Kids

There is deep public concern about this issue. Eighty-seven percent of consumers with a child in the household avoid doing business with companies they do not believe protect their privacy.[30] Eighty-nine percent of Americans believe it is extremely or very important to keep personal information about their kids private from corporate tracking.[31] And almost eight out of ten believe that companies should get permission from teens aged 13 to 15 before collecting personal information about them or sending them targeted advertisements.[32]

This public concern is beginning to translate into political consensus. There is bipartisan agreement that children should not be tracked without their parents' consent or even their knowledge, and growing bipartisan support for the notion that teens deserve similar protections.[33] And there is bipartisan agreement that student data should be used to improve education, not to sell products or amass permanent profiles.[34] Common Sense Media supports the principles that kids and teens should be free of tracking, and that affirmative express consent should be required before their personal information, including geolocation, is collected, or before profiles are created about them and behavioral advertisements served.

B. Privacy Legislation Should Require Data Brokers to Limit Collection from and about Children and Teens

The FTC Data Broker Report notes that data brokers are collecting information about minors, and the one plausible explanation for such collection is to prevent fraud. The use of a child's or teen's data for fraud prevention purposes is one thing. But in order to flag a purchase for fraud, all that is necessary to know is the age associated with the purchaser (or device or ID) making the transaction. It is not necessary to know that the purchaser is also partial to cowboy cartoons, has recently asked puberty-related questions on a health site, or is progressing in an interactive book well behind grade-level expectations, indicating a likelihood of a learning disability. Nonetheless, this information may be collected.[35]

Legislation should require data brokers to refrain from collecting personal information from or about children and teens without affirmative express, informed consent. The principles underlying COPPA, which requires parental consent before online collection of personal information from children under 13, should apply equally to information collected offline from children and information collected and compiled by data brokers from or about children.[36] Teens, likewise, deserve the opportunity to opt-in to data brokers collecting, compiling, and profiling their personal information.

Accordingly, Common Sense Media proposes the enactment of privacy legislation, enforceable by the FTC, that incorporates the following principles:

1) Consumer-facing entities that share child or teen data with third parties such as data brokers should provide notice to their customers, and should obtain affirmative, express opt-in consent from either a parent (for children under 13) or a teen before they collect or share information from or about a child or teen.[37] This is consistent with the FTC Data Broker Report's legislative recommendation that customer-facing sources obtain "express affirmative consent" from consumers before sharing their sensitive information with data brokers for marketing purposes. [38]
2) If a data broker knows or reasonably should know it is collecting information from a child under 13, it should stop collecting, until and unless it has affirmative, express parental consent. This is consistent with COPPA's framework, and would prevent any backdoor methods of collecting personal information, including persistent identifiers, "finger prints," or other methods that allow for highly detailed profiles of children. To the extent data brokers collect information from or about children, it should be used only to safeguard the child, such as prevention of fraud and identity theft.
3) If a data broker knows or reasonably should know it is collecting information from a teen, it should stop collecting, until and unless is has the teen's affirmative express and informed consent.

CONCLUSION

Big data shapes our lives in ways both large and small. It brings numerous benefits and efficiencies. But it should not be used to label or limit kids. We thank the FTC for considering how big data is categorizing consumers, and the inclusionary and exclusionary impacts of big data, in its workshops, reports, and recommendations. The particularly powerful impacts that big data may have on children and teens should be further explored and considered in these proceedings. We look forward to working with the FTC and other policymakers and stakeholders to ensure that children and teens can reap the benefits of big data while avoiding its risks.

Respectfully submitted,
James P. Steyer
CEO and Founder Common Sense Media

End Notes

[1] FTC, Data Brokers: A Call for Transparency and Accountability 21 (May 2014) ("FTC Data Broker Report").

[2] FTC, Protecting Consumer Privacy in an Era of Rapid Change 47, 60 (Mar. 2012) ("FTC 2012 Privacy Report"). (stating that when sensitive data such as "children's information is involved É the likelihood that data misuse could lead to embarrassment, discrimination, or other harms is increased," and that, "companies that target teens should consider additional protections."). See also FTC Data Broker Report at 55 (noting that principles underlying the Children's Online Privacy Protection Act may apply equally in offline contexts, and that teens often fail to appreciate long-term consequences of posting data online).

[3] FTC Data Broker Report, supra note 1, at 55.

[4] See Common Sense Media, Comments on Big Data and the Consumer Privacy Bill of Rights (Aug. 5, 2014), available at http://www.ntia.doc.gov/files/ntia/common sense media 0.pdf.

[5] A quarter of children have an online presence before being born. See, e.g., Business Wire Press Release, Digital Birth: Welcome to the Online World – AVG Study Finds a Quarter of Children Have Online Births Before Their Actual Birth Dates (Oct. 6, 2010), http://www.businesswire.com/news/home/20101006006722/en/Digital-BirthOnline-World.

[6] Twice as many young children used mobile in 2013 than just two years prior, and 38% of toddlers under age two have used a mobile device in the last two years. See Common Sense Media, Zero to Eight: Children's Media Use in America 2013 11 (Oct. 28, 2013), available at https://www.commonsensemedia.org/file/zerotoeightfinal2011pdf-0/download. One in four teens are cell-mostly Internet users, versus the 15% of adults overall, and among teen smartphone owners, that number is one in two. Pew Research Center & Berkman Center for Internet & Society, Teens and Technology 2013 (Mar. 13, 2013), available at

http://www.pewinternet.org/files/oldmedia//Files/Reports/2013/PIP_TeensandTechnology2013.pdf.

[7] FTC Staff, Mobile Apps for Kids: Disclosures Still Not Making the Grade (Dec. 2012).

[8] Ninety percent of teens have used social media. Common Sense Media, Social Media, Social Life: How Teens View Their Digital Lives 9 (June 26, 2012), available at https://www.commonsensemedia.org/file/socialmediasociallife-final-061812pdf-0/download.

[9] A recent research study found that teens' use of Facebook increased in the last two years. Reed Albergotti, Survey: Teens Say They Are Using Facebook More, Wall St. J. Digits Blog (June 24, 2014, 6:00 AM), http://blogs.wsj.com/digits/2014/06/24/survey-teens-say-they-are-using-facebook-more/.

[10] FTC 2012 Privacy Report, supra note 2, at 70.

[11] Pew Research Center & Berkman Center for Internet & Society, Teens, Social Media, and Privacy 2 (May 21, 2013), available at http://www.pewinternet.org/files/2013/05/PIP_TeensSocialMediaandPrivacy_PDF.pdf.

[12] Executive Office of the President, Big Data: Seizing Opportunities, Preserving Values (May 2014) ("White House 2014 Big Data Report").

[13] Id. at 25.

[14] The only stated purpose of such inclusion was for fraud prevention. FTC Data Broker Report, supra note 1, at 21.

[15] Id.

[16] Data brokers' sources are myriad and opaque. It is doubtful that all sources are "suppressing" information related to children and teens, especially given the vast number of third-party trackers that are targeting children for advertising and profiling. For instance, in May of 2014, TRUSTe found 1,110 third-party trackers, including 644 unique tracking organizations, on the top 40 websites used by kids. TRUSTe found an average of two dozen trackers on preschool and education sites, and even more on kids' entertainment and gaming sites. Press Release, TRUSTe, New Study Finds 644 Unique Third Party Trackers (Jun. 19, 2014), http://www.truste.com/about-TRUSTe/pressroom/news-study-finds-644-unique-third-party-trackers. It is unclear if these trackers provide their information to ad networks, data brokers, or both; regardless, they are all part of a sharing ecosystem. See, e.g., Display Advertising Technology Landscape, LUMA Partners LLC (Dec. 31, 2010), http://cdn.theatlantic. com/static/mt/assets/science/display_advertising_ecosystem_011011-1024x741.png

[17] White House 2014 Big Data Report, supra note 12, at 8.

[18] FTC Data Broker Report, supra note 1, at 29.

[19] See, e.g., Kate Kaye, Acxiom Acquires LiveRamp to Boost Offline-to-Online Data Capability, Advertising Age (May 14, 2014), available at http://adage.com/article/datadriven-marketing/acxiom-buys-liveramp-offline-onlinedata-capability/293212/.

[20] Ninety-percent of data was created in the last two years. See Edith Ramirez, Chairwoman, FTC, Speech at the Media Institute: Protecting Consumer Privacy in a Big Data Age (May 8, 2014).

[21] E.g., Danielle Keats Citron & Frank A. Pasquale, The Scored Society: Due Process for Automated Predictions, 89 Wash. L. Rev. 1 (2014); Pam Dixon & Robert Gellman, The Scoring of America: How Secret Consumer Scores Threaten Your Privacy and Your Future (Apr. 2, 2014), available at http://www.worldprivacyforum.org/wpcontent/uploads/2014/04/WPF_Scoring_of_America_April2014_fs.pdf.; Senate Committee on Commerce, Science, and Transportation, Office of Oversight and Investigations Majority Staff, A

Review of the Data Broker Industry (Dec. 18, 2013), available at http://www.commerce.senate.gov/ public/?a=Files.Serve&File_id=0d2b3642-6221-4888-a631-08f2f25 5b577.

[22] Dixon, Gellman, supra note 21, at 8; FTC Data Broker Report, supra note 1, at 21.

[23] Sarah Sparks, Data System Flags Dropout Risks by 1st Grade, Education Week (Aug. 6, 2013), available at http://www.edweek.org/ew/articles/ 2013/08/07/37firstgrade-2.h32.html; Stephanie Simon, Big Brother, Meet the Parents, Politico (June 5, 2014), available at http://www.politico.com/ story/2014/06/internet-data-mining-children107461.html; Charles Duhigg, How Companies Learn Your Secrets, N.Y. Times Magazine (Feb. 16, 2012).

[24] Edith Ramirez, Chairwoman, FTC, Keynote Address at the Technology Policy Institute Aspen Forum: Privacy Challenges in the Era of Big Data: A View from the Lifeguard's Chair (Aug. 19, 2013); Ramirez, supra note 20.

[25] Citron, Pasquale, supra note 21, at 4.

[26] Id. at 33.

[27] Citron and Pasquale describe another frightening scenario involving a recent college graduate: she can't get a job after graduation, gets a low "employability" score on this basis, finds only part-time work which reduces her credit score, and then suffers more because of her low credit score, never finding a full-time job. Id. at 32.

[28] FTC 2012 Privacy Report, supra note 2, at 59-60; FTC Data Broker Report, supra note 1, at 55. See also The White House, Consumer Data Privacy in a Networked World: A Framework for Protecting Privacy and Promoting Innovation in the Global Digital Economy 15 (Feb. 2012); and White House 2014 Big Data Report, supra note 12, at 25.

[29] See, e.g., legislative and best practice recommendations in FTC Data Broker Report, supra note 1.

[30] 2014 TrustE Kids Privacy Index, supra note 16. This is particularly problematic because not a lot of consumers do believe companies protect their privacy. A recent Gallup poll found that only 1 in 5 consumers has a lot of trust that businesses will protect their privacy. See John Fleming & Elizabeth Kampf, Few Consumers Trust Companies to Keep Online Info Safe (June 6, 2014), http://www.gallup.com/poll/171029/few-consumers-trust-companies-keep-online-info-safe.aspx.

[31] Memorandum from Anzalone Liszt Grove Research, Americans Concerned about Privacy from Corporate and Government Surveillance (Mar. 31, 2014), available at http://media.wix.com/ugd/c4876a_e8f4ee3b207344 d9aac9a3403118ca9c.pdf.

[32] Id. By requiring teens' permission as the default, companies can allow teens to pause, consider consequences, and get more information. As the FTC has explained, setting more privacy-protections by default "can function as an effective 'speed bump' for this audience and, at the same time, provide an opportunity to better educate teens about the consequences of sharing personal information." FTC 2012 Privacy Report, supra note 2, at 60.

[33] See Do Not Track Kids Act of 2013, introduced by Senators Edward J. Markey (D-Mass.) and Mark Kirk (R-Ill.) and Representatives Joe Barton (R-Texas) and Bobby L. Rush (D-Ill.), S. 1700 and H.R. 3481. This bill would require that websites and online services directed to teens ages 13 to 15, or who know they are collecting personal information from teens aged 13 to 15, obtain their consent before collecting their personal information, including geolocation. The bill would also allow children and teens to remove personal information via an "eraser button."

[34] See Protecting Student Privacy Act of 2014, introduced by Senators Edward J. Markey (D-Mass.) and Orrin Hatch (R-Utah), and co-sponsored by Senators Mark Kirk (R-Ill.) and John Walsh (D-Mont.), S. 2690.

[35] If onboarding is occurring, the device profile might also include information about local ice cream store preferences, or matinee movie visits.

[36] Cf. FTC Data Broker Report, supra note 1, at 55.

[37] The FTC Data Broker Report recommended legislation requiring that consumer-facing sources obtain affirmative express consent before they collect sensitive information, "such as certain health information." FTC Data Broker Report, supra note 1, at 52. Relatedly, Chairwoman Edith Ramirez and Commissioner Julie Brill also recommended that data brokers should take reasonable steps to assure themselves that their sources obtained data with notice and choice, "including express affirmative consent for sensitive data." Id. at 52 n.91. And Commissioner Brill separately supported "[a] requirement that the sources of data broker information used for marketing purposes provide consumer control over collection—express affirmative consent for sensitive information collection, notice and choice for other information... ." Statement of Commissioner Julie Brill, Data Brokers: A Call for Transparency and Accountability C-4 (May 27, 2014).

[38] See Supplement to Statement of Commissioner Julie Brill (May 27, 2014) (summarizing Commission legislative recommendations), available at http://www.ftc.gov/system/files/documents/public_statements/311541/140527databrokerrptbrill.pdf

In: The Use of Big Data
Editor: Diana Simpson

ISBN: 978-1-63485-318-7

Chapter 8

COMMENTS OF LAURA W. MURPHY, DIRECTOR, WASHINGTON LEGISLATIVE OFFICE, AMERICAN CIVIL LIBERTIES UNION. WORKSHOP ON "BIG DATA: A TOOL FOR INCLUSION OR EXCLUSION?"*

Chairwoman Edith Ramirez Federal Trade Commission Room 438
600 Pennsylvania Avenue, NW Washington, DC 20580

Dear Chairwoman Ramirez:

The American Civil Liberties Union appreciates the opportunity to file this comment in follow-up to the FTC's recent workshop, "Big Data: A tool for inclusion or exclusion?" We write to urge the Federal Trade Commission ("FTC"), as well as the Consumer Financial Protection Bureau (CFPB") and other federal agencies to enforce existing anti-discrimination law in the area of online credit marketing. For nearly 100 years, the ACLU has been our nation's guardian of liberty, working in courts, legislatures, and communities to defend and preserve the individual rights and liberties that the Constitution and the laws of the United States guarantee everyone in this country. The ACLU works both to safeguard individuals' rights to privacy and to ensure full equality for members of historically marginalized groups, including people of color,

* This is an edited, reformatted and augmented version of comments offered October 27, 2014 in response to a request from the Federal Trade Commission in preparation of a public workshop on September 15, 2014.

women, immigrants, the disabled, and lesbian, gay, and transgendered people. Our work on privacy issues, in recent years, has centered on the importance of regulating and securing the vast quantities of data about individuals generated as we move through the digital landscape. The ACLU has also worked at the junction of these privacy and equality issues before, most recently as a signatory, along with other civil rights groups, to the Civil Rights Principles for the Era of Big Data.[1]

In considering the implications of big data, we are particularly concerned about the behavioral targeting, which has the potential to significantly reinforce existing economic disparities between racial groups. Such targeting causes individuals to see different advertisements, potentially offering them different products or different prices. Because decisions about which advertisements to display are in some cases based on data about race or factors closely linked to race, we are in danger of segregating the consumer experience on the web. Yet the web has enormous potential as a marketplace free from the history of segregation and disparity that plagues geographical space, and the agencies should help ensure that online commerce harnesses that potential.

I. The Equal Credit Opportunity Act Prohibits Discriminatory Online Marketing Practices

The Equal Credit Opportunity Act ("ECOA")[2] provides the agencies with powerful tools to combat discriminatory marketing of credit products. The ECOA prohibits creditors from discriminating against applicants for credit with respect to "any aspect of a credit transaction . . . on the basis of race, color, religion, national origin, sex or marital status, or age . . ."[3] Intentional discrimination and practices that disproportionately impact protected classes are equally impermissible under the ECOA, as implemented by Regulation B.[4] In other words, creditors may not use race-based criteria to screen or target certain applicants, nor may they use "outwardly neutral . . . practices" that lead to "a significantly adverse or disproportionate impact on persons of a particular [race] produced by the defendant's facially neutral acts or practices."[5]

Advertising and marketing practices are subject to regulation under the ECOA. The ECOA's prohibition against discriminatory credit transactions extends beyond the approval or denial of credit applications, to include "*every aspect* of an applicant's dealings with a creditor regarding an application for credit or an existing extension of credit,"[6] including the marketing that leads to the initiation of that application or extension. Certain targeted marketing practices—like pushing harmful products toward protected groups, or beneficial products away from them—can constitute intentional discrimination.[7] Additionally, marketing practices that unjustifiably cause disproportionate harm to protected groups violate the ECOA.[8] Separately, Regulation B makes clear that creditors may not use advertising or marketing to "discourage on a prohibited basis a reasonable person from making or pursuing an application."[9]

The ECOA governs online marketing and advertising with no less force. In fact, as data-based advertising techniques allow for new forms of targeted marketing, the risk of discrimination grows. Data brokers use information from "public records, social media sites, online tracking, and retail loyalty card programs to build 'modeled' profiles of individuals, which include inferences and predictions about them."[10] As the FTC has observed, some of these models "primarily focus on minority communities with lower incomes, such as 'Urban Scramble' and 'Mobile Mixers'Éwhich include a high concentration of Latino and African-American consumers with low incomes."[11] Some segments are explicitly race-based, such as "African-American Professional"[12] or "Native American Lifestyle."[13] Other factors considered by data brokers are less explicit, but serve as proxies for race—such as "purchase behavior data" sorted by consumers interested in "Kwanzaa/African-Americana Gifts."[14] Data brokers also offer the ability to 'append' additional information about consumers for retailers and other clients including race, age, gender, religion and ethnicity.[15]

This kind of data creates significant potential for discriminatory marketing practices, and, in the field of lending, such practices violate the ECOA.[16] For instance, if a bank were to show mortgage advertisements featuring a higher interest rate to users that, as a result of data, it believed to be African-American, that targeting would constitute impermissible intent-based discrimination. Or, if advertisers were to show website viewers individualized advertisements based in part on neighborhood-level credit score data,[17] such that creditworthy African-Americans end up receiving credit on less favorable terms than their similarly-situated white counterparts, that marketing practice would have a disparate impact in violation of the ECOA. Similarly, if direct marketers of credit offers remove individuals living in certain neighborhoods from their lists,[18] this practice may impermissibly discourage a reasonable person from making an application for credit on a protected basis, and it may also create an illegal disparate impact.

In short, providers of credit are prohibited from using race or factors closely linked to race to market lower quality products to members of protected racial groups, or to exclude them from the marketing of higher quality products. Evidence exists that data brokers hold and sell lists that enable this kind of discrimination.[19] More investigation of how lenders use that data in marketing is sorely needed, and the FTC and CFPB should take the actions described below to address and prevent violations.

II. The FTC and the CFPB Have the Tools to Investigate and Enforce the ECOA's Prohibition on Discriminatory Online Marketing

We commend the FTC for using its authority under Section 6 of the Federal Trade Commission Act ("FTCA") to study data broker practices and to issue its report this spring.[20] Through that process, the FTC has already gathered significant information relevant to determining whether extant marketing practices violate the ECOA. For instance, the FTC has obtained information concerning which types of personal data are collected, generated, or stored by data brokers, including racial or ethnic information; how this data is sold in products and services, and what those products and services look like; which customers buy these products and services; and how agreements with those customers may limit the use of the data.[21] Thus, the FTC is well-equipped to determine whether the data brokers it investigated are enabling marketing practices that violate the ECOA.

The FTCA arms the FTC with unfairness authority, allowing it to bring enforcement actions against entities within its jurisdiction that use unfair practices in commerce.[22] The FTCA specifically states that "[i]n determining whether an act or practice is unfair, the Commission may consider established public policies as [relevant] evidence."[23] The ECOA, with its discriminatory effects test, is one such policy.[24] Thus, the FTC may use its unfairness authority to take action against a data broker that sells a product which enables lenders to violate the ECOA. The FTC can bring such an action despite the fact that data brokers are not themselves creditors under the ECOA.[25] Further, the FTC can also enforce the ECOA directly against non-bank lenders, and it should do so where the online marketing practices of these lenders violate the ECOA.[26]

The CFPB is also empowered to gather information about potential violations of the ECOA in this arena. It can issue civil investigative demands[27] seeking information, and, like the FTC, it can require the entities it regulates to submit reports or answers in writing to specific questions.[28] But the CFPB can also monitor and prevent such practices through its supervision of the banks within its jurisdiction.[29] In order to make clear to banks that discriminatory online marketing practices violate the ECOA, the CFPB should amend the ECOA baseline review modules contained within its examination manual[30] to specifically seek information about the use of protected class data in online marketing of credit products. If information obtained through investigation and compliance review reveals ongoing violations of the ECOA, the CFPB should take immediate enforcement action. The CFPB can and should bring suit against any bank or non-bank entity, like a payday lender or auto lender, that violates the ECOA with its online marketing practices.[31]

* * * *

In sum, the agencies are currently equipped with the authority and the tools to fight marketing discrimination as it plays out in new and pernicious ways online. They should act now in order to prevent discrimination from contaminating access to credit in the digital realm. Please contact Naureen Shah, legislative counsel at the ACLU Washington Legislative Office, at nshah@aclu.org or (202) 675-2327 with any questions.

Sincerely,
Laura W. Murphy Director
ACLU Washington Legislative Office
Rachel Goodman Staff Attorney
ACLU Racial Justice Program

End Notes

[1] Civil Rights Principles for the Era of Big Data, The Leadership Conference on Civil and Human Rights http://www.civilrights.org/press/2014/civil-rights-principles-big-data.html (last visited Oct. 14, 2014).

[2] 15 U.S.C. § 1691; see also 12 C.F.R. § 202.1.

[3] 15 U.S.C. § 1691(a).

[4] "The Act and regulation may prohibit a creditor practice that is discriminatory in effect because it has a disproportionately negative impact on a prohibited basis, even though the creditor has no intent to discriminate and the practice appears neutral on its face, unless the creditor practice meets a legitimate business need that cannot reasonably be achieved as well by means that are less disparate in their impact." 12 CFR Pt. 1002 Supp. I Sec. 1002.6(a)—2 (2014) (official staff interpretation).

[5] Ramirez v. Greenpoint Mortgage Funding, Inc., 268 F.R.D. 627, 640 (N.D. Cal. 2010) (quoting Budnick v. Town of Carefree, 518 F.3d 1109, 1118 (9th Cir. 2008) (internal marks omitted). See also Estate of Davis v. Wells Fargo Bank, 633 F.3d 529, 539-40 (7th Cir. 2011) (recognizing disparate impact claim under ECOA); Haynes v. Bank of Wedowee, 634 F.2d 266, 272 n.5 (5th Cir. 1981) (noting that ECOA regulations endorse use of the disparate impact test) (citing 12 CFR § 202.6(a) n.7); Barrett v. H & R Block, Inc., 652 F. Supp. 2d 104, 108 (D. Mass. 2009) (noting that many circuit and district courts have concluded that disparate impact claims are permissible under the ECOA) (citing Miller v. Am. Express Co., 688 F.2d 1235, 1239-40 (9th Cir. 1982); Bhandari v. First Nat'l Bank of Commerce, 808 F.2d 1082, 1101 (5th Cir. 1987), vacated and remanded on other grounds, 492 U.S. 901 (1989); Golden v. City of Columbus, 404 F.3d 950, 963 n.11 (6th Cir. 2005) (dictum); Miller v. Countrywide Bank, N.A., 571 F.Supp.2d 251 (D. Mass. 2008)), reconsidered on other grounds sub nom, Barrett v. Option One Mortgage Corp., 2012 WL 4076465 (D. Mass. Sept. 18, 2012); M & T Mortgage Corp. v. White, 736 F. Supp. 2d 538, 574 (E.D.N.Y. 2010) (noting that ECOA claims may be prosecuted on the basis of disparate impact) (citing LeBlanc–Sternberg v. Fletcher, 67 F.3d 412, 425 (2d Cir. 1995); Powell v. American General Finance, Inc., 310 F.Supp.2d 481, 487 (N.D.N.Y. 2004)); Hargraves v. Capital City Mortgage Corp., 140 F. Supp. 2d 7, 20-23 (D.D.C. 2000) (recognizing disparate impact claim under ECOA); CFPB Bulletin 2012-04 at 2 (April 18, 2012), available at http://files.consumerfinance.gov/f/201404_cfpb_bulletin_lending_discrimination.pdf ("The applicability of disparate impact doctrine, also known as the 'effects test,' to credit transactions is reflected in the legislative history of the ECOA.").

[6] 12 C.F.R. § 202.2(m) (emphasis added).

[7] U.S. ex rel. Cooper v. Auto Fare, Inc., No. 3:14-CV-0008-RJC, 2014 WL 2889993, at *3 (W.D.N.C. June 25, 2014) (placing car dealerships in predominately African-American neighborhoods provided some evidence of intentional discrimination); M & T Mortgage Corp. v. White, 736 F. Supp. 2d 538, 576 (E.D.N.Y. 2010) (advertising in heavily minority neighborhoods could show some degree of intentional targeting); Hargraves v. Capital City Mortgage Corp., 140 F. Supp. 2d 7, 21-22 (D.D.C. 2000) (evidence regarding, inter alia, defendants' advertisements in black communities supported intentional discrimination claim); United States v. Am. Future Sys., Inc., 571 F. Supp. 551, 562 (E.D. Pa. 1982) (credit card marketing program targeting white, female college students discriminated on the basis of race, in violation of the ECOA), aff'd, 743 F.2d 169 (3d Cir. 1984).

[8] See, e.g., Alleyne v. Flagstar Bank, FSB, No. CIV.A. 07-12128-RWZ, 2008 WL 8901271, at *5 (D. Mass. Sept. 12, 2008) (claim that black borrowers were more likely than white borrowers to obtain mortgages through higher cost brokers because of defendant's choices regarding the location of its offices, sufficiently articulated a causal connection between the challenged policies and the disparate impact alleged); Nat'l Ass'n for Advancement of Colored People v. Ameriquest Mortgage Co., 635 F. Supp. 2d 1096, 1104 (C.D. Cal. 2009) (plaintiff's allegation of marketing policy leading to disparate impact was sufficient to state cause of action under the ECOA); Jackson v. Novastar Mortgage, Inc., 645 F. Supp. 2d 636, 647 (W.D. Tenn. 2007) (allegation that company targeted minority sub-prime borrowers via

advertisements, in combination with other policies alleged, was sufficient to state cause of action under ECOA); Matthews v. New Century Mortgage Corp., 185 F. Supp. 2d 874, 883 (S.D. Ohio 2002) (finding that plaintiffs sufficiently alleged cause of action under the ECOA by claiming defendants "target[ed] single, elderly women for allegedly predatory loans."); Johnson v. Equicredit Corp. of Am., 2002 WL 448991, at *4 (N.D. Ill. Mar. 22, 2002) (Facts indicated that the defendant "target[ted] neighborhoods comprised primarily of minorities and impose[d] predatory credit terms on them, which result[ed] in discrimination based on race and color" thus plaintiff sufficiently pled a cause of action under the ECOA).

[9] 12 C.F.R. § 202.4(b). See also CFPB Consumer Laws and Regulations: ECOA at 3 (June 2013), available at http://files.consumerfinance.gov/f/201306_cfpb_laws-and-regulations_ ecoa-combined-june-2013.pdf ("For example, a creditor may not advertise its credit services and practices in ways that would tend to encourage some types of borrowers and discourage others on a prohibited basis.").

[10] Robinson + Yu, Civil Rights, Big Data, and an Algorithmic Future 8 (Sept. 2014), available at http://bigdata.fairness.io/wp-content/uploads/2014/09/Civil_Rights_Big_Data_and_Our_ Algorithmic-Future_2014- 09-12.pdf.

[11] FTC, Data Brokers: A Call for Transparency and Accountability 20 (May 2014), available at http://www.ftc.gov/system/files/documents/reports/data-brokers-call-transparency-accountability-report-federaltrade-commission-may-2014/140527databrokerreport.pdf [hereinafter, "FTC Data Brokers Report"].

[12] Id. at 21. See also id. at Appendix B-3 (listing demographic data considered by brokers, including "Race & Ethnicity").

[13] Id. at Appendix B-5.

[14] Id. at Appendix B-6.

[15] Id. at 24.

[16] Indeed, as the Senate Commerce Committee has warned, some data brokers' products "likely appeal to companies that sell high-cost loans and other financially risky products." U.S. Senate Committee on Commerce, Sci., and Trans., A Review of the Data Broker Industry: Collection, Use and Sale of Consumer Data for Marketing Purposes 26 (2013), available at http://www.commerce.senate.gov/public/?a=Files.Serve&File_id=0d2b3642-6221-4888-a631-08f2f255b577.

[17] Pam Dixon & Robert Gellman, World Privacy Forum (WPF), The Scoring of America: How Secret Consumer Scores Threaten Your Privacy and Your Future 37 (2014), available at http://www.worldprivacyforum.org/wpcontent/uploads/2014/04/WPF_Scoring_of_ America_April2014_fs.pdf (including "Summarized credit score or modeled credit score by neighborhood" on list of consumer data available for purchase).

[18] What Information Do Data Brokers Have on Consumers, and How Do They Use it?, S. Comm. on Commerce, Sci., and Transp., 113th Cong. 3 (2013) (testimony of Pam Dixon, World Policy Forum), available at http://www.worldprivacyforum.org/wpcontent/uploads/ 2013/12/WPF_PamDixon_CongressionalTestimony_DataBrokers_2013_fs.pdf ("Data brokers sell lists of people who live in or near trailer parks so that these undesirable consumers can be targeted for suppression.").

[19] See supra notes 12-15.

[20] FTC Data Brokers Report, supra note 11, at ii.

[21] Id. at Appendix A.

[22] 15 U.S.C. § 45(a)(2).

[23] 15 U.S.C. § 45(n).

[24] 12 CFR Pt. 1002 Supp. I Sec. 1002.6(a)—2 (official staff interpretation); see also Md. Code Ann., Com. Law § 12-704.

[25] See F.T.C. v. Accusearch, Inc., 06-CV-105-D, 2007 WL 4356786 (D. Wyo. Sept. 28, 2007) (finding website selling telephone records illegally-obtained by others to be proper target of unfairness action because business depended on illegal actions) aff'd, 570 F.3d 1187 (10th Cir. 2009)

[26] 15 U.S.C. § 1691c(c). See also Letter from J. Reilly Dolan, Associate Director, Division of Financial Planning Practices, Federal Trade Commission, to Patrice Alexander Ficklin, Assistant Director, Fair Lending & Equal Opportunity, Consumer Financial Protection Bureau at note 3 (Mar. 4, 2014), available at http://www.ftc.gov/system/files/documents/reports/federal-trade-commission-enforcement-activities-relatedcompliance-regulation-b-equal-credit/140603cfpbficklin.pdf.

[27] 12 C.F.R. § 1080.6.

[28] 12 U.S.C. § 5512(c)(4)(B)(ii).

[29] 12 U.S.C. § 5515(b)(1) ("The Bureau shall have exclusive authority to require reports and conduct examinations on a periodic basis of [insured depository institutions and credit unions with more than $10,000,000,000 in assets] for purposes of (A) assessing compliance with the requirements of Federal consumer financial laws; (B) obtaining information about the activities subject to such laws and the associated compliance systems or procedures of such persons; and (C) detecting and assessing associated risks to consumers and to markets for consumer financial products and services."); 12 U.S.C. § 5516(b) ("The Director may require reports from [insured depository institutions and credit unions with less than $10,000,000,000 in assets] as necessary to support the role of the Bureau in implementing Federal consumer financial law, to support its examination activities . . . and to assess and detect risks to consumers and consumer financial markets."). See also CFPB Depository Institutions Based on 6/30/14 Total Assets, available at http://files.consumerfinance.gov/f/201409_cfpb_depository-institutions-list.pdf (list of depository institutions and depository affiliates under CFPB supervision as of June 30, 2014).

[30] CFPB Examination Procedures: Equal Credit Opportunity Act (July 2013), available at http://files.consumerfinance.gov/f/201307_cfpb_ecoa_baseline-review-module-fair-lending.pdf.

[31] 12 U.S.C. § 5564(a); § 5514(a)(1).

In: The Use of Big Data
Editor: Diana Simpson

ISBN: 978-1-63485-318-7

Chapter 9

COMMENTS OF BEN SZOKA, PRESIDENT, TECHFREEDOM. WORKSHOP ON "BIG DATA: A TOOL FOR INCLUSION OR EXCLUSION?"*

COMMENTS OF TECHFREEDOM[1] & THE INTERNATIONAL CENTER FOR LAW & ECONOMICS[2]

dis]crim]i]na]tion noun \dis-ˌkri-me-ˈnã-shen\

1. the practice of unfairly treating a person or group of people differently from other people or groups of people
2. the ability to recognize the difference between things that are of good quality and those that are not
3. the ability to understand that one thing is different from another thing[3]

- Merriam Webster

At last Jane began, and though the first bars were feebly given, the powers of the instrument were gradually done full justice to. Mrs. Weston had been

* This is an edited, reformatted and augmented version of comments offered October 31, 2014 in response to a request from the Federal Trade Commission in preparation of a public workshop on September 15, 2014. Additional comments were provided by Tom Struble, Legal Fellow, TechFreedom; Geoffrey A. Manne, Executive Director, International Center for Law & Economics; Ben Sperry, Legal Fellow, International Center for Law & Economics.

delighted before, and was delighted again; Emma joined her in all her praise; and the pianoforte, with every proper discrimination, was pronounced to be altogether of the highest promise.

- Jane Austen, EMMA (1815)[4]

INTRODUCTION AND SUMMARY

To the American ear, there is perhaps no uglier word than "discrimination." The mere mention brings to mind Bull Connor, turning police dogs and fire hoses onto Martin Luther King, Jr.'s non-violent demonstrators against Jim Crow in Birmingham, back in the 1962. Or perhaps subtler manifestations of racism. We all want America to be that nation King spoke of, where everyone "will not be judged by the color of their skin, but by the content of their character."[5]

Yet this is precisely what "Big Data" offers: by studying correlations in larger data sets, "data scientists" can craft algorithms that distinguish better between superficial attributes like race, sex, and sexual orientation and deeper attributes like reliability, honesty, credit-worthiness and other aspects of the "content of our character." In short, Big Data may mean less of the Bull Connor kind of discrimination and more of the kind that would have seemed natural to Jane Austen's readers (Merriam-Webster's second definition). This is precisely what credit scoring did: replacing the old system where bankers made lending decisions based on the banker's personal judgment - and biases - with one that discriminated between good and bad credit risks, regardless of superficial attributes or the simple social proximity between banker and borrower.[6]

Of course, no data set, no matter how big, is perfect; no algorithm will ever perfectly predict anyone's character. Machines make decisions based on probabilities, and there will always be anomalies, so there will always be mistakes. Federal and state lawmakers have enacted a variety of laws that govern how data is used to make decisions about credit, insurance, employment, housing and so on. The Federal Trade Commission ("FTC" or "Commission") has long played a key role in enforcing many of these laws.

This topic amply deserves the FTC's attention - indeed, it deserves more careful consideration than the FTC has given it thus far. Neither the FTC's initial request for comments nor the workshop itself sufficiently focused the attention of experts from the FTC, other government agencies, industry, civil rights advocates, discrimination law experts, economists, constitutional scholars and so on. The workshop suffered from a number of procedural failures, which can and should be avoided in the future. Most notably, the workshop:

1. Was unnecessarily politicized and lacking in the bipartisanship that allows the FTC, at its best, to rise above the normal clamor of Washington politics.
2. Failed to include representative expertise across the range of discrimination law, including from the FTC's own Division of Financial Practices, civil rights advocates, and discrimination law experts.
3. Lacked technical rigor, such as peer review of the study presented by the FTC's chief technologist, and a full discussion of the specific tradeoffs in regulating Big Data by outside technical experts and data scientists.[7]
4. Made no mention of the critical First Amendment implications of regulating Big Data's use for marketing purposes.
5. Failed to include representative expertise on the impact of potential regulation on competition values, which could have drawn from the FTC's own Bureau of Competition.
6. Included no economists who could discuss properly the benefits of Big Data for consumers, and for competition or question the reigning assumption that Big Data will be used even it does not facilitate more accurate predictions, the idea that greater accuracy itself is a harm, or that price discrimination is harmful to consumers overall, or to the disadvantaged in particular.

As a result, the workshop failed to provide the building blocks needed to answer the basic legal questions of what the FTC could, or should, do about concerns raised around Big Data with its existing legal authority, where legal gaps might exist, what Congress should do (if anything), or what self_ regulatory or multistakeholder processes could do to fill in such gaps in ways that would actually make consumers better off.

UNNECESSARY POLITICIZATION

One of the FTC's strengths is that, unlike executive branch agencies (e.g., the Department of Justice), it is bipartisan: with a Chairman and two Commissioners nominated by the President from his own party, and two Commissioners chosen (in practice) by the Senate leader of the opposite party. Nothing better removes the cloud of partisanship that hovers over so many policy debates in Washington than having a Commissioner of the opposite party speak at an event on what might be considered a controversial topic. The FTC has done this for many other workshops - for example, Commissioner Ohlhausen keynoted last year's Internet of Things workshop.[8]

Yet in the Big Data workshop, only Democratic Commissioners spoke about their concerns, as neither Commissioner Wright nor Commissioner Ohlhausen, nor any of their staff attorneys, appear to have been invited to participate in any way. Further, the first speaker on the first panel was a Democratic Congressional staffer[9] whose boss, Senator Jay Rockefeller, has demonstrated less willingness to listen to input from the other side of the aisle - indeed, from anyone that does not already agree with him - than any other Senate Commerce Committee Chairman in recent memory. Needless to say, no Republican Congressional staffer participated - and we are not aware of any having been invited.[10]

Unfortunately, this extreme partisanship set the tone throughout the day of an unbalanced and incomplete view of the topic. As noted above, most of the first words uttered at the workshop by the FTC's Chair cast Big Data in a sinister light, using emotionally charged language.[11] This partisan approach leads one to wonder whether the FTC has already made up its mind about the prospect of Big Data discrimination, and whether the other process failures described below were intentional.

LACK OF EXPERTISE ON DISCRIMINATION

The FTC's Bureau of Consumer Protection (BCP) is already responsible for enforcing a variety of laws governing discrimination, including the Equal Credit Opportunity Act, Truth-in-Lending Act, Fair Credit Reporting Act, and Fair and Accurate Credit Transactions Act of 2003. BCP's Division of Financial Practices (DFP), as the FTC unit that has long enforced these laws, thus has a wealth of expertise directly relevant to the subject of this workshop.

Yet the Division of Privacy and Identity Protection (DPIP) failed to include anyone from DFP to speak on the FTC's experience with these laws, where gaps might exist, what lessons should be learned from the FTC's enforcement experience, and so on. DPIP might have, for example, included a DFP representative as a co-moderator to facilitate discussion - since having dual moderators is a common practice for FTC workshops.[12]

Indeed, the agenda was notably lacking in expertise in discrimination law. The only panelist from a discrimination law enforcement agency was Carol Miaskoff from the Equal Employment Opportunity Commission ("EEOC").[13] Notably absent was a representative from the Department of Justice's Civil Rights Division, the leading federal anti-discrimination agency. Ms. Miaskoff was asked little more than "Is the law sufficient?" - a question that the workshop did not actually resolve.[14]

The only full-time representative of a civil rights organization participating was Dr. Nicol Turner-Lee of the Minority Media Telecommunications Council, a specialty organization. By contrast, the Division of Financial Practices' recent "Fraud Affects Every Community" workshop included no less than nine representatives from civil rights groups, most of whom had specific expertise in discrimination law.[15]

The unfortunate result from all of this is that this Workshop failed to answer what should have been the key questions addressed: (1) what lessons can be learned from the prior history of enforcing non- discrimination laws; (2) can existing laws continue to ensure non-discrimination in the wake of the rise of Big Data; and (3) if there are gaps in the laws that need to be filled in, what should new legislation look like?

LACK OF TECHNICAL AND STATISTICAL RIGOR

In her opening remarks, Chairwoman Ramirez cited "real world examples of possible risks,"[16] including three studies. Each could mark an intriguing beginning of research into how to ensure that Big Data is, as the FTC's Workshop title suggests, a tool for inclusion - but only a beginning. The workshop did little to advance discussion of these early forays, either by subjecting them to additional technical/statistical scrutiny or by integrating them into discussion by experts in other fields.

The first, conducted by Microsoft Research's Kate Crawford in 2013, illustrated vividly what should be intuitively obvious: Big Data can produce disparate outcomes if it is not "Big" enough.[17] Crawford studied Boston's use of the Street Bump smartphone app to empower citizens to report service needs (e.g., potholes), concluding that relying solely on reporting through the app could skew city services towards wealthier areas, where users might be more likely to have a smartphone and use it in this fashion.[18] Of course, this is no more an argument against using Big Data than was it an argument against opinion polling when, in 1936, pollsters famously predicted that Republican Alf Landon would trounce Franklin Roosevelt based on polling using telephone records - which, obviously (in hindsight), skewed towards Republican voters.[19] The answer, then as now, is to be aware of the limitations of any data set and the need to adjust inferences accordingly. Indeed, this is precisely how the Street Bump team addressed the problem after Crawford's study: they monitored their product in the field and then made adjustments when they learned of its disparate effect.[20] If anything this vindicates the use-and-iterate approach that is the essence of Silicon Valley's success. Thus, the remedy is even Bigger Data to cure these data gaps, as Daniel Castro and Nicol Turner-Lee discussed at the workshop, or at least adjusting the model to account for the bias of the data. Michael Spadea briefly made this point at the FTC's workshop,[21] but since the FTC failed to include data ethicists or any additional data scientists in the workshop, the discussion of the critical question of how to ensure that Big Data is used *well* was not continued.

The second study cited by the Chairwoman was conducted by Latanya Sweeney, the FTC's Chief Technologist, before joining the FTC. In 2013, Sweeney concluded that online searches for typically black names were significantly more likely to show ads for services referencing arrest records than were searches for typically white names.[22] Yet Sweeney herself was cautious about the implications of her study, warning that it "raises more questions than it answers[,]"[23] - in particular, as to whether "advertising technology exposes racial bias in society and how ad and search technology can develop to assure racial fairness."[24] For example, a 1997 Department of Justice study concluded that black males have a 28% likelihood of being incarcerated at some point in their lives, compared to only 4% for white males.[25] This statistic has devastating implications for black communities, and should cause a serious re- examination of the criminal justice system in America and a re-consideration of our disastrous "War on Drugs." But blaming Big Data for exposing this problem is a misdirection of energy - especially when the discussion of Sweeney's study avoids specifics about what, if anything, should be done about cases where Big Data puts too clear a mirror to society's inequities. Is this actually a Big Data problem? Or are advertisers simply bidding on black names because the market for their services is disproportionately focused on black names because of wildly disproportionate incarceration rates (and the broad public awareness of those disproportionalities)?[26] A proper discussion of this issue would require data ethicists and First Amendment experts, as discussed below.[27]

Also, in the middle of the workshop, Sweeney presented research conducted by graduate students.[28] Their research, apparently very preliminary, showed that minority audiences were more likely to receive offers for more "criticized" credit cards and less likely to receive offers for more highly "praised" credit cards. This research, apparently very preliminary, was not peer-reviewed, nor did Sweeney address basic questions about her methodology.[29] Despite the opportunity to blog about the students' study on an official FTC blog *after* the Workshop,[30] key questions remain unanswered: Just how common were these objectionable ads (for criticized cards)? How many times did her researchers have to hit refresh in their study? What was the ratio of unobjectionable ads to objectionable ads? Just how rigorous of a metric is online praise of credit cards to assess ads against? Without answers to these questions, it is impossible to assess just how significant the problem of discriminatory advertising might be.

Even this would not be the end of the story. As discussed below, the next important question would still remain unanswered: To what extent did such marketing actually shape outcomes? Are other mechanisms readily available for consumers to find credit card offers? The more easily consumers are able to compare credit cards based on their credit score, the less important discriminatory marketing will be - indeed, the less likely it will happen at all, because it will likely not be profitable - and the more likely it is that existing laws governing credit scores will be adequate to protect consumers.

LACK OF DISCUSSION OF THE FIRST AMENDMENT

Among the many reasons why traditional discrimination law focuses on eligibility decisions (uses), rather than marketing, is that the First Amendment protects marketing as a form of speech - both for commercial and non-commercial purposes.[31] Any attempt to expand traditional discrimination law to marketing must ultimately survive First Amendment review. The most obvious responses to concerns about Big Data are also the most inconsistent with America's unique protection of free speech.

For example, Sweeney's study of arrest record ads might be used to suggest that the U.S. should suppress publication of arrest records, as

Germany's highest court did in a landmark 1973 decision[32] that has led Europe to attempt to impose a "Right to Be Forgotten" online.[33] This kind of suppression of truthful information would be difficult to justify, given American courts' strong insistence that the best response to objectionable or problematic speech is *more* speech, not less.[34] That could mean speech by civil rights groups or even the government itself directed towards employers to caution them against drawing unfair inferences from the appearance of arrest record ads in response to searches for black names. Or it could mean civil rights or other minority groups helping their communities manage their online reputations so that effective counter-speech appears on search results for their names, such as a LinkedIn profile - the modern equivalent of a résumé. Neither Sweeney nor any other panelist discussed the kind of benefits that courts generally recognize as flowing from these types of speech, such as potentially making those whose names are associated with arrest records aware of the need and possibility for them to use such search services themselves - for example, to seal juvenile arrest records where state laws make that possible, to correct errors in their arrest records, to become aware of potential confusion with someone of the same name, etc. Having an arrest record search service ad appear next to your name may well harm your job prospects, at least with a potential employer who lacks the sophistication necessary to understand that the ad does not necessarily reflect on you. But the greater harm might well be that employers will use such services anyway, and potential employees from minority communities may not be aware of this possibility and thus fail to do what they can to mitigate such harms.

This is precisely the kind of analysis that the First Amendment requires. Yet only once was the First Amendment and its concomitant benefits even mentioned at the workshop, and then only obliquely. In response to Danah Boyd's call for greater consumer control over marketing ("transparency and the tools and the mechanisms with which to hold ... systems of power accountable"[35]), David Robinson responded:

> I think there are ... legislative and ultimately constitutional questions about how far the FCRA-style model could be extended into the marketing world that I think really do force us to - and I also - let's - you know, law and regulation have a valuable role to play, but so does - but so does corporate citizenship potentially.[36]

This remark merely hints at the way the First Amendment analysis shapes regulation of speech in general, including marketing: forcing the government to work its way up a layered approach to addressing problems that generally begins with education, user empowerment, self-regulation and enforcement of existing laws. Given the importance piece that free speech principles should play in assessing consumer protection regulation,[37] the FTC's failure to have a First Amendment expert or even any discussion of the First Amendment left a critical hole in the overall discussion.

A thorough First Amendment analysis of this issue must also grapple with the implications of the Supreme Court's recent decision in *Sorrell v. IMS Health*, recognizing that data itself deserves First Amendment Protection. As Justice Kenney put it, writing for the majority,

> Facts, after all, are the beginning point for much of the speech that is most essential to advance human knowledge and to conduct human affairs. There is thus a strong argument that prescriber-identifying information is speech for First Amendment purposes. 38

LACK OF ECONOMIC RIGOR

An equally critical, and probably more pressing, analytical hole was the lack of economic discussion during the workshop. In the Big Data workshop, the FTC included only a single economist, Alessandro Acquisti, whose work has principally focused on a specific subset of economics: behavioral experiments designed to show how users make real choices about privacy.[39] This is certainly a useful area of expertise, but it in no way compensated for the workshop's failure to include an economist (or a few economists) who could have commented on the tradeoffs at play in regulating big data.[40] The FTC has an entire Bureau of Economics ("BE") full of talented economists who could have offered greater economic rigor - yet none of them were included in this workshop. Indeed, the Division of Privacy and Identity Protection ("DPIP") has not included a BE economist, or any other economist (besides Acquisti), in any of its recent workshops - including those on the Internet of Things, Facial Recognition, Consumer Generated and Controlled Health Data, Alternative Scoring Products, and Mobile Device Tracking. Each of these workshops would have benefitted from the inclusion of an economist focused on the economics of information markets.

Many of the questions raised at the Big Data workshop were essentially economic questions. Some of the panelists (primarily from industry) offered sensible responses, providing a first approximation of what an economist might have said - but there was no one who could really delve into the issues properly. Among other economic questions, the FTC missed an opportunity to develop economic rigor on five key issues:

1. Is greater granularity in targeting a harm, a benefit, or both?
2. How will market forces play out to encourage accuracy or tolerate inaccuracy?
3. What are the economic benefits (as well as costs) of price discrimination?
4. To what extent and at what cost (if any) can consumers' overcome potentially troubling aspects of Big Data marketing techniques?
5. What are the likely effects on competition from increased use of Big Data - and potential regulations of it?

Only by answering these questions can the FTC be sure that it is prioritizing the allocation of its limited resources on things that will actually benefit consumers. The FTC's procedural failings in crafting its initial request for comments and the agenda for the workshop are primarily what led to the substantive failures described below.

HOW WELL DO MARKET FORCES DRIVE ACCURACY?

What, exactly, is the problem the Commission is worried about here? In his comments filed before the workshop, James Cooper made a critical point that should have framed the entire workshop: "because the reduction in private information improves the efficiency of markets, the ability of big data to make more granular classifications - either through firm sorting or consumer signaling - should be considered a benefit rather than a harm."[41]

The conclusion need not have been taken as a given by the FTC's workshop. But the workshop should have been driven almost singularly by investigation of the question of trade-offs inherent in the collection and use of data: At least as much time should have been devoted to understanding the *benefits* of Big Data in overcoming discrimination and improving economic outcomes as was spent seeking to highlight the possible risks that it presents. Having a few industry representatives share anecdotes and voice their points of view is no substitute for the kind of rigorous discussion driven by economists or other experts of trade-offs that should inform a law enforcement agency - especially one with such a distinguished history of leadership in law and economics.

Much of the discussion at the workshop revolved around speculation that Big Data would proliferate, even where it did not offer effective discrimination in the traditional sense of the word (i.e., accurate predictions of salient interests and characteristics, like credit-worthiness), thus causing, unintentionally, invidious discrimination based on race, sex, or other sensitive factors. Pam Dixon and Bob Gellman summarized this concern in their comments:

> Analytics tools will continue to come down in price, just as consumer data has become a commodity item. Widespread and inexpensive data and analytics have the potential to allow broader use of predictive analytics. Consumer scores may proliferate, especially in the absence of any need for accuracy, fairness, or transparency. Consumer scoring may expand just because it is cheap and fashionable. Merchants themselves may have little ability to judge the accuracy of consumer scoring.[42]

There may be some truth in this. But just *how much* truth is far from clear. How many businesses will really use consumer scoring "just because it is cheap and fashionable[?]"[43] Why should we not expect that the use of consumer scoring will depend primarily on its efficacy? If a consumer scoring tool claims to allow merchants to better predict who will buy their product, why would merchants pay for it if it doesn't work - or doesn't work as well as other tools? At the same time there are well-known costs to engaging in invidious discrimination, whether it is intentional or not.[44] As Gary Becker famously demonstrated, those businesses that do not have a "taste" for discrimination - that, in other words, seek to minimize costs and maximize revenues without regard for the race, sex, etc. of their customers - will suffer from discrimination in the market. It is rational to conclude that such businesses will work to ferret out those costs.[45]

It may well be true that individual merchants "may have little ability to judge the accuracy of consumer scoring," but markets do not work through isolated individuals, bumping against each other like frenzied atoms flying about in some kind of plasma. Instead, markets of all kinds work through intermediaries: Few individual consumers really understand how cars work or can discriminate effectively among cars in the many complicated dimensions of a vehicle's performance - yet they can rely on countless third parties to filter information about quality to them, from Consumer Reports to Car and Driver Magazine.[46] These third parties were clearly represented at the workshop, but there was no assessment on how their important work has disciplined the market - a subject so important that it has given birth to an entire subfield of economics focused on information and reputation markets.[47] Individuals may be ignorant, yet the system may be rational - not perfectly, of course, but rational enough for good features delivered cost-effectively to succeed over time in the ongoing competitive process. Similarly, it is implausible to expect that merchants will buy consumer scoring - or any other product - merely because it is "cheap and fashionable."[48] They will buy it, if at all, because it works. The difficult question, hinted at by Dixon, Gellman and other commenters, but never really developed in an analytically rigorous way, boils down to this: To what extent can we rely on market forces to ensure that consumer scoring is accurate?

EFFECTS ON COMPETITION

The FTC has a dual mandate: to protect consumers from unfair and deceptive practices while also protecting competition. This is reflected in the FTC's division into two enforcement bureaus: the Bureau of Consumer Protection and the Bureau of Competition. Marketing has long been understood to drive competition, such as by allowing new entrants to overcome the heavy advantages of incumbents by cost-effectively identifying and communicating to customers likely to be interested in their products. Yet there was essentially no discussion of competition at the Big Data Workshop.

This is especially problematic because, as discussed below, the FTC's Unfairness Policy Statement requires the FTC to weigh effects on competition in any use of its unfairness authority:

> To justify a finding of unfairness the injury must satisfy three tests. It must be substantial; it must not be outweighed by any countervailing benefits to consumers or competition that the practice produces; and it must be an injury that consumers themselves could not reasonably have avoided.[49]

Thus, as discussed below, failing to weigh the effects on competition misses both a critical dimension of policy analysis and a part of the FTC's own standards for exercising its Section 5 authority.

IS PRICE "DISCRIMINATION" REALLY A PROBLEM?

Much of the concern about Big Data seems to be that it will facilitate *price* discrimination - or, to use a less charged term, price differentiation. Had there been even a single economist at the workshop with expertise beyond the narrow experimental economics of privacy, she would surely have explained that differential pricing is frequently a good thing: tailoring prices more closely to an individual's willingness to pay means that more transactions will take place than otherwise would have, with more consumers having access to the product and more consumers' desires being satisfied.[50] And price differentiation generally means that the poor pay less, not more, for the same goods. That's precisely why it was so extraordinary when, in late 2012, a Wall Street Journal study led by privacy activist Ashkan Soltani (recently named to be the FTC's new chief technologist)[51] found that Staples might be charging higher online prices to consumers who lived farther away from a Staples store - which would generally mean higher prices for poorer consumers:

> What economists call price discrimination - when companies offer different prices to different people based on their perceived willingness to pay - is commonplace and can be beneficial.... But using geography as a pricing tool can also reinforce patterns that e- commerce had promised to erase: prices that are higher in areas with less competition, including rural or poor areas. It diminishes the Internet's role as an equalizer.
>
> In the Journal's examination of Staples' online pricing, the weighted average income among ZIP Codes that mostly received discount prices was roughly $59,900, based on Internal Revenue Service data. ZIP Codes that saw generally high prices had a lower weighted average income, $48,700.[52]

For an economist, this highly anecdotal study would be merely the beginning of a larger inquiry. In particular, an economist would ask the obvious question: If customers are already shopping online, why would their proximity to a physical store matter? If they're willing to make purchases online, why would they not comparison-shop to check prices on Staples' *online* competitors? In other words, could consumers not easily circumvent such price differentiation? If so, why would we expect price differentiation to be effective?

This point was made by several industry representatives at the workshop. But it is a more complicated point that deserves greater discussion among specialists in the economics of information. The theoretical basis for concern about price differentiation appears to be that advertisers will use Big Data to take advantage of consumers through a greater information asymmetry, charging each consumer as much as he or she appears willing to bear. This idea is predicated on the idea that Internet users undervalue their data and overvalue the benefits of the content they receive access to.

This information asymmetry story has superficial plausibility - consumers in real-world markets never have the perfect information that certain models presume. But businesses also fail to have perfect information, and this fact is glossed over by critics. The market process is useful because it incentivizes participants to gain information efficiently as the costs and benefits of decisions are borne by each decision-maker herself.[53] Further, whatever information asymmetry persists is not likely in the favor of even most informed business. No one knows more about a consumer's preferences than the consumer herself. All the tracking in the world will, at best, allow online advertising networks to play catch-up. It is surely overstated to claim that businesses in possession of information, even that enabled by Big Data, will be at an informational advantage compared to the consumers about whom they are supposedly informed. Indeed, consumers are often armed not only with their own ability to inform themselves, but also by companies seeking to provide information services about pricing and services through crowd surfing and other means, as popular apps like Gas Buddy and Yelp have shown.

Another plausible-sounding argument about the harm of price differentiation is that because major advertising networks are able to collect a great deal of data about their users for analysis, businesses could segment consumer groups based on certain characteristics and offer different deals. The resulting price differentiation could lead to many consumers paying more than they would have in the absence of Big Data. Therefore, it has been argued, Big Data facilitates price differentiation, and that harms consumer welfare.

This argument misses a large part of the story, though. The flip side is that price differentiation could have benefits to those who receive *lower* prices from the scheme than they would have in the absence of Big Data. If this group is as big as or bigger than the group that pays higher prices, then it is difficult to state with any certainty that the practice leads to a reduction in consumer welfare, even if this can be divorced from total welfare.

Further, this analysis fails to consider the dynamic efficiencies of price differentiation, as suggested above. In a static model of third-degree price differentiation, some buyers receive lower prices (and purchase higher quantities), while other buyers receive higher prices (and purchase lower quantities). Thus, the net impact of price differentiation on output is ambiguous.[54] But, in a dynamic model, price differentiation may often be pro-competitive because the profits provide incentives for entry and allow for additional investments in innovation and increasing product variety, expanding retail outlets, or research and development.[55] Price differentiation may allow for increased competition to all consumers, including previously unreached poorer consumers - a pro-competitive outcome.[56] And contrary to the received wisdom,[57] economists have more recently noticed that price differentiation is present even in competitive markets.[58]

While critics of Big Data have focused on the possible negative effects of price differentiation to one subset of consumers, they usually ignore the positive effects of businesses being able to expand output by serving previously underserved consumers. It is unlikely that a business relying on metrics would want to serve only those who can pay more by charging them a lower price, while charging those who cannot afford it a larger one, as some of the anecdotes at the workshop suggested. If anything, price differentiation would likely promote egalitarian outcomes by allowing companies to offer lower prices to poorer segments of the population, which can be identified by data collection and analysis.

In an error cost framework, courts and antitrust regulators should refrain from declaring conduct anticompetitive unless the likelihood of procompetitive outcomes is extremely low.[59] It may be difficult for the FTC to differentiate positive price differentiation from negative price differentiation. Here, it seems unlikely that the price differentiation "facilitated" by Big Data is anti-consumer welfare. Big Data helps drive the Internet ecosystem, and many businesses that previously did not compete with each other do now compete in the same Internet markets in an effort to offer the best deal to consumers through targeted advertising. It seems just as likely, if not more so, that Big Data is increasing consumer welfare by helping businesses find consumers interested in their products and serving up more relevant advertisements to those consumers - thus increasing the amount of positive sum transactions overall.

Lack of Legal Rigor

In the end, economic and technical rigor is useful because it helps to define what problem government needs to solve - and how to ensure that government intervention in the marketplace does more to help consumers than to harm them. Unfortunately, here, too, was a missed opportunity to explore the key legal questions raised by the workshop - specifically:

1. How should the FTC use its existing Section 5 authority over Big Data?
2. What gaps exist in the discrimination laws already enforced by the FTC and other federal agencies, and by states, regarding credit, lending, employment, housing, etc.?

SECTION 5: UNFAIRNESS

The Workshop featured surprisingly little discussion of the FTC's broad Section 5 authority over practices it deems unfair. The only real explanation of how unfairness might apply to potentially discriminatory uses of Big Data came from Lee Peeler, a 33-year veteran of the Deputy Director of the Bureau of Consumer Protection and Associate Director of the Division of Advertising Practices.[60]

First, as Peeler notes, this requires identifying a substantial harm.[61] In his comments filed before the workshop, law professor Dennis Hirsch argues that Section 5's "legal framework fits nicely with the issues that big data presents. As to the first factor, denial of employment, a loan or a similar benefit or opportunity can constitute a substantial harm."[62] These are, of course, examples of things already covered by existing discrimination law, which would therefore qualify easily as substantial injuries under 15 U.S.C. § 45(n), which provides that, in determining whether a given act or practice is unfair, the "Commission may consider established public policies as evidence to be considered with all other evidence," although "[s]uch public policy considerations may not serve as a primary basis for such determination."[63] The FTC's 1980 Unfairness Policy Statement explains that:

> To the extent that the Commission relies heavily on public policy to support a finding of unfairness, the policy should be clear and well-established. In other words, the policy should be declared or embodied in formal sources such as statutes, judicial decisions, or the Constitution as interpreted by the courts, rather than being ascertained from the general sense of the national values. The policy should likewise be one that is widely shared, and not the isolated decision of a single state or a single court.[64]

In other words, before the FTC uses unfairness authority beyond the scope of existing laws and court decisions, it must clearly demonstrate consumer injury, which requires far more careful analysis than it has performed thus far. An FTC report or consent decree would not, for example, qualify as "established public policy." Nor would laws that regulate credit, lending, employment and so on to protect against discrimination based on prohibited factors like race and gender suffice to allow the FTC to regulate marketing based on those same factors using Section 5. The point is not that regulation is necessarily inappropriate, but that Section 5 is not a blank check for the FTC to decide whether and how to regulate.

Second, the FTC must show that the unfair practice was not reasonably avoidable by consumers. As Peeler notes, this could be difficult to do where the conduct at issue is marketing rather than eligibility decisions already governed by existing discrimination law. Before bringing an unfairness case, the FTC

> would need to look at whether the ad is targeted to a specific group, but also what's the consumer group's access to alternative products, how easily can the group go on and find alternative products at better prices or at better terms?[65]

As discussed above, no one at the FTC workshop, or in filed comments, actually demonstrated that consumers could not reasonably find alternatives to the marketing they received. Yet this is precisely the burden the FTC would bear in any enforcement action predicated on unfairness. To the contrary, the marketplace appears to indicate that consumers are quite adept at comparison shopping across channels (a.k.a., "showrooming"), using the Internet to find bargains not clearly offered (e.g., by utilizing popular coupon code aggregators and interest rate comparison sites), and more. Thus, it is not enough to presume, as Dennis Hirsch does that:

> most consumers will not understand data analytics, predictive profiles and how these growing practices will affect them. They cannot "reasonably avoid" the harm through their own actions in the marketplace.[66]

Finally, the FTC must weigh harms against countervailing benefits to consumers and, as noted above, to competition. This includes "the various costs that a remedy would entail. These include not only the costs to the parties directly before the agency, but also the burdens on society in general in the form of increased paperwork, increased regulatory burdens on the flow of information, reduced incentives to innovation and capital formation, and similar matters."[67] Hirsch proposes that:

> The third component - whether these harms outweigh "countervailing benefits to consumers or to competition" - is exactly what society needs to sort out. It needs to identify core values - opportunity, free will, equality - and weigh them against the efficiencies and social benefits that big data can provide. The third prong provides a vehicle through which the FTC can undertake this crucial balancing.[68]

Hirsch is correct that harms need not necessarily be financial to be "substantial," but they cannot be conjectural - and they must be sufficiently clear that they can be weighed meaningfully against countervailing benefits. As the Unfairness Policy Statement notes,

> The Commission is not concerned with trivial or merely speculative harms. In most cases a substantial injury involves monetary harm, as when sellers coerce consumers into purchasing unwanted goods or services or when consumers buy defective goods or services on credit but are unable to assert against the creditor claims or defenses arising from the transaction. Unwarranted health and safety risks may also support a finding of unfairness. Emotional impact and other more subjective types of harm, on the other hand, will not ordinarily make a practice unfair."[69]

The FTC thus bears a heavy evidentiary burden in defining non-monetary harms. This is not to say that values like "opportunity, free will [and] equality" are inappropriate objects of government intervention in the marketplace. We have, for example, an *Equal* Employment *Opportunity* Commission. But these values have been protected (and balanced with other competing values) through legislation enacted by democratically elected lawmakers in Congress - not by a vote of three unelected bureaucrats at the FTC.

And, of course, attempting to shoehorn non-monetary harms into Section 5 is precisely what got the FTC in trouble with Congress in the 1970s. The FTC became essentially a second national legislature, attempting to regulate a broad range values based on its assertions about public policy - from pollution to the advertising of sugared cereals to children to labor practices. A heavily Democratic Congress responded furiously in 1980, briefly shuttering the agency, imposing additional procedural safeguards on its rulemaking powers under the 1975 Magnuson-Moss Warranty Improvements Act, and forcing it to issue the Unfairness Policy Statement to constrain its authority. Congress clearly expected the FTC to establish a robust factual record around each of the factors of unfairness - and for the FTC's balancing of those factors to be subject to judicial review - not least because this is what the FTC itself promised in the Unfairness Policy Statement:

> The present understanding of the unfairness standard is the result of an evolutionary process. The statute was deliberately framed in general terms since Congress recognized the impossibility of drafting a complete list of unfair trade practices that would not quickly become outdated or leave loopholes for easy evasion. The task of identifying unfair trade practices was therefore assigned to the Commission, subject to judicial review, in the expectation that the underlying criteria would evolve and develop over time. As the Supreme Court observed as early as 1931, the ban on unfairness "belongs to that class of phrases which do not admit of precise definition, but the meaning and application of which must be arrived at by what this court elsewhere has called 'the gradual process of judicial inclusion and exclusion.[70]

Congress's revisions to Magnuson-Moss clearly demonstrate just how high a bar it intended to set for the FTC to meet before the agency declared a practice unfair - the more abstract the injury, the greater the evidence that would be required. Of course, in practice, the FTC has abandoned Magnuson-Moss rulemaking altogether, preferring instead to regulate unfair and deceptive acts an practices through a mix of case-by-case enforcement (i.e., in cutting-edge areas of law, through unadjudicated consent decrees) and workshops and reports that roughly imitate the rulemaking process but produce only vague recommendations based on loose analysis of records formed around open-ended questions rather than specific queries or proposals - much like the one at issue here.

If the FTC concludes that Big Data creates some consumer injury that cannot adequately be addressed through existing laws, it has essentially four legally sound options:

1. Build a factual record adequate to justify the evidentiary requirements of Magnuson-Moss;
2. Build a similarly rigorous record but on a smaller scale, within the context of a specific fact pattern, and bring enforcement actions, at

least some of which get litigated, thus ensuring that courts check the agency's discretion in extending Section 5 into a new area of law;
3. Ask Congress for legislative authority over that practice, including the ability to issue rules tailored to that problem with the expedited rulemaking processes used by most agencies; and
4. Urge industry and other affected stakeholders (e.g. in the civil rights community) to convene a multistakeholder process to produce a code of conduct enforceable by the FTC.

In all four cases, but particularly the first three, the FTC would need to do far more than it has done in this process to produce an evidentiary record explaining why new regulation (or self-regulation) is necessary and why it would, on net, benefit consumers.

The FTC has two other options, which would be legally unsound and unwise, as a policy matter:

1. Issue a report that does not actually explain the need for new regulation (or even self- regulation), or explore the trade-offs at stake, but which nonetheless pressures industry to adopt certain practices that are not legally required - extrapolating from the FTC's recent "Privacy by Design" principles, these might be dubbed "Equity by Design" principles; and
2. Begin bringing Section 5 enforcement actions against companies that are willing to settle such actions out of court, thus avoiding judicial review but nonetheless enforcing "Equity by Design" principles as *de facto* regulations, or "soft law" - or, as some Commissioners have proudly admitted, "common law of consent decrees.h1[71]

Of course, the FTC may conclude that, like Mrs. Sweeney and her fellows' studies, the record generated by this workshop raises more questions than it answers. The proper response in that case would be to issue a request for comments more akin to a Notice of Inquiry ("NOI"). Instead of attempting to distill a consensus from the patchy record generated by comments filed this proceeding, such an NOI would ask clearer questions about what, precisely, it is that the FTC thinks might fall through the gaps of existing law, and what the trade-offs involved in various approaches to regulating such practices would be. The more of an evidentiary basis an agency can point to as proof of the existence of a problem, the more it can explain what seem to be the shortcomings in existing law, and the more helpful will be the responses received by the agency - not only in preparing to write a report, but even in picking speakers and topics for a workshop.

CONCLUSION

The Commission has limited resources. It can hold only so many workshops per year. Just as it must prioritize enforcement actions, it must also prioritize its policymaking exercises - and focus them on clearly defined problems. The purpose of workshops, of course, is to gather answers, but if the Commission cannot even clearly articulate the questions it is trying to answer, it risks wasting its own time and the time of the many organizations that respond to its request for comments - time that could have been spent responding to clear, focused questions on this topic, or on other pressing topics.

For example, identity theft is the clearest consumer protection problem facing the agency and has long been the leading source of complaints to the agency. Yet the FTC has not held a comprehensive workshop on this topic since 2007.[72]

Finally, the Commission should remember that it holds an enormous bully pulpit. It can certainly use that bully pulpit for good. Indeed, one of the most valuable things the Commission does is its competition advocacy work, filing on behalf of consumers to advocate the removal of barriers to competition - such as its recent comments to the D.C. Taxicab Commission opposing regulations that make it difficult for new entrants like Uber and Lyft to compete with regulated taxis.[73] Such work relies for its effect on the FTC's moral authority as a defender of competition. The FTC has used the same authority in the consumer protection context to encourage self-regulatory efforts, such as the Digital Advertising Alliance's regulation of online advertising and data use.

But anytime the FTC talks about the "risks" (Chairwoman Ramirez's term) posed by new technologies, it inevitably shapes the public discourse about that topic. Given the extreme sensitivity of this topic - the deep emotional legacy of Bull Connor-style discrimination in America - the FTC should tread carefully in this area. It ought not be shy about asking difficult questions, but it should ask them not merely for the sake of asking them - and frame them in a way that actually produces clear, specific answers. Otherwise, the FTC risks inflaming public sentiment against a technology that the FTC itself admits has enormous potential help consumers. At worst, this could be a kind of technopanic - a subset of the moral panic well documented by social scientists and first defined by British sociologist Stanley Cohen in the 1970s:

> panic as a moment when a condition, episode, person or group of persons emerges to become defined as a threat to societal values and interests; its nature is presented in a stylized and stereotypical fashion by the mass media; the moral barricades are manned by editors, bishops, politicians and other right-thinking people; socially accredited experts pronounce their diagnoses and solutions; ways of coping are evolved or resorted to .. . Sometimes the panic passes over and is forgotten, except in folklore and collective memory; at other times it has more serious and long-lasting repercussions and might produce such changes as those in legal and social policy or even the way the society conceives itself.[74]

Mercatus scholar Adam Thierer has written extensively about technopanics, warning against the threat inflation that drives policymakers to overreach or misdirect their reactions to new technologies, rather than to calmly weigh the costs and benefits, both seen and unseen.[75] In particular, Thierer warns against the resort to the precautionary principle, which heavily weights seen costs over unseen benefits, and drives public reaction in a feedback loop of increasingly panicked reaction to new unsettling new technologies.[76]

To ensure that Big Data fulfills its promise as "a tool for inclusion," for positive discrimination in the best sense of that word, the FTC must itself be more discriminating in its approach to the tradeoffs posed by Big Data, and the difficult questions of how to regulate its use beyond existing laws.

End Notes

[1] Berin Szoka is President of TechFreedom, a nonprofit, nonpartisan technology policy think tank. He can be reached at bszoka@techfreedom.org. Tom Struble is a Legal Fellow at TechFreedom. He can be reached at tstruble@techfreedom.org.

[2] Geoffrey A. Manne is the founder and Executive Director of the International Center for Law and Economics (ICLE), based in Portland, Oregon. He is also a Lecturer in Law at Lewis & Clark Law School, and a Senior Fellow at TechFreedom. He can be reached at gmanne@laweconcenter.org. Ben Sperry is ICLE's Associate Director. He can be reached at bsperry@laweconcenter.org.

[3] Merriam-Webster Dictionary (last visited Oct. 31, 2014), available at http://www.merriam-webster.com/dictionary/discrimination.

[4] JANE AUSTEN, EMMA (1815), available at http://www.gutenberg.org/files/158/158-h/158-h.htm.

[5] Martin Luther King, Jr., "I Have A Dream" Speech Delivered at the Lincoln Memorial in Washington, DC (Aug. 28, 1963), available at https://www.youtube.com/ watch?v=3vDWWy4CMhE.

[6] See generally Loretta J. Mester, What's the Point of Credit Scoring?, BUS. REV. (Sept.–Oct. 1997), available at https://www.phil.frb.org/research-and-data/publications/business-review/1997/september-october/brso97lm.pdf (discussing the history of credit scoring in the U.S. and its modern applications to lending decisions).

[7] See, e.g., Fed. Trade Comm'n, Big Data: A Toolfor Inclusion or Exclusion?: Transcript, at 269 (Sept. 15, 2014) [Transcript], available at http://www.ftc.gov/system/files/documents/public events/313371/bigdata-transcript- 9 15 14.pdf ("Mr. Castro: So, I'd say, you know, I think this is definitely the start of the conversation. We need many more voices here. I think it's interesting. Today's workshop has been fantastic, but, you know, across town, there's a predictive analytics government conference going on with some of the best predictive analytics data scientists in the country, and they're not in the room. So, you know, we need them here. They certainly should be part of the conversation.").

[8] Maureen K. Ohlhausen, Commissioner, Fed. Trade Comm'n, Remarks at the Internet of Things Workshop in Washington, DC (Nov. 19, 2013), available at http://www.ftc.gov/public-statements/2013/11/remarks-commissioner-maureen-k-ohlhausen-ftc-internet-things-workshop.

[9] Fed. Trade Comm'n, Big Data: A Tool for Inclusion or Exclusion?: Agenda (Sept. 15, 2014), available at http://www.ftc.gov/news-events/events-calendar/2014/09/big-data-tool-inclusion-or-exclusion.

[10] See id.

[11] See Edith Ramirez, Chairwoman, Fed. Trade Comm'n, Opening Remarks at the FTC Big Data Workshop: Framing the Conversation, 3 (Sept. 15, 2014), available at http://www.ftc.gov/system/files/documents/videos/big-data-tool-inclusion-or-exclusion-part-1/ftc big data workshop - transcript segment 1.pdf ("[The] worry is that existing disparities will be exacerbated. Is this discrimination? In one sense, yes. By its nature that's what Big Data does in the commercial sphere. It analyzes vast amounts of information to differentiate data at blinding speed. But is it unfair or biased or illegal [discrimination]? If so[,] can steps be taken to level the playing field? Those are the questions that we will be exploring today.").

[12] See, e.g., Fed. Trade Comm'n, Fraud Affects Every Community: Agenda (Oct. 29, 2014), available at http://www.ftc.gov/news-events/events-calendar/2014/10/fraud-affects-every-community.

[13] See id.

[14] See Transcript at 162–213 (surveying the current legal landscape, but not answering whether the existing laws are sufficient or whether new legislation is needed).

[15] Fed. Trade Comm'n, Fraud Affects Every Community: Agenda (Oct. 29, 2014), available at http://www.ftc.gov/news-events/events-calendar/2014/10/fraud-affects-every-community.

[16] Transcript at 11.

[17] Kate Crawford, The Hidden Biases in Big Data, Harv. Bus. Rev. (Apr. 1, 2013), available at http://blogs.hbr.org/2013/04/the-hidden-biases-in-big-data/.

[18] Id.

[19] See, e.g., Nat'l Constitution Staff, Five Biggest Political Polling Mistakes in U.S. History, CONST. DAILY (Oct. 2, 2012), available at http://blog.constitutioncenter.org/2012/10/five-biggest-political-polling-mistakes-in-u-s-history/.

[20] Transcript at 259–60.

[21] Id.

[22] Latanya Sweeney, Discrimination in Online Ad Delivery, at 34 (Jan. 28, 2013), available at http://papers.ssrn.com/sol3/papers.cfm?abstract id=2208240

[23] Id.

[24] Id. at 1.

[25] See U.S. Dept. of Justice, If 1991 Incarceration Rates Continue, One in Twenty U.S. Residents Could Be Imprisoned During Their Lifetimes (Mar. 6, 1997), available at http://www.bjs.gov/content/pub/press/LLGSFP.PR.

[26] See, e.g., Wikipedia, Race in the United States Criminal Justice System (last visited Oct. 31, 2014), available at http://en.wikipedia.org/wiki/Race in the United States criminal justice system.

[27] See infra, Lack of Discussion of the First Amendment.

[28] Transcript at 155–61.

[29] See id.

[30] Latanya Sweeney, Online Ads Roll the Dice, BLOGS: TECH@FTC (Sept. 25, 2014), available at http://www.ftc.gov/news-events/blogs/techftc/2014/09/online-ads-roll-dice

[31] See Cent. Hudson Gas & Elec. Corp. v. Pub. Serv. Comm'n of New York, 447 U.S. 557 (1980).

[32] See John Schwartz, Two German Killers Demanding Anonymity Sue Wikipedia's Parent, N.Y. Times (Nov. 12, 2009), available at http://www.nytimes.com/2009/11/13/us/ 13wiki.html (reporting about a recent dispute regarding the online publication of arrest records in Germany, and quoting a lawyer from Berlin, Julian Häppner, discussing the applicable 1973 ruling from Germany's highest court).

[33] See Court of Justice of the European Union, Press Release No. 70/14: An Internet Search Engine Operator is Responsible for the Processing that it Carries Out of Personal Data Which Appear on Web Pages Published by Third Parties (May 13, 2014), available at http://curia.europa.eu/jcms/upload/docs/application/pdf/2014- 05/cp140070en.pdf.

[34] See, e.g., Snyder v. Phelps, 131 S. Ct. 1207 (2011).

[35] Transcript at 69.

[36] Id. at 69–70.

[37] Maureen K. Ohlhausen, 100 is the New 30: Recommendations for the FTC's Next 100 Years, 21 GEO. MASON L. REV. 1131 (2014), available at http://www.georgemasonl awreview.org/doc/Ohlhausen.pdf.

[38] See Sorrell v. IMS Health Inc., 131 S. Ct. 2653, 2667 (2011); see also TechFreedom, TechFreedom Files Amicus Brief in Sorrell v. IMS Health (Mar. 31, 2011), available at http://techfreedom.org/post/58428716508/techfreedom_files_amicus_brief_in_sorrell_v_im s_health.

[39] See, e.g., Alessandro Acquisti & Jens Grossklags, What Can Behavioral Economics Teach Us About Privacy?, DIGITAL PRIVACY: THEORY, TECHNOLOGIES AND PRACTICES (Taylor & Francis Group, 2007), available at http://www.heinz.cmu.edu/ ~acquisti/papers/ Acquisti_Grossklags_Chapter_Etrics.pdf.

[40] See Ohlhausen, 100 is the New 30, supra note 37.

[41] James C. Cooper, Comment: Office of Science and Technology Policy, Big Data Study (Mar. 31, 2014), available at http://www.ftc.gov/system/files/documents/publiccomments/2014/07/00011-92278.pdf.

[42] Pam Dixon & Robert Gellman, The Scoring of America: How Secret Consumer Scores Threaten Your Privacy and Your Future, WORLD PRIVACY FORUM (Apr. 2, 2014), available at http://www.ftc.gov/system/files/documents/public comments/2014/08/00014-92369.pdf.

[43] Id.

[44] GARY S. BECKER, THE ECONOMICS OF DISCRIMINATION (1957).

[45] Id.

[46] See, e.g., Consumer Futures, The Rise of the Consumer Empowering Intermediary, CTRL–SHIFT (Jan. 2014), available at http://www.consumerfutures.org.uk/files/2014/01/The-Rise-of-the-Consumer-Empowering- Intermediary-Ctrl-Shift.pdf.

[47] Gary E. Bolton, et al., Cooperation Among Strangers with Limited Information About Reputation, 89 J. of Pub. Econ. 1457 (2005), available at http://bit.ly/1EdqQaY.

[48] Dixon & Gellman, The Scoring of America, supra note 42.

[49] Michael Pertschuk, Chairman, Fed. Trade Comm'n, et al., FTC Policy Statement on Unfairness (Dec. 17, 1980) [Unfairness Policy Statement], available at http://www.ftc.gov/public-statements/1980/12/ftc-policy-statement- unfairness (codified at 15 U.S.C. § 45(n)).

[50] See, e.g., Arthur C. Pigou, Discriminating Monopoly, in THE ECONOMICS OF WELFARE (1938). The conclusion is even more true in the presence of high fixed costs. See, e.g., Hal Varian, Differential Pricing and Efficiency, 1 First Monday (August 5, 1996), available at http://firstmonday.org/ojs/index.php/fm/article/view/473/829.

[51] Fed. Trade Comm'n, Federal Trade Commission Appoints Ashkan Soltani as Chief Technologist (Oct. 21, 2014), available at http://www.ftc.gov/news-events/press-releases/2014/10/federal-trade-commission-appoints-ashkan- soltani-chief.

[52] Jennifer Valentino-Devries, et al., Websites Vary Prices, Deals Based on Users' Information, WALL ST. J. (Dec. 24, 2012), available at http://online.wsj.com/articles/SB10001424127887323777204578189391813881534.

[53] See F. A. Hayek, The Use of Knowledge in Society, 35 AM. ECON. REV. 519 (1945).

[54] See, e.g., Joshua D. Wright, Missed Opportunities in Independent Ink, CATO SUP. CT. REV., at 348 (2005-2006), available at http://object.cato.org/sites/cato.org/files/serials/files/supreme-court-review/2006/9/wright.pdf.

[55] Id. at 350.

[56] Id.

[57] See William M. Landes & Richard A. Posner, Market Power in Antitrust Cases, 94 HARV. L. REV. 937, 977 (1981).

[58] See, e.g., 70 ANTITRUST L.J. 593 (2003) (symposium articles discussing competitive price discrimination).

[59] Frank H. Easterbrook, The Limits of Antitrust, 63 TEX. L. REV. 1 (1984). The error cost model is well-accepted in the antitrust law and economics literature. See, e.g., RICHARD A. POSNER, ANTITRUST LAW, at ix (2nd ed. 2001); C. Frederick Beckner & Steven C. Salop, Decision Theory and Antitrust Rules, 67 ANTITRUST L.J. 41 (1999); David S. Evans & A. Jorge Padilla, Designing Antitrust Rules for Assessing Unilateral Practices: A Neo-Chicago Approach, 72 U. CHI. L. REV. 73 (2005); Luke Froeb et al., Vertical antitrust policy as a problem of inference, 23 INT'L; J. INDUS. ORG. 639 (2005); Keith N. Hylton & Michael Salinger, Tying Law and Policy: A Decision-Theoretic Approach, 69

ANTITRUST L.J. 469 (2001); Geoffrey A. Manne & Joshua D. Wright, Innovation and the Limits of Antitrust, 6 J. COMPETITION L. & ECON. 153 (2010).

[60] Transcript at 174–78.

[61] Id. at 176.

[62] Dennis Hirsch, Public Comments Submitted for: The Federal Trade Commission, in Big Data: A Tool for Inclusion or Exclusion? Workshop, Project No. P145406, 2 (Aug. 15, 2014), available at http://www.ftc.gov/system/files/documents/public comments/2014/08/00025-92435.pdf.

[63] 15 U.S.C. § 45(n).

[64] Unfairness Policy Statement, supra note 49.

[65] Transcript at 176–77.

[66] Dennis Hirsch, Unfair! Or is it? Big Data and the FTC's Unfairness Jurisdiction, WESTIN RES. CENTER PRIVACY PERSPECTIVES (July 31, 2014), available at https://privacyassociation.org/news/a/unfair-or-is-it-big-data-and-the-ftcs-unfairness-juris diction/.

[67] Unfairness Policy Statement, supra note 49.

[68] Hirsch, Unfair! Or is it?, supra note 66.

[69] Unfairness Policy Statement, supra note 49.

[70] Unfairness Policy Statement, supra note 49.

[71] See Julie Brill, Commissioner, Fed. Trade Comm'n, Privacy, Consumer Protection, and Competition: A Speech Delivered at the 12th Annual Loyola Antitrust Colloquium (Apr. 27, 2012), available at http://www.ftc.gov/sites/default/files/documents/public statements/privacy-consumer-protection-and- competition/120427loyolasymposium.pdf ("Yet our privacy cases are also more generally informative about data collection and use practices that are acceptable, and those that cross the line, under Section 5 of the Federal Trade Commission Act creating what some have referred to as a common law of privacy in this country.").

[72] See Fed. Trade Comm'n, Proof Positive: New Directions for ID Authentication (Apr. 23, 2007), available at http://www.ftc.gov/news-events/events-calendar/2007/04/proof-positive-new-directions-id-authentication. The FTC did hold a workshop on data security in 2009, but focused on the international dimensions of the issue, not the data security and identity theft in the U.S. See Fed. Trade Comm'n, Securing Personal Data in the Global Economy: Agenda (Mar. 16, 2009), available at http://www.ftc.gov/sites/default/files/ documents/ public events/securing-personal-data-global- economy/agenda.pdf.

[73] Fed. Trade Comm'n, FTC Staff Submits Comments to DC Taxicab Commission on Proposed Passenger Motor Vehicle Transportation Rules: Press Release (June 12, 2013), available at http://www.ftc.gov/news-events/press- releases/2013/06/ftc-staff-submits-comments-dc-taxicab-commission-proposed.

[74] STANLEY COHEN, FOLK DEVILS AND MORAL PANICS: THE CREATION OF THE MODS AND ROCKERS, 9 (London, UK: MacGibbon and Kee, 1972).

[75] Adam Thierer, Technopanics, Threat Inflation, and the Danger of an Information Technology Precautionary Principle, MERCATUS CENTER WORKING PAPER NO. 12–09 (Feb. 2012), available at http://mercatus.org/sites/default/files/publication/technopanic-Thierer.pdf.

[76] Id.

In: The Use of Big Data
Editor: Diana Simpson
ISBN: 978-1-63485-318-7

Chapter 10

BIG DATA AND DIFFERENTIAL PRICING*

Executive Office of the President

EXECUTIVE SUMMARY

Big data refers to the ability to gather large volumes of data, often from multiple sources, and with it produce new kinds of observations, measurements and predictions. Commercial applications of big data deserve ongoing scrutiny given the speed at which both the technology and business practices are evolving. One of the many questions raised by big data is whether companies will use the information they harvest to more effectively charge different prices to different customers, a practice that economists call price discrimination. Economics suggests that many forms of differential pricing, such as senior citizen discounts at the box office or tiered pricing for air travel, can be good for both businesses and consumers. However, the combination of differential pricing and big data raises concerns that some consumers can be made worse off, and have very little knowledge why. This report finds that many companies already use big data for targeted marketing, and some are experimenting with personalized pricing, though examples of personalized pricing remain fairly limited. While substantive concerns about differential pricing in the age of big data remain, many of them can be addressed by enforcing existing antidiscrimination, privacy, and consumer protection laws. In addition, providing consumers with increased transparency

* This is an edited, reformatted and augmented version of report released February 2015.

into how companies use and trade their data would promote more competition and better informed consumer choice.

INTRODUCTION

Understanding the customer is a core principle of good marketing, and over time companies have developed a wide variety of tools for doing so. These tools range from surveys to focus groups, rewards programs and the quarterly sales meeting. For many companies, big data and consumer analytics are an increasingly important part of this tool kit.

In the marketing context, big data refers to the ability to gather large volumes of data, often from multiple sources, and use it to produce new kinds of observations, measurements and predictions about individual customers. Much of what companies learn through big data is used to design products and services that deliver more value to the individual consumer. At the same time, if sellers can accurately predict what a customer is willing to pay, they may set prices so as to capture much of the value in a given transaction, especially when they face little competition.

This report considers the implications of big data and customer analytics for the American consumer, with a particular emphasis on how these tools might be used for differential pricing. The report strives to provide an economic perspective on these issues, focusing on the underlying technology, how it is used, the potential costs and benefits for both buyers and sellers, and the kinds of policies that can best promote efficiency, equity, and innovation in this space.

Big data clearly holds both promise and peril for the individual consumer. As the Executive Office of the President's 2014 report *Big Data: Seizing Opportunities, Preserving Values* recently observed, "It is one thing for big data to segment consumers for marketing purposes, thereby providing more tailored opportunities to purchase goods and services. It is another, arguably far more serious, matter if this information comes to figure in decisions about a consumer's eligibility for... employment, housing, health care, credit or education" (Podesta et al. 2014). This report explores these issues, beginning with an overview of the economics of differential pricing. It goes on to describe how sellers are using big data to create personalized marketing campaigns and pricing strategies, and how buyers are responding. The concluding section considers how big data and personalized pricing fit into our existing framework of antidiscrimination and consumer protection laws.

I. The Economics of Differential Pricing

Differential pricing, or what economists call "price discrimination," is the practice of charging customers different prices for the same product. While this sounds unfair, many forms of differential pricing generate few objections. For example, venues like movie theaters that charge a price of admission may offer discounts to particular groups, such as children, senior citizens, or members of the military. Business travelers often pay a higher price for the same plane ticket or hotel room if they purchase closer to the date of travel. And a variety of big-ticket items – products ranging from a new car to a university education – have a list price, but offer individualized discounts that vary from one customer to the next.

In each of these examples, the seller's goal is to raise prices for those willing to pay more, without losing another group of more price-sensitive customers. That is the general idea behind differential pricing – to set prices based on demand, or what customers are willing to pay, rather than costs.

Economics textbooks usually define three types of differential pricing. Personalized pricing, or first-degree price discrimination, occurs when a seller charges a different price to every buyer. Individually negotiated prices, such as those charged by a car dealer, are an example of personalized pricing. Quantity discounts, or second-degree price discrimination, occur when the per-unit price falls with the amount purchased, as with popcorn at the movie theater. Finally, third-degree price discrimination occurs when sellers charge different prices to different demographic groups, as with discounts for senior citizens.

Big data has lowered the costs of collecting customer-level information, making it easier for sellers to identify new customer segments and to target those populations with customized marketing and pricing plans. The increased availability of behavioral data has also encouraged a shift from third-degree price discrimination based on broad demographic categories towards personalized pricing. Nevertheless, differential pricing still presents several practical challenges. First, sellers must figure out what customers are willing to pay. This can be a complex problem, even for companies with lots of data and computing power. A second challenge is competition, which limits a company's ability to raise prices, even if it knows that one customer might be willing to pay more than another. Third, companies need to prevent resale by customers seeking to exploit price differences. And finally, if a company does succeed in charging personalized prices, it must be careful not to alienate customers who may view this pricing tactic as inherently unfair.

When differential pricing is possible, economic theory suggests that it can produce both costs and benefits. The main benefit is that when sellers have some market power, differential pricing allows them to expand the size of the market. For example, matinee prices encourage large families and music lovers on a tight budget to take in a show. If a theater were prohibited from using this type of differential pricing, it might decide to keep prices high and leave some seats empty. This would mean less profit for the theater and fewer people getting entertained.

Similarly, financial aid packages help universities bring in more tuition by charging the list price to those who can afford it, while educating more students who might be excluded if need or merit-based financial aid were prohibited. These forms of differential pricing typically generate few objections because they appeal to customers' sense of fairness – companies charge a bit more to the least price-sensitive customers, who can probably afford it, and a lower price to those who cannot.

On the other hand, one cost of differential pricing is that it can produce incentives to inefficiently degrade product quality. Early railroad operators, for example, sought to increase profits by charging wealthy customers more for passage but did not have a good way of determining which customers were willing to pay more. As a response, some railroads chose to provide no roof on third-class carriages in order to increase the difference in quality (and price) between a first- and third-class ticket. The modern equivalent might be disabling features built into a car or a smartphone, or degrading the speed of an Internet connection, in order to create high and low-end versions of the same product (see box on versioning). In each case, sellers can profit at the expense of high-end customers by degrading the low-end product, even if it is costly to reduce overall quality.

What Is Versioning?

Firms often produce multiple versions of a product to encourage consumers to self-select into groups that pay different prices, even when it would be more cost efficient to sell a single design. For example, at one time IBM sold two versions of its LaserPrinter Series E, where the only difference between them was a chip that made the low-priced version print more slowly (Deneckere and McAffee 1996). While intentionally disabling some features of a product to facilitate price-discrimination seems perverse, it can nevertheless increase welfare for both firms and consumers if it allows the seller to reach a larger number of customers who would not otherwise be served.

Versioning is especially prevalent with information goods such as books, films, or software because the costs of reproduction are typically small relative to the price. For these products, companies often release multiple versions over time (e.g. hardcover, paperback, and e-book) or add and remove features (e.g. bonus tracks or concurrent user limitations) as part of their product-line strategy.

It is difficult to predict how big data will influence the prevalence of versioning. If it becomes easier to predict individual customers' willingness to pay and charge different prices for an identical product, versioning may be replaced by personalized pricing. On the other hand, versioning has the benefit of reducing concerns about inequity that arise with personalized pricing, and big data may facilitate versioning strategies based on "mass customization," particularly for information goods that can be customized at relatively little incremental cost.

Another concern with differential pricing is that it transfers value from consumers to shareholders, which generally leads to an increase in inequality and can therefore be inefficient from a utilitarian standpoint. This is particularly true in settings where there is no competition, and few consumers would exit the market, even if a firm raised prices dramatically.

Ultimately, whether differential pricing helps or harms the average consumer depends on how and where it is used. In a competitive market with transparent pricing, the benefits are likely to outweigh the costs.[1] For example, while there is lots of differential pricing in airline ticket sales, the Internet has made it relatively easy for many travelers to compare prices and itineraries across airlines and to select the best deal for any given trip. Some studies even suggest that differential pricing can intensify competition relative to uniform pricing, by allowing high-margin sellers to compete more aggressively for price-sensitive customers who might otherwise buy from a lower-priced rival.[2]

Even in the absence of competition, consumers have several tools that can be used to undermine differential pricing. One of those tools is collective action, through negotiating group discounts. Another tool is arbitrage, or the ability to become a seller. For example, if a seller offers the same product in two cities (or through two distribution channels) at very different prices, an entrepreneurial buyer could purchase several copies in the low-price market and resell them at a profit in the high-price market, so long as the price difference exceeds the cost of transportation.

Ultimately, differential pricing seems most likely to be harmful when implemented through complex or opaque pricing schemes designed to screen out unsophisticated buyers. For example, companies may obfuscate by bundling a low product price with costly warranties or shipping fees, using "bait and switch" techniques to attract unwary customers with low advertised prices and then upselling them on different merchandise, or burying important details in the small print of complex contracts.[3] When these tactics work, the economic intuition that differential pricing allows firms to serve more price-sensitive customers at a lower price-point may even be overturned. If price-sensitive customers also tend to be less experienced, or less knowledgeable about potential pitfalls, they might more readily accept offers that appear fine on the surface but are actually full of hidden charges.

Finally, it is worth noting that the preceding discussion focused on "value-based" pricing, where prices reflect differences in consumers' *willingness to pay* for a particular good or service. That is what most economists mean by differential pricing. However, sellers may also charge prices that reflect differences in the *cost* of serving different groups of buyers. This type of "risk-based" pricing arises most commonly in insurance markets, where prices reflect the risk that an individual will experience the outcome covered by an insurance policy. Big data encourages risk-based pricing by enabling more fine-grained measurement of various risks, for example through tracking individual driving behaviors.[4]

Risk-based pricing can improve economic efficiency by discouraging risky behavior, such as when individuals with a history of traffic accidents are charged more for auto insurance. It can also make insurance more widely available by reducing adverse selection, which occurs when only high-risk individuals enroll at a given (uniform) price. At the same time, differential pricing in insurance markets can raise serious fairness concerns, particularly when major risk factors are outside an individual customer's control, with health insurance an obvious example.

In general, risk-based pricing favors less risky customers, whereas value-based pricing favors those who are more price-sensitive. Nondiscrimination policies are one way to promote fairness for high-risk buyers. However, those policies can re-introduce adverse selection problems unless they are accompanied by rules or subsidies that encourage low-risk buyers to remain in the market.[5]

The remainder of this report is primarily focused on value-based pricing, which has different economic motivations and implications from risk-based pricing. However, the impact of big data on risk-based pricing remains an important area for further discussion.

II. Big Data and Personalized Pricing

To understand how big data enables personalized pricing, it is useful to start with an overview of the technology. Computers have long been used to collect sales data, organize customer lists, and identify market segments. The features of big data that promise to make it more informative, however, are the increased scale of the underlying databases, the increasing variety of customer-level observations and measures, and the speed with which data are now harvested, traded, and deployed.

Two broad trends are driving the increased application of big data to marketing and consumer analytics. The first trend is the widespread adoption of new information technology platforms, of which the Internet and the smartphone are the most important. These platforms provide access to a wide variety of applications such as search engines, maps, blogs, and music or video streaming services. These new applications, in turn, create new ways for businesses to interact with consumers that produce new sources and types of data. For example, it is now possible to track:

- a user's location via mapping software
- their browser and search history
- whom and what they "like" on social networks like Facebook
- the songs and videos they have streamed
- their retail purchase history
- the contents of their online reviews and blog posts.

Sellers can also utilize these new types of information to make an educated guess about consumer characteristics. For example, some web sites use a computer's Internet Protocol (IP) address to guess the user's location.[6] Others might use the items in a virtual shopping basket to infer a buyer's gender, or the history of web sites that a user has browsed to guess at their income or health status.[7]

To some extent, this new ability to measure a consumer's digital footprint depends upon a company's relationship with that consumer. For example, when an Internet user visits a web site, the owner of the site may place a file called a "cookie" onto the user's computer, enabling the site to keep track of information about the user's interactions with the site. Over time, cookies can be used to build a long-term picture of an individual's Internet browsing history, and that information can be shared across sites (see box: What is a Cookie?). However, it is considerably easier to track customer behaviors on web sites or mobile applications that require users to create an account and log into that account with each use. In addition to simplifying online tracking, account holders typically provide personal information that a site can use to link them with other external information sources.

What Is a Cookie?

A cookie is a small text file that a web site can place on a user's computer. Each time a user loads a particular web site, the cookie is sent to that site. This allows web sites to "remember" certain information, such as what pages a user has already visited, or whether they are currently logged in to the site. Internet browsers generally allow users to set various permissions that control whether cookies are allowed on their computer.

Cookies were created by programmers working for Netscape in 1994, and the name is a reference to "magic cookies" – a term used to describe a piece of data that a program receives and then retransmits unchanged. Today, cookies are used for a wide variety of purposes, most notably tracking customers across multiple sites in order to send them behaviorally targeted advertising.

Cookies are not regulated in the United States. However, in 2009 the European Union modified its e-Privacy directive to regulate cookies. In particular, the Directive told EU member states to pass laws requiring users to "opt in" or provide consent before placing a cookie on their computer.

The second trend driving the application of big data to marketing is the growth of the ad-supported business model, and the creation of a secondary market in consumer information. Companies like Google and Facebook, both of which earn much of their revenue by selling targeted marketing opportunities, demonstrate the commercial potential of ad-supported Internet platforms.[8] The ability to place ads that will be targeted to a specific audience based on their personal characteristics makes consumer information increasingly valuable to businesses. This has fostered a growing industry of data brokers and information intermediaries that buy and sell customer lists and other data used by marketers to assemble a digital profile of individual consumers.

Given sufficient data, sellers can try to predict how buyers will behave in response to different prices and pricing schemes. While randomized experiments are one approach, non-experimental tools and techniques for predicting consumer behavior are also evolving rapidly. Predictive modeling is not a simple problem. However, companies have large incentives to refine these tools, since even small improvements can have a large impact on profitability, particularly for companies with a large customer base. For example, a 2014 recent study by Benjamin Shiller estimates the increase in profits if Netflix were to use behavioral data for personalized pricing. He finds that differential pricing based on demographics (whereby Netflix would adjust prices based on a customer's race, age, income, geographic location, and family size) could increase profit by 0.8 percent, while using 5,000 web browsing variables (such as the amount of time a user typically spends online or whether she has recently visited Wikipedia or IMDB) could increase profits by as much as 12.2 percent.

The potentially large benefits of personalized pricing lead naturally to the question of whether many companies are actually engaging in the practice. The remainder of this section examines how both sellers and buyers are adapting to the rapid diffusion of big data in the context of personalized marketing.

What Sellers Are Doing?

Although a few studies have tried to detect differential pricing online, current knowledge is mainly anecdotal. Companies naturally protect information about pricing strategies for competitive reasons, and perhaps also for fear of a customer backlash. Nevertheless, the anecdotes suggest that we have not yet entered an era of widespread personalized pricing. Rather, sellers are using online and offline pricing practices that fall into three broad categories: (1) exploring the demand curve, (2) steering and differential pricing based on demographics, and (3) behavioral targeting and personalized pricing.

Exploring the Demand Curve

Experiments are a powerful way of learning about demand and consumer behavior, even in the absence of big data. As a consequence, marketers often conduct "A/B Tests" that randomly assign customers to one of two possible price conditions. These experiments are technically a form of differential pricing, since they result in different prices for different customers, even if they are "nondiscriminatory" in the sense that all customers are equally likely to face the higher price.

Offline businesses have long been able to explore the demand curve by testing prices in different stores or randomizing offers via direct mail. The Internet, however, provides a much better platform for running demand experiments quickly and effectively. For example, a recent study identified hundreds of thousands of "seller experiments" on eBay, where an identical item was listed multiple times by the same seller at different prices or with different auction parameters, presumably to learn how those variables influence demand for the underlying product (Einav et al 2011).

While such price experiments are common, they can still become controversial. For example, in 2000 users discovered that Amazon.com was conducting price tests and complained about paying different prices for the same DVD. Amazon's CEO Jeff Bezos apologized in a news release that same year indicating that the tests were random and promised that "We've never tested and we never will test prices based on customer demographics."[9]

Even if sellers do not wish to randomize prices across potential buyers at a point in time, it is often possible to collect similar data by raising and lowering prices for all customers over very brief time intervals. For example, if customers who arrive at a website at 10 am face a lower price than those who arrive at 10:15 am, and buy correspondingly more of a given product, the seller has discovered valuable information about the demand curve without technically offering different prices to its customers. To provide an example indicating that this phenomenon happens, the following chart shows two years of prices for a particular children's toy on Amazon.com. While these frequent price changes are not necessarily experiments, they will certainly provide information about consumer demand for this item.

Source: Thetractor.com.

Steering

Steering is the practice of showing different products to customers in different demographic groups. In the online environment, steering occurs when a web site alters its search results based on information about a potential customer. Like third-degree price discrimination, steering uses information about potential buyers, but not at the individual level.

Both steering and differential pricing can happen with or without a customer's knowledge. As one example, Dell Computer's web site might offer the same laptop to different types of buyers (e.g. government, academic, individual, and business users) at different prices. This type of differential pricing is easily observed because buyers are asked to identify what group they belong to. On the other hand, customers may not be aware that some Internet retailers vary prices or steer customers to different products based on a computer's Internet address, which provides a proxy for their geographic location, or based on the type of device they are using.[10]

Computer scientists from Northeastern University recently found evidence of either steering or differential pricing at 4 out of 10 general merchandise web sites and 5 out of 5 travel web sites. Although this suggests widespread differential pricing, the same study found that these practices affected a very small number of products – less than 2 percent of the sampled products on each site in the study (Hannak et al 2014). Thus, the overall picture to emerge from this study is that experimentation with steering and differential pricing is a common practice across web sites, but for a relatively limited set of products.

One reason why steering and third-degree discrimination are not more prevalent could be that it is difficult to infer much about Internet users without access to personal information. Variables such as the type of operating system, a user's IP address, or whether they are using a mobile device may contain some information about willingness to pay but are imperfect proxies at best. For this reason, much of the interest in big data and differential pricing has focused on data that captures individual users' browsing, search, purchase, or other behaviors.

Behavioral Targeting and Personalized Pricing

Behavioral targeting and personalized pricing use customer-specific information to target advertisements or tailor prices for a set of products. Historically, this kind of personalization required a human, such as a salesperson who could negotiate the price of each car or appliance. However, big data and electronic commerce have reduced the costs of targeting and first-degree price discrimination.

Loyalty programs provided some of the first applications of big data to personalized pricing. When a buyer joins a loyalty program, they typically provide some personal information and consent to a seller tracking their purchases. In return, the buyer typically receive some type of benefit such as seat upgrades or free flights from an airline frequent flier program, or price discounts on specific items from a grocery store. Sellers use loyalty programs to customize their marketing. Some retailers also partner with companies that aggregate data from loyalty programs and use it to create customized coupons, which are printed on the back of receipts that a customer receives at the cash register or point of sale. Firms that specialize in this type of personalization claim that data-driven analysis can increase the redemption rates on such coupons from 1 percent for non-personalized coupon offers to as much as 25 percent for highly-targeted coupons.[11]

Widespread adoption of the Internet and smartphones is producing many new types of behavioral data that can be used for targeted marketing. For example, online advertisers use browsing data collected from ad networks and third party cookies to send users targeted ads. Thus, someone who spends lots of time at a travel web site reading about Hawaii might begin to see advertisements for flights to Honolulu or hotels in Waikiki when they are later reading the news on another site in the same network. Many web services also use behavioral data to make customized recommendations. For example, Amazon recommends books, Netflix recommends movies, and Apple and Google recommend music based on customers' purchase and consumption patterns.

While behavioral targeting has been widely reported, there is relatively little evidence of personalized pricing on the Internet. For example, the Northeastern study described above found no evidence of personalization based on user-specific information at any of the 10 general merchandise web sites in the study and could only discern behavioral discrimination at 1 out of 5 travel sites. Likewise, recent reports on the data broker industry produced by the Federal Trade Commission in 2014 and the Government Accountability Office in 2013 contained no specific references to examples of personalized pricing.

The relative scarcity of personalized pricing examples suggests that companies are moving slowly or remaining quiet, perhaps due to fears that consumers will respond negatively, but also because the methods are still being developed. For example, a new story about using big data to identify and target customers who are pregnant produced a number of headlines containing terms like "creepy."[12] At the same time, the story led practicing statisticians to point out that marketers are typically very cautious with this type of prediction, because when big data suggests that a customer is 75 percent pregnant, the 25 percent risk of marketing to a "false positive" customer is unacceptably high.[13]

The fact that companies have not yet embraced personalized pricing does not mean that sellers share the same general concerns as their customers. Consumer groups typically object to the fact that many buyers are only vaguely aware of what a website might know about them or how that information could be used. They also argue that in settings where the cost of a mistake is high, individuals should be able to ensure the accuracy of their data. Sellers appear more concerned with the reliability of statistical models and the potential reputational impact of their pricing practices. Nevertheless, companies' reputational concerns may reflect a belief that consumers will view personalized pricing as unfair if the data are not reliable, if the buyer did not opt-in to the data collection process (as with loyalty programs), or if price differences are not framed as discounts (as with coupons).

What Buyers Are Doing?

While much of the interest in big data and differential pricing has focused on sellers, buyer behaviors are also revealing. In particular, three broad trends suggest that concerns about big data and personalized pricing are not stifling consumer activity on the Internet. Those trends are: (1) the rapid growth of electronic commerce, (2) the proliferation of consumer-empowering technologies, and (3) the slow uptake of privacy tools.

E-Commerce

Americans are using the Internet to shop in rapidly growing numbers, suggesting that consumers believe they are getting a good deal on the Internet, regardless of any differences in the pricing practices of online and offline retailers. The U.S. Census estimates that e-commerce has increased from 2 percent of total U.S. retail sales in 2004 to 6 percent in 2014. Moreover, electronic commerce revenue is currently growing at a rate of 16 percent per year in the United States, more than three times the 5 percent growth rate in overall retail sales (Borgie 2014).

Consumer Technology

In the online environment, consumers have a variety of tools that may help them find a better price if they are concerned about steering or differential pricing. The simplest of these tools is the search engine. For example, the following chart shows the weekly frequency of worldwide Google searches that include the phrase "best price." The strong seasonality suggests that consumers are using the Internet for price comparisons during the run-up to holiday season, and perhaps more so during the recession.

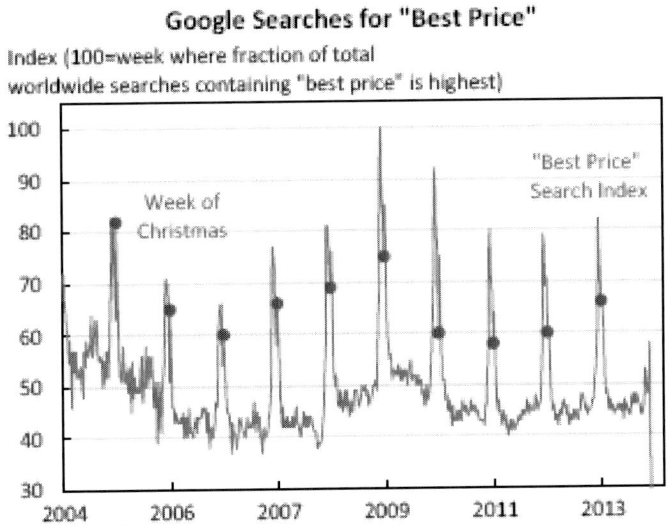

Source: Google Trends.

Price comparison and price-tracking sites are another type of buyer-empowering technology. Price comparison sites, such as Travelocity, Expedia, or PriceGrabber, show the current price of similar items at many different online sellers at a point in time, making it easier for buyers to see the full range of prices. Price tracking sites provide the price that a single online seller offers for one item over time and can issue alerts to a potential buyer if the price falls below some threshold.[14]

The Internet has also strengthened the ability of arbitrageurs to undermine differential pricing by making it easier for buyers to become sellers. In particular, if a seller charges widely divergent prices to customers in different markets, it creates an opportunity for someone to buy at the low price and undercut the seller in the high-priced market. For example, a student named Supap Kirtsaeng created a substantial business out of importing foreign edition textbooks from Thailand and re-selling them on eBay. Websites like Amazon and Craigslist create similar opportunities. In Kirtsaeng's case, textbook sellers challenged his legal right to import the copyrighted works, thereby highlighting a more general point – our intellectual property and contract laws, trade rules and safety regulations can all influence consumer bargaining power by placing limitations on re-sale.[15]

Privacy Tools

Finally, it is worth noting the relatively low adoption rates for some widely available consumer privacy tools. For example, most browsers allow users to set policies for accepting different types of cookies used to track their web surfing behavior. While there does not appear to be any systematic study of this behavior, a test by one Internet Service Provider (ISP) found that 96 to 97 percent of its users allow some cookies and 85-90 percent allow third-party cookies.[16] Similarly, users can opt out of targeted advertising on many web sites by clicking on a small triangular icon but often decline to do so.[17]

Privacy advocates suggest that users are unaware of these tools and unaware that advertisers are gathering and aggregating data about their Internet use. On the other hand, this could be "rational ignorance" on consumers' part, reflecting a view that the cost of engaging with details of privacy settings outweighs the benefits gained. Evidence on this topic is mixed, perhaps reflecting the rapidly evolving technical and commercial landscape. Some older surveys support the claim that many Internet users don't understand how their data are being gathered and used (Turrow, Feldman and Meltzer 2005). However, a 2014 survey by the Pew Research Center finds that 55 percent of Americans are "willing to share some information about [themselves] with companies in order to use online services for free" at the same time as 64 percent believe that government could do more to regulate what advertisers do with their personal information (Pew Research Center 2014).

III. Toward a Policy Framework

Economists typically see value-based pricing as a tool for expanding the size of the market by charging more to those willing to pay and less to those who are not. While this practice may seem unfair to those who pay a higher price, buyers often have tools for fighting back, especially in a competitive market. Moreover, anecdotal evidence suggests that while many sellers use the Internet to explore the demand curve, few make widespread use of personalized pricing, at least for the moment.

Nevertheless, the combination of big data and differential pricing does raise serious concerns. For example, big data may facilitate discrimination against protected groups, and when prices are not transparent, differential pricing could be conducive to fraud or scams that take advantage of unwary consumers. This final section of the report considers how big data and differential pricing relate to existing antidiscrimination and consumer protection laws that might address these issues.

Antidiscrimination

Big data naturally raises concerns among groups that have historically been victims of discrimination. Given hundreds of variables to choose from, it is easy to imagine that statistical models could be used to hide more explicit forms of discrimination by generating customer segments that are closely correlated with race, gender, ethnicity, or religion. Moreover, the term "price discrimination" may lead to concerns about economic injustice, even if the profit motive is different from, and in many cases fundamentally inconsistent with, the sort of prejudice that our antidiscrimination laws seek to prohibit.

To understand how big data is likely to affect historically disadvantaged groups, it helps to distinguish between disparate treatment and disparate impact. In the marketing context, disparate treatment occurs when a seller uses race, religion, or some other consumer characteristic as a proxy for demand. This practice can be efficient, producing gains for both seller and buyer, even if it is annoying (or worse) for members of a targeted group. The premise of big data is that when marketers have a wide variety of behavioral data to choose from, they will find imperfect proxies such as race or religion to be less useful. In other words, big data aims to reduce the rate of "false positive" cases that potentially make disparate treatment a problem.

Disparate impact occurs when some practice has an adverse impact on a protected group, even if the practice was not intended to be discriminatory. For high-stakes markets such as credit and employment, laws like the Civil Rights Act of 1964 and the Fair Credit Reporting Act (FCRA) are used to prevent disparate outcomes.[18] In principle, big data could lead to disparate impacts by providing sellers with more variables to choose from, some of which will be correlated with membership in a protected class. However, big data also provides new tools for detecting problems, both before and perhaps after a discriminatory algorithm is used on real consumers. For example, it is often straightforward to conduct statistical tests for disparate impact by asking whether the prices generated by a particular algorithm are correlated with variables such as race, gender or ethnicity. Put differently, in markets where it is important to prevent disparate impact, big data can be used to enforce existing antidiscrimination laws more effectively, thereby obviating the need for broader restrictions on its use.

Finally, it is important to keep in mind that if historically disadvantaged groups are more price-sensitive than the average consumer, profit-maximizing differential pricing should work to their benefit. This argument does, however, come with two caveats. First, it assumes competition is held constant. Minority groups may pay higher prices because they are underserved, so that sellers who do business with them face less competition and can more easily raise prices. But in that case, policy should focus on encouraging competition rather than limiting differential pricing. Second, as described above, risk-based pricing generally favors less risky customers, as opposed to those who are more price sensitive. This suggests that policies to prevent inequitable application of big data should focus on risk-based pricing in high-stakes markets such as employment, insurance, or credit provision. While the antidiscrimination provisions of existing laws such as the FCRA and Civil Rights Act should apply to these settings, ongoing scrutiny is warranted given the rapid changes in both technology and business practices.

Consumer Protection

In a competitive market with transparent pricing, value-based pricing is unlikely to harm the average consumer, who can easily compare offers and switch sellers. However, when sellers obfuscate by bundling a low product price with costly warranties or shipping fees, use "bait and switch" tactics to attract customers with false promises, or bury important details in the small print of complex contracts, differential pricing can cross the line into fraudulent behavior. In such cases, Section 5 of the Federal Trade Commission Act generally provides the FTC with sufficient authority to prohibit "deceptive acts or practices."

Some consumer advocates suggest that we should go further and limit the use of personalized pricing to offline settings or require its disclosure to buyers.[19] Economic reasoning suggests that differential pricing, whether online or offline, can benefit both buyers and sellers, as described above. Thus, we should be cautious about proposals to regulate online pricing – particularly if we believe that online markets are particularly competitive. Proposals to require seller disclosure are less worrisome. In general, rules requiring disclosure that prices or search results may vary across users should be based on a comparison of the compliance costs and the expected benefits from increased transparency. However, in assessing the benefits, we should recognize that buyers have strong incentives to seek out a good price, and that they may come to expect personalized pricing in specific online settings, just as they do offline.

A final issue that is often conflated with differential pricing, but represents a valid concern in its own right, is privacy. While many questions about privacy rights fall outside the scope of this report, it is important to note that big data involves the aggregation, sale, and use of large amounts of personal information, often in ways that individual consumers know very little about.[20] Much of this activity facilitates personalized tracking and targeting, which create value by helping sellers better identify and serve buyers' needs. However, many users may not want some kinds of information, such as visits to health or finance-related web sites, to be tracked without their explicit consent. In some cases, individuals may also have a greater interest in the accuracy of their information than the companies handling it.

Concerns over privacy, data quality, and fairness are especially salient when considering risk-based pricing. In particular, big data may cause risk-based pricing strategies to target consumers based on factors outside their own control. The challenge for policy in this area will be to promote the application of big data where it can discourage excessive risk-taking and help solve adverse selection problems, while preventing unfair discrimination against consumers who have little control over newly-measureable risk factors.

One way to limit unfair or inaccurate applications of big data might be to give consumers greater control over their information. Data brokers claim that strong property rights over personal information could produce large transaction costs that would undermine valuable applications of big data. Economic theories also suggest that such property rights would not fully resolve the privacy problem. For example, adverse selection issues could re-emerge through voluntary disclosure of information.[21] Nevertheless, a property rights approach to privacy seems particularly appealing where big data leads to concerns about fairness in the application of risk-based pricing strategies, and information intermediaries may have insufficient incentives to ensure the accuracy of personal information.

In practice, various self-regulatory efforts, such as the Individual Reference Services Group, which lasted from 1997 to 2001, have failed to produce consistent rules or widely adopted norms regarding consumer access to or control over the information used in personalized marketing. Thus, in their recent reports on the activities of data brokers and information resellers, both the Federal Trade Commission and the Government Accountability Office have suggested a need to rethink existing frameworks for regulating consumer privacy and the acquisition and use of big data in the marketing context.

CONCLUSION

Economists have studied differential pricing for years, and while big data seems poised to revolutionize pricing in practice, it has not altered the underlying principles. In particular, value-based pricing generally benefits sellers who earn more profit and buyers who would otherwise be priced out of the market, at the expense of less price-sensitive customers who end up paying a higher price. Risk-based pricing favors the least costly customers, as opposed to the most price-sensitive but can produce similar market-expanding benefits in the presence of adverse selection and may also discourage excessive risk-taking in some settings, although it can raise serious fairness concerns in others. Competition, collective purchasing, and arbitrage can all limit sellers' ability to implement differential pricing.

How might big data change differential pricing in practice? In many ways, it remains too early to tell. Broadly speaking, big data seems likely to produce a shift from third-degree price discrimination based on broad demographic categories towards personalized pricing and individually targeted marketing campaigns. A review of the current practices suggests that sellers are now using big data and digital technology to explore consumer demand, to steer consumers towards particular products, to create targeted advertising and marketing offers, and in a more limited and experimental fashion, to set personalized prices. At the same time, buyers are making use of the Internet and the variety of choices and tools it provides to ensure that they get a good deal.

Concerns with differential pricing are often entangled with related concerns about competition or consumer privacy. In many cases, policy should be able to address these issues individually. In particular, where differential pricing harms a protected group or crosses the line into fraudulent behavior, our existing antidiscrimination, competition, and consumer protection laws provide a variety of tools to correct the problem. However, given the speed at which both the technology and business practices are evolving, commercial applications of big data deserve ongoing scrutiny, particularly where companies may be using sensitive information in ways that are not transparent to users and fall outside the boundaries of existing regulatory frameworks.

REFERENCES

Armstrong, Mark. 2006. "Recent Developments in the Economics of Price Discrimination." Advances in Economics and Econometrics: Theory and Applications: Ninth World Congress.

Borgie, Lana. 2014. "Trends in Producer Prices between E-commerce and Brick-and-mortar Retail Trade Establishments." Bureau of Labor Statistics 3, no. 18. http://www.bls.gov/opub/btn/volume-3/trends-in-producer-prices-between-ecommerce-and-brick-and-mortar-retail-trade-establish ments.htm.

Cackley, Alicia Puente. 2013. "Information Resellers: Consumer Privacy Framework Needs to Reflect Changes in Technology and the Marketplace." September. United States Government Accountability Office.

Corts, Kenneth. 1998. "Third-Degree Pricing Discrimination in Oligopoly: All-Out Competition and Strategic Commitment" The RAND Journal of Economics 29, no. 2.

"Do Many Users Turn off Cookies?" Webmasters Stack Exchange. http://web masters.stackexchange.com/questions/58210/do-many-users-turn-off-cookies.

Deneckere, Raymond J., and R. Preston McAfee. 1996. "Damaged Goods." Journal of Economics & Management Strategy 5, no. 2 http://www2.econ.iastate.edu/faculty/langinier/teaching2005/615-fall2005/paper-hom2/damagegoods.pdf.

Einav, Liran, Theresa Kuchler, Jonathan D. Levin, and Neel Sundaresan. 2011. "Learning from Seller Experiments in Online Markets." National Bureau of Economic Research Working Paper No. 17385. http://www.nber.org/papers/w17385.

Ellison, Glen and Sarah Fischer Ellison. 2009. "Search, Obfuscation and Price Elasticities on the Internet." Econometrica 77, no. 2.

Hannak, Aniko, Gary Soeller, David Lazer, Alan Mislove, and Christo Wilson. 2014. "Measuring Price Discrimination and Steering on E-commerce Web Sites." http://www.ccs.neu.edu/home/cbw/pdf/imc151-hannak.pdf.

Hermalin, Bejamin and Michael L. Katz. 2006. "Privacy, Property Rights and Efficiency: The Economics of Privacy as Secrecy." Quantitative Marketing and Economics 4, no. 3.

Hossain, Tanjim, and John Morgan. 2006. "...Plus Shipping and Handling: Revenue (Non) Equivalence in Field Experiments on EBay." Advances in

Economic Analysis & Policy 6, no. 2. http://faculty.haas.berkeley.edu/rjmorgan/ebay.pdf.

Pew Research Center. 2014. "Public Perceptions of Privacy and Security in the Post-Snowden Era." November. http://www.pewinternet.org/2014/11/12/public-privacy-perceptions/

Podesta, John, Penny Pritzker, Ernest J. Moniz, John Holdren, and Jeffrey Zients. 2014. "Big Data: Seizing Opportunities, Preserving Values." Executive Office of the President. http://www.whitehouse.gov/sites/default/files/docs/big_data_privacy_report_5.1.14_fi nal_print.pdf.

Varian, Hal. 1997. "Versioning Information Goods." Digital Information and Intellectual Property. http://people.ischool.berkeley.edu/ ~hal/Papers/version.pdf.

Varian, Hal. 1985. "Price Discrimination and Social Welfare." The American Economic Review 75, no. 4. http://www.jstor.org/stable/1821366.

Ramirez, Edith, Julie Brill, Maureen K. Ohlhausen, Joshua D. Wright, and Terrell McSweeny. 2014. "Data Brokers: A Call for Transparency and Accountability." Federal Trade Commission. http://www.ftc.gov/system/files/documents/reports/data-brokers-call-transparency-accountability-report-federal-trade-commission-may-2014/140527databrokerreport.pdf.

Shiller, Benjamin Reed. 2014. "First-Degree Price Discrimination Using Big Data." http://benjaminshiller.com/images/First_Degree_PD_Using_Big_Data_Apr_8,_2014.pdf. Turow, Joseph, Lauren Feldman, and Kimberly Meltzer. 2005. "Open to Exploitation: America's Shoppers Online and Offline." A Report from the Annenberg Public Policy Center of the University of Pennsylvania. http://repository.upenn.edu/cgi/ viewcontent.cgi?article=1035&context=asc_papers. Government Accountability Office. 2013. "Information Resellers: Consumer Privacy Needs to Reflect Changes in Technology and the Marketplace." http://www.gao.gov/assets/660/658151.pdf.

INDEX

C

D

E

I

J

Q

R

S

T

U

V

W

Y